The TUDOR QUEENS *of* ENGLAND

DAVID LOADES

MJF BOOKS
NEW YORK

Published by MJF Books
Fine Communications
322 Eighth Avenue
New York, NY 10001

The Tudor Queens of England
LC Control Number: 2009940526
ISBN-13: 978-1-60671-002-9
ISBN-10: 1-60671-002-8

Printed in the United States of America.

WCM   10   9   8   7   6   5   4   3   2   1

Contents

Illustrations

For Judith,
wife, sovereign and friend

Introduction: Image and Reality

A medieval queen was not a ruler. The imagery of power was exclusively masculine and very largely military. A king led his soldiers into battle, executed the brutal sentences of justice upon criminals and played war games with his nobles and companions. The ideal Christian prince was a crusader, the father of strong sons, tough and wise. It was his first duty to protect his realm in arms and to be leader and patron of those who fought. He was also the protector of the Church – that is of those who prayed – and of those who laboured, traded or otherwise lived under the shelter of his shield. His councillors and clerks were either nobles, who shared his value systems, or celibate clergy. God had been incarnate in the form of a man, and the whole bible, particularly the Old Testament, was heavily androcentric.[1] Women were seen mainly in relation to men – the symbolism of Adam's rib being frequently invoked. A woman complemented her husband, bearing his children, tempering his severity, sustaining his virtue – and of course flattering his ego. Women were believed to be intellectually inferior to men, physically weaker and morally more fragile. The ideal woman was chaste, obedient and patient. A woman held no office in the public domain, and her virtue was judged against her own kind, not in relation to men. Her role model was the Virgin Mary, the mother of God and the only woman to have accomplished the miraculous feat of being a mother and a virgin simultaneously. At the same time every woman was also Eve, a source of temptation and potentially of the betrayal of God. This seems to have been primarily a clerical perception, and arose from the extremely negative attitude of the medieval Church towards sexuality. Female sexuality was mysterious and fascinating but also evil if not strictly controlled. Without the discipline that man imposed upon her, any woman might be a whore or a witch – or both. In the middle of the sixteenth century John Knox (not, admittedly, a sympathetic witness) could write:

> Of which words it is plain that the Apostle meaneth (in 1 Corinthians 11) that woman in her greatest perfection should have known that man was Lord above her … in her greatest perfection woman was created to be subject to man. But after her fall and rebellion committed against God, there was put upon her a new necessity, and she was made subject to man by the irrevocable sentence of God, pronounced in these words:

I will greatly multiply thy sorrow and thy conception, with sorrow shalt thou bear thy children, and thy will shall be subject to thy man; and he shall bear dominion over thee ...[2]

And he went on to quote Tertullian: 'Thou are the porte and gate of the Devil. Thou art the first transgressor of God's law ...' In spite of Tertullian, this was sharper and more hostile than the prevailing medieval view and Christine de Pisan was not alone in presenting her contemporaries in a positive light. In the right circumstances (within marriage), motherhood was a noble calling, but it was strictly under male control and one of the prime reasons for the extreme hostility to extra-marital sex was that it exemplified female nature operating outside that control. The single mother was like the masterless man, operating beyond the conventional discipline of society.

Both the canon and the common law reflected these perceptions. The woman who had extra-marital sex, whether or not she had borne a child, was a suitable subject for penance and was liable to be ostracized – especially by other women. She was also liable to be without support because men were notoriously reluctant to admit their responsibility for such matters; she was thus a burden on the Church's charitable resources. Fornication was by far the commonest reason why women were cited before the ecclesiastical courts. Where the man could be identified he would be cited as well but often he seems to have avoided detection. In theory the distinction between rape and fornication was very clear. The former was a crime under the common law for which the death penalty could be imposed; the latter was a sin by both parties for which the woman usually carried the responsibility. The trouble was that then (as now) the practical distinction lay not in the commission of the act but in the attitude of the woman – which was no less problematic to establish than it is today. Women were certainly protected against predatory males as far as the law was concerned but the uncertainties of prosecution remained formidable, especially if the guilty party was well protected by patronage. In terms of property, the law made a clear distinction between married and unmarried women. The latter, whether virgins or widows, had full control over whatever they might possess, whether it were lands or moveable goods, and were protected against depredations in the same way that men were. In other words the *femme seul* was a proper person in the eyes of the law.[3] Not so the married woman, or *femme couvert*. She had no existence apart from her husband and any property that she took into the marriage remained vested in him for the duration of his life, unless it were protected by some special trust or other covenant. Her only safeguard was that her husband could not dispose of any such property without her consent, but it could not descend to her own heirs until after his death. She could not testify against him in court and her position was in every sense dependent.

If an aristocrat died without male heirs then his property could descend to his daughter or be equally divided if there was more than one. His title, however, if he had one, became extinct. This was a reflection of the military origins of such dignities and of the consideration that no woman could perform military service in person. A woman could transmit a claim but it was entirely at the discretion of the monarch whether such a claim was recognized – and usually it was not. Of course if the same aristocrat died without heirs of any kind then his property also returned to the Crown by a process known as *escheat*. In the sixteenth century it was possible for a woman to hold a title of nobility in her own right by special creation but in the two cases where this happened – the Earldom of Salisbury (Margaret Pole) and the Marquisate of Pembroke (Anne Boleyn) – the heritability of the title was not tested as both were extinguished by attainder. No woman held such a title during the fifteenth century. From these limitations the royal dignity itself stood apart. In France the so-called Salic Law not only prohibited a woman from holding the Crown, but also barred all claims transmitted through the female line. That was not the case in England and both the Yorkists and the Tudors based their claims primarily on the female line of descent. The possession of the Crown itself, however, had never been tested. In the twelfth century the Empress Matilda had made such a claim and had been recognized by some but had never secured effective possession and had never been crowned. This issue came to the fore during the reign of Henry VIII and was actually put to the test on the death of Edward VI in 1553, when both the potential claimants were women. As we shall see, the consequences were to preoccupy lawyers and councillors alike when Mary, the successful claimant, announced her intention to marry.

The problem was that a ruling queen was forced by her position into being a surrogate male but was simultaneously a woman and perceived as being subject to all the traditional limitations of her sex. This created challenges both to her ingenuity and to her sense of identity and made her a completely different creature from a Queen Consort, who was primarily a wife. The latter did not exercise *dominium*, but was both ideologically and politically integral to the proper deployment of her husband's authority.[4] What she held was a status rather than an office but, if she acted discreetly and respected the perceptions of those about her, she could supply vital elements in her husband's kingship that might otherwise be lacking. As Jacobus de Casalis wrote in *The Game and Play of Chess*:

A Quene ought to be chaste, wyse, of honest peple/well mannered and not curious in nourishynge of her children/her wysedom ought not only tappere in fact and workes, but

also in speakynge that is to wete that she be secrete and telle not suche thynges as ought
to be holden secrete ... A Quene ought to be well mannered & amonge all she ought to
be tymerous and shamefast ...[5]

In other words she should show all those qualities that were held to be virtues
in contemporary women, but to an enhanced degree because of her unique
position. Most important, perhaps, was her role as mediator and intercessor.
Here the image of the Virgin was particularly significant because of the Church's
emphasis upon the supernatural intercession that she was perceived to offer.
Stories of Mary interceding for otherwise hopeless sinners were legion and the
sight of a human queen, on her knees and with her hair unbound before her stern
and unbending lord had an irresistible appeal. When Catherine interceded for the
perpetrators of the Evil May Day in 1517 she was acting out a trope, as indeed
Henry was in responding. There was also more than a suggestion that – just as
the Queen was acting out a human role in this drama – so the King was acting
out a Divine mercy. A foreign queen had a double responsibility in this respect.
Not only could she intercede in this conventional sense but she was also the
natural mediator between her husband and her own kindred. Both Catherine
de Valois and Margaret of Anjou were supposed to be not only mediators but,
in their marriages, symbols of peace and reconciliation. It was the wedding,
after all, which made a queen, just as it was the coronation that made a king.
When a queen was crowned, it was not only a recognition of her position but
also an enhancement of her husband's power and a way of emphasizing that
she was no longer an ordinary noblewoman. It was because their wedding had
been quiet to the point of being secret that, on 30 September 1464, Elizabeth
Woodville was led into the chapel of Reading Abbey by the Duke of Clarence
and the Earl of Warwick 'and openly honoured as Queen by the Lords and all
the people'.[6]

Because Elizabeth of York had her own claim to the kingdom, a claim that
had to be subsumed in that of her husband, her marriage to Henry VII in 1486
was choreographed with especial care and medallions were struck. It was a rite
of passage for the kingdom, as well as for Elizabeth. She was crowned on St
Katherine's day and William Capgrave's life of St Katherine was not slow to make
the same point, that 'government by a woman is unfeasible' and that consequently
it was the King's position that mattered.[7]

Of course a foreign queen could also serve a quite different purpose if
circumstances demanded it. She could be a lightening conductor for hostility and
frustration. When the expected peace with France failed to follow the marriage of
Henry VI and Margaret of Anjou in 1445, the unfortunate young woman found

herself blamed. Margaret was to be particularly vulnerable in this respect because circumstances forced her into a role of political leadership that was supposed to be alien to her nature. In 1462, when she found herself struggling to maintain the cause of her increasingly deficient husband, she was fiercely denounced by Yorkist propagandists for bringing in Frenchmen and Scots 'to destroy utterly the name, the tongue and all the bloude Englyshe of this oure saide Realme ...'[8]

Margaret was caught in a trap, because she was forced to appear as Henry's agent at a time when he was virtually incapable of helping himself – and there was no way in which her image could conform to the political reality.

A queen was supposed to be chaste because only by such means could the integrity of the royal line be protected, but the most important of all her functions was to bear her husband children. If she was deficient in other ways, skilful image brokers could conceal the fact, but no amount of spin could disguise her failure to produce an heir. Hence the ceremony that attended a royal lying in. This was the classic opportunity to display successful queenship, and churchings and Christenings were public and splendid events. Childbirth was the ultimate female mystery and even comparatively humble gentlewomen would retire from view, accompanied by a midwife and one or two female servants. Queens did the same on a grander scale. However in their cases the stakes were much higher and the possibilities of fraud or substitution proportionately greater. Consequently, although no man (unless he were a physician) could be present at the birth itself, visits from royal officials during the period of confinement were common. In 1555 Mary's phantom pregnancy gave rise to all sorts of scandalous rumours and her condition was clearly as much of a mystery to contemporaries as it has remained ever since – but no one had the temerity to accuse their sovereign of adultery. When Anne Boleyn had a miscarriage in February 1536, her enemies were quick to attribute it to sexual misconduct but it would have been high treason to have levelled similar accusations against Mary – and not even John Foxe attempted to do so. The unfortunate Margaret of Anjou was so accused, although not at the time of Prince Edward's birth. As evidence of Henry's mental incapacity began to mount after 1453 it began to be doubted whether he could ever have fathered a son and as young Edward's place in the scheme of Lancastrian monarchy became more evident and immediate their Yorkist rivals had every incentive to impugn his legitimacy. That was unusual; the careful observance of all the correct rituals of motherhood was normally sufficient to protect the Queen from such slanders and to guarantee the subsequent enhancement of her status.

The queen who was also the mother of a male heir was doubly fortunate. Not only had she fulfilled her highest duty – she had enhanced her husband's authority to an immeasurable extent and demonstrated that God looked favourably upon his government. The political role of the Queen Consort thus depended to some extent upon her womanhood but it also varied with circumstances and with her own personality. A queen who was the mother of a royal prince could not expect the same control over his upbringing that an ordinary gentlewoman had. Despite the Holy Family imagery she did not breastfeed him – that being the responsibility of a specially appointed wet nurse. Very often a separate household was established for him almost from the time of his birth. The queen was consulted but all appointments were made by the King, even when the child was 'among the women' in accordance with the custom of the time. Anne Boleyn does not even seem to have been consulted when her daughter Elizabeth was weaned and contact between them seems to have been confined to regular visits. When Margaret's son, Prince Edward, was created Prince of Wales in March 1454 he was less than a year old and, although his Council was a political and administrative institution rather than a domestic one, Queen Margaret was influential in its creation. Edward IV's son, also Edward, was promoted at about the same age in 1471 and his mother was, very unusually, formally admitted as a councillor and is alleged to have dominated that body, which was one of the reasons why the Duke of Gloucester viewed her with suspicion in 1483. Arthur was slightly older when he was promoted in 1489, and the then Queen, Elizabeth of York, is not known to have played any part. By the time that Henry became Prince, in 1504, she was dead and there were no more princes of Wales within the period, the next being the eldest son of James I in 1610. The only Queen Consort to bear a son during the sixteenth century was Jane Seymour and she did not live to play any part in his upbringing. Elizabeth of York was protective of her elder daughter, Margaret, and is alleged to have persuaded her husband not to marry her for diplomatic reasons before the canonical age of co-habitation, which was 12. Margaret was actually 13 when she married James IV of Scotland in a purely political match and Elizabeth seems to have supported that – or at least she did not oppose it.

A queen also continued, to some extent, to be defined by her own family. Catherine de Valois made little of her royal blood after her marriage and took as her second husband a mere household servant, while Margaret of Anjou was alternately bedevilled and rescued by hers. No one was allowed to forget that she was of the Ducal House of Anjou. Catherine of Aragon actually served as her father's accredited ambassador in England between her marriages to Arthur and Henry and was the symbol of an alliance by which the King set great store in the early years of his reign. When he was trying to get rid of her in 1527, it was her family, in the person of the Emperor, Charles V, who stood in his way and forced him into one of the defining actions of his reign. However, paradoxically the two most important consort families were not foreign but domestic. The Greys and the Woodvilles owed their spectacular rise entirely to the marriage of Elizabeth to Edward IV. The familiar picture of the antagonism between the Queen's kindred and Richard of Gloucester in 1483 is almost entirely the creation of Tudor propaganda but the elevation of Elizabeth's father as Earl Rivers in 1466 and of her son Thomas Grey as Earl of Huntingdon in 1471 and Marquis of Dorset in 1475 were sufficiently factual and reflect a deliberate attempt on Edward's part to build up his wife's family into a significant political force. Her successor, Elizabeth of York, had no need of such patronage. Had it not been for her gender, she would have had a better claim to the Crown than her husband; on the other hand, if she had been born male she might have gone the same way as her brothers. Her marriage to Henry VII was celebrated for years as the reconciliation of the great rivalry of Lancaster and York and she continued to use the white rose as her badge for the rest of her life. In her son and daughters ran the blood of both royal families, and through her elder daughter, Margaret, it was conveyed to the Scottish royal house of Stuart.

Edward IV's patronage of the Woodvilles was reflected in a paler way in the manner with which Henry VIII dealt with the kindred of his second, third, fifth and sixth wives. Sir Thomas Boleyn became Earl of Wiltshire in 1529, Edward Seymour Earl of Hertford in 1537 and William Parr Earl of Essex in 1543 as a result of his marriages to Anne, Jane and Catherine. The Duke of Norfolk, who was Catherine Howard's uncle, did not gain any further promotion when she shared the royal bed, but for about two years his ascendancy at court and in the council was unchallenged. Unfortunately what went up could also come down. The Boleyns were ruined by Anne's alleged infidelities and the Howards by Catherine's real ones. William Parr was never a figure of much significance but Edward Seymour, as the uncle of Prince Edward, the cherished heir to the throne, was an important national figure in the last years of Henry's life and more particularly during the minority of his son. Henry VIII's marital adventures confused the image of queenship. No one could claim that Anne Boleyn was either meek or patient. Unlike Margaret of Anjou, she was not forced into a political role by the incapacity of her husband. She chose it, and created a formidable clientage over which the King had only imperfect control – which was one of the main reasons for her downfall. Nor could anyone plausibly describe Catherine Howard as chaste and not even the most flattering courtier could apply the image of the Virgin Mary to her without arousing unseemly mirth. Catherine Parr was a queen in a more traditional mould. Although neither virgin nor mother, she recreated the King's shattered family and by her wisdom and discretion helped to temper the unpredictability of his increasingly uncertain temper. She was as chaste, wise and well mannered as even Jacobus de Cassalis could have wished and she was the last of her kind for over half a century.

A ruling queen was a completely different creature and with the accession of Mary in 1553 we enter a new world. The situation was not unprecedented in Europe. Isabella of Castile offered a recent and obvious example but that was in a different legal system and few Englishmen would have known much about her. A woman had never governed England and there were uncertainties both of image and of expectation. In the case of a Queen Consort, who exercised temporary power, her husband defined the position. When Edward IV went to France in 1475, he left Elizabeth as governor in his place and when Henry VIII did the same in 1513 he left the government in the hands of Queen Catherine. The same applied in 1544, with a different Catherine but the same process. However that was at the King's discretion and if he was incapacitated, or died leaving his heir a minor, the same conditions did not apply. When Henry VI collapsed in 1453, the Duke of York became Protector and when Edward died in 1483, leaving his sons under age, he named his brother the Duke of Gloucester as Protector. After Henry VIII's death in 1547 the council named the Duke of Somerset as Protector and no one suggested that the position should have gone to the Queen Dowager. John Knox was not alone in believing that the rule of women over men was unnatural and contrary to the Law of God, but that was not the prevailing view.[9] It is impossible to say what might have happened in 1553 if Mary had been challenged by a man with a plausible claim but, in the event, her only rival was another woman whose claim was by general consent inferior. Unfortunately there was no consensus about the nature of Mary's claim. The Queen herself believed that her right lay in the fact that she was Henry's only legitimate child and that was a view shared by her Habsburg kindred and by most of Catholic Europe. Her subjects, however, believed for the most part that her entitlement lay in the dispositions that Henry had made by statute in 1543 and in his last will and testament.

This hardly mattered for the purpose of seeing off Jane Grey in July 1553 but it was important thereafter, as we shall see. Mary was crowned as though she had been a king, convened parliament, established her Council and acted in every respect as her father or grandfather would have done. For the time being she even acted as Supreme Head of the Church, although it soon became apparent that the title offended her conscience. As a *femme seul*, she was in command of her own private lordship and her lawyers, at least, were comfortable with that thought. The imagery that was developed on her behalf, most of it admittedly in Europe rather than in England, made the best of her unexpected emergence from affliction to power. She was the helpless virgin triumphing over the strong man armed – the woman clothed with the sun, and so on.[10] This successfully blended femininity with success, but was hardly imagery for the exercise of power. That no one ventured to produce, and Mary herself clearly had no idea what form it should take. Unlike Edward, she could not even attempt to strike her father's pose. She then compounded her problems by deciding to marry. There were good reasons for this, the most compelling being her need for an heir, but she also sought to use marriage to provide for the security of her realm, and to reinforce the religious policy upon which she was determined. She set about this in the same way that a King would have done – she took advice where she pleased (in this case mainly from Simon Renard, the Imperial ambassador) made up her own mind, and then announced her decision. This took her councillors aback, but only because they were expecting her to be 'shamfast' and to take her lead from them. In choosing her mate, Mary had acted like a man, but there the similarities came to an end. By converting herself from a *femme seul* into a *femme couvert* she was muddying the waters horribly.

If the realm was a *dominium*, or lordship, as most believed, would it pass to her husband in full ownership for the duration of his life, as would be the case with a private lordship? She had made it clear almost from the beginning that her intended husband was Prince Philip of Spain, the only son of her cousin the Emperor Charles V. This was not well received in England and the problems that would have arisen in any case in respect of a King Consort were redoubled by the unpopularity of her choice. If there were no children, and she predeceased him, did he remain king for the remainder of his natural life? If there were children, and Mary died while they were underage, did he automatically become regent? During their marriage, what control would he exercise over her person and the resources of the kingdom? A conventional marriage suggested pessimistic answers to all these questions. The trouble was that the roles of a wife and of a sovereign were not really compatible. A queen could hardly be a petitioner and intercessor in her own country, let alone a humble and dutiful helpmate. She could be chaste and discreet, but hardly silent – and what if her duty compelled her to fall out with her royal spouse? Some of these problems were resolved by the treaty that accompanied the marriage agreement, which was negotiated by Charles rather than Philip, and gave him very little independent authority in England.[11] If there was an heir, he would be regent in the event of the Queen's death but only until the normal age of majority and if she died childless his interest in the realm would cease. Philip was not pleased and many Englishmen believed that such conditions would be unenforceable, but in theory the treaty completed an acceptable relationship. The more limited legal problem was resolved by a statute in Mary's second parliament that 'ungendered' the Crown and declared that a queen's authority was identical with that of a king.[12]

Despite all these precautions, Mary never really came to terms with her predicament, as we shall see. Nor could she ever find an image with which she was comfortable. If she had ever become a mother she might have used the Virgin as a role model but that was not to be. Neither a virgin nor a mother, she was also a wife who, for most of her married life, was left to cope on her own. Philip was at her side for only about 15 months of their four-year marriage. While he was present they appeared together in studied equilibrium, but while he was absent she was rather at a loss to express her status. Praise for her religious policies, particularly from the clergy, was strong but unfocused. Her portraits show her magnificently dressed but otherwise nondescript – neither regal nor iconic. The only image that survives of her after her marriage is the one she would least have wanted and in many ways the unfairest – that of Bloody Mary, the arch persecutor and religious bigot. Mary was a woman of puritanical conscience and no imagination or sense of humour. She had also spent so much of the formative part of her life acting out the role of a suffering servant that she was unable to adjust to power when she found herself possessing it. Her failure to bear a child was probably critical in this as in other ways and left her after 1555 with a role that she could live (as she had to) but could not express.

Her half-sister and successor Elizabeth was a total contrast in every respect save one – she was also a woman thrust into a role normally played by men. The sad example of Mary's failed marriage – and even more the problems that it had created – may have deterred her from following the same route or it may not, we do not know. What we do know is that her whole attitude, both to the exercise of power and to its imagery, was quite different. Mary had been hesitant, traditional in her conception of a woman's place in the scheme of things, and uncertain of her image, but Elizabeth relished the challenge and took politics by the scruff of the neck. She was probably both more intelligent and better educated than her sister and was well aware that intellectually she had the edge of almost everyone around her. That was why she was able to fill her court and administration with men of such extraordinary ability. While recognizing that she was operating in a man's world, she had no time at all for the traditional notion that some matters were beyond a woman's competence. Whereas Mary had regarded her sex as a liability, and potentially a crippling one, Elizabeth used hers as weapon. Quite aware that she was strikingly good looking, she set out to fascinate and tease the men with whom she had to deal in a way that her sister would have regarded with incredulous horror. Women were supposed to be unstable and procrastinating – very well, she would delay and change her mind until they were all dancing with frustrated rage – knowing perfectly well that only she could make the necessary decisions. Let them wait! Whether her famous courtships were genuine or simply political ploys we do not know and it is quite likely that she was not sure herself. Only in her dealings with Robert Dudley did the fundamental conflict between the woman and the Queen become apparent, and then the Queen won, at considerable cost.[13] Like Mary, her religious conscience was highly developed, but whereas God told Mary that she must restore the old faith and eliminate heresy, He told Elizabeth that He had entrusted a realm and a church to her and that she would be answerable to Him for both. Let no one presume to usurp her authority.

If Elizabeth had ever married – as every man at her court (and most women) expected her to – she might well have become mired in the same conceptual and political bog but by not sharing her bed she avoided sharing her power. By not being a wife she was free to act as a king – and even donned armour at the time of the Armada to address her troops assembled at Tilbury. No man could have governed in her inimitable style – certainly not her successor James I – because even in her old age (when it had become somewhat grotesque) she never ceased to play the game of courtly love. Politics eventually came to wear the masque of charade but woe betide anyone who presumed upon the old lady's indulgence, as the Earl of Essex found to his cost. In some respects Elizabeth's imagery was frozen in time, because it was always depicting the idea rather than the real woman. Her portraits, and there are hundreds of them, are iconic, stylized. Whether they bear any relation to the real woman is almost irrelevant. She was Deborah, Astrea, Belphoebe and many other biblical or mythical figures. Above all, she was a figure of mystery and power – mysterious as only a woman could be in a world of men. As the prospects of marriage receded, even in the eyes of the most optimistic, virginity became her trade mark. She never exploited the Blessed Mary to provide a role model – that would not have suited her Protestant conscience; rather, she became an iconic virgin herself – a woman whose physical integrity became a symbol for the inviolability of her country. By remaining a *femme seul*, Elizabeth was able to develop a female style of monarchy that was quite distinct from the traditional male style to which all Queen Consorts were subjected, but just as effective.

It would be easy in this post-feminist world to contrast the triumphant reign of Elizabeth with the downtrodden consorts of Edward IV or Henry VIII and to conclude that the latter were poor specimens of womanhood. That would be a serious mistake because their circumstances were quite different and the tasks that they performed quite distinct. Consorts were always seen as aspects of their husbands and contributors to his *maiestas*, never as people in their own right. They might, as was the way with women of all social classes, have great influence over their husbands, but any action that resulted was always his responsibility, not hers An intelligent woman with ideas of her own thus faced a dilemma, as was the case with both Margaret of Anjou and Anne Boleyn. Margaret paid with her reputation and Anne with her life. It was in motherhood and in intercession that a Queen Consort found her fulfilment, and both were distinctively female accomplishments. No king could bear his own child and a consort who failed in this respect, like Catherine of Aragon, was liable to pay a high price. The idea of marriage as a free and equal partnership was alien to the medieval mind. It was a state that men entered into with their own interests in mind and within which the woman had a defined and subordinate role. She was judged by the skill with which she discharged that role. In principle a ruling queen was a man, discharging a male function, which was why combining rule with marriage was so schizophrenic and why Elizabeth's balancing act was so uniquely successful. No female ruler actually became a mother until the time of Queen Anne, over a century after Elizabeth's death – and by then the world had changed so much that her consort did not have to be recognized as king. Anne's frequent and futile pregnancies were an affliction but did not affect the way in which she was regarded, which was more as a figurehead than as an effective head of state. Elizabeth would have been horrified by the transformation. Victoria was also born into a culture of marital subordination and although her influence upon her ministers was considerable she was more an imperial symbol and icon than an effective governor. Her constitutional position was by then so clearly defined that her husband, in a neat role reversal, was consigned to the supportive role previously occupied by female consorts. Outside the bedroom, the customs of marriage did not apply to the Crown. Victoria's daughters helped to define the royal houses of Europe and her long widowhood left a symbolic trail that long outlived her. The present Queen and her consort have been totally defined by constitutional propriety and since Victoria's death the British monarchy has been constrained to reinvent itself not once but several times. The gulf that separates Elizabeth II from Elizabeth I is as great as that which separated the first Elizabeth from Catherine de Valois.

1

The Queen as Trophy: Catherine de Valois

Catherine was the youngest daughter of Charles VI of France and his consort, Isabella of Bavaria. She was born in Paris on 27 October 1401 at the Hotel de St Pol, which was used almost as a retreat when her father's mental illness was particularly severe. Her upbringing was eccentric, being marked by periods of neglect and even privation as her father was not in touch with reality and her mother was pursuing her own agenda.[1] At one point she was even abducted by her uncle, Louis of Bavaria, but on that occasion the King recovered his reason at the critical time. Isabella was imprisoned at Tours and Catherine was placed temporarily in other hands but she never seems to have borne her mother any ill will for her erratic behaviour. She had been called into political service long before she was old enough to be aware of what was happening and before her second birthday was betrothed to Charles, the grandson and heir of Louis, Duke of Bourbon. However, Charles died in 1409 and even before that Henry IV of England had been proposing a peace settlement to be sealed by a marriage between Catherine and his own heir, Henry of Monmouth. However, there were a number of stumbling blocks in the way of such a settlement, not least Henry's claim to the Crown of France and the scale of the bride's dowry, which the English king is alleged to have set at two million crowns. Charles VI offered 450,000, and the negotiation came to nothing.

When Henry IV died on 20 March 1413, the issue was still unsettled but his successor, who was still unmarried and 25 years old, was keen to continue the quest and in January 1414 vowed that he would wed no other. France, however, was in a state of almost constant crisis, with the Burgundians and the Armagnacs at each other's throats. The king was again mentally ill and only occasionally fit to conduct business. It seems that Henry may well have had it in mind to secure his bride by capture rather than negotiation because he was obviously anxious to take advantage of France's problems. He entered into an alliance with John the Fearless of Burgundy for that purpose in 1414. On 13 August 1415 he attacked on the flimsiest of pretexts and laid siege to Harfleur. Shortly after he won his great victory at Agincourt, and began the systematic conquest of Normandy. Negotiations for peace and marriage alike disappeared from view.

With the King incapacitated and the Queen discredited, the government of France was temporarily in the hands of the Constable, Bernard of Armagnac. The royal family was in almost total eclipse. Two successive dauphins had died and the third, Charles, was as yet too young to assume any responsibility. John the Fearless had held aloof from the Normandy campaign but as the English increasingly gained the upper hand so his relations with Henry became closer. In May 1418, operating in the name of the Queen, he seized Paris, and with it the formal government of what was left of France. The Dauphin, Charles, however, had escaped from Paris and, showing no signs of his father's debility, in spite of his youth, set himself up as regent at Bourges. From there he controlled (more or less) a large area in the centre of the country. In order to resolve this deadlock, an agreement with the official government in Paris now became increasingly desirable from Henry's point of view and on 7 May 1419 envoys were appointed to negotiate such a settlement. Catherine, now 18, seems to have been present at these discussions, together with her mother who is alleged to have exercised great influence over her. Once again the size of the dowry was a sticking point. Meanwhile John of Burgundy was also negotiating with the Dauphin because, clearly, an agreement that included him would be preferable to one that did not. He was strong enough to make a considerable nuisance of himself if he were excluded. However, on 10 September 1419, the two had a blazing row on the bridge at Montereau, as a result of which the Duke was set upon and murdered by the Dauphin's followers. Charles was not actually present when this happened but was generally (and reasonably) held responsible. This put paid to any chance of a tripartite settlement and since the rest of the royal family, including Catherine, was under the control of Philip of Burgundy, John's son and heir, the way to a more limited agreement was now open. At the same time Philip's animosity to the Dauphin could be taken for granted.

The resulting Treaty of Troyes, signed in May 1420, has been represented as the nadir of French fortunes. Although in one guise the Duke of Burgundy was a great nobleman of France and could not unreasonably negotiate on the King's behalf, at the same time he was also an independent ruler in alliance with the King's enemy. The ambiguities of the French political system were as much to blame for the humiliation at Troyes as Charles VI's weakness. Henry V agreed to give up the title 'King of France' in return for recognition of his sovereignty over those territories which he already controlled. Henry and Charles would both continue for the time being to rule their respective realms but if Charles should die first the King of England would succeed him, and any child born to Henry's union with Catherine would inherit both kingdoms. The text of the treaty reads (in part):

First it is agreed between our said father of France and us, that for as much as by the bond of matrimony made for the good of peace between us and our most dear and beloved Katherine, daughter of our said father and of our most dear mother Isabel his wife, those same Charles and Isabel are made our father and mother, and honour them as such, and as it fitteth such and so worthy a prince and princess, to be honoured especially before all other temporal princes of this world ...[2]

At the same time, instead of demanding a dowry, Henry agreed to fund his queen to the extent 40,000 ecus a year from the realm of England, which amounted to some £7,500; that being what 'Queens of England hitherto were wont to take and have', with an additional 20,000 francs from his lands in France if he should predecease her.[3] The English lands were to be assigned principally out of the Duchy of Cornwall and the Earldom of Chester. The Estates General, the Sorbonne and the City of Paris all endorsed the treaty. A few days later, on 2 June 1420, Henry and Catherine met for the first time and were betrothed. Although Shakespeare's famous account of their meeting is fiction there does seem to have been a genuine chemistry between them, which was just as well because a few days later they were married. The ceremony was performed in the parish church at Troyes by the Archbishop of Sens and their honeymoon was spent recovering the town of Sens from the Armagnacs, which when taken was restored to the Archbishop with considerable bloodshed. Philip of Burgundy said of Catherine at this point that 'she had passionately longed to be espoused to King Henry, from the moment that she saw him ...', which would suggest that she had first set eyes on him at the abortive meeting in 1419, although they had not actually met.[4] After their turbulent honeymoon the bride seems to have returned briefly to her parents, who were at Bray-sur-Seine, until the time of their state entry into Paris, which occurred in December.

The Treaty of Troyes was a realignment of forces rather than a genuine peace, because the Dauphin remained (understandably) unreconciled and was quite strong enough to continue waging war in defence of his own position. How, his propagandists complained, could Catherine claim to transmit a claim to the throne of France to her heirs while he was still alive? That was not, of course, the point, because it was Henry who was recognized as Charles's heir, not his daughter. The Salic Law, in any case, would have prohibited any claim transmitted by her but it was a telling point for a French audience anxious to work up a head of steam against the 'betrayal of the fleur de lys'. So the war continued and although Catherine was established with a generous English household (for which Henry paid) she was not expected to accompany her husband on campaign, remaining instead at Bray-sur-Seine, where Henry was a frequent visitor. Her time came when there were triumphs to be celebrated and, although the Dauphin won some victories against lesser English commanders, the King himself proved well-nigh invincible. He did not need to conquer Paris, but he did need to make his presence felt there; consequently, after several months of campaigning, he made a ceremonial entry, accompanied by his queen in December 1420. They kept Christmas at the Louvre with great pomp. Whatever efforts Henry might have made to teach his wife English – and it would hardly have been necessary because he spoke perfect French – she had not yet visited his homeland. However that was remedied on 27 December when they cut short their Christmas celebrations and set sail for England.

The king was now out to impress. He was 'with triumph come from France' and was given a suitably enthusiastic welcome by his devoted subjects. In the wake of the Southampton plot, he needed to establish that he was unchallenged in England as well as victorious in France and to impress his wife with the completeness of his control.[5] At the same time (although obviously this was not said) his wife was a trophy of the successful war. She was 19 years old and by all accounts extraordinarily beautiful. They entered London together on 21 February and she was crowned at Westminster on 24 February. This was Catherine's moment of high exposure to the social and political elite of England. Henry deliberately did not attend, leaving her to preside at the coronation banquet and to bear the full weight of the elaborate ceremonial, every last detail of which was solemnly recorded in Fabyan's Chronicle.[6] They then went off on progress to the north of England, where Henry was again at great pains to display his trophy, until Catherine returned to Westminster in May. It must have been during this progress that their child was conceived. Catherine spent the summer and autumn of 1421 becoming more visibly pregnant. With so dominant a husband, she had little political role and seems to have been content to busy herself with works of piety and other 'female concerns', like managing the love affairs of her friend King James of Scotland. It seems that she did not even administer her own estates. No accounts survive to provide an indication, and such evidence as there is suggests that the King's officers continued to be in charge and simply paid over to her Steward the proportion of their revenues that the marriage treaty required. How the Steward then disbursed that money we do not know. Presumably Catherine paid for the staff and upkeep of those houses which had been allocated to her, but whether she was also expected to pay for her residence at court when in her husband's company is not clear. Despite his obligations under the treaty of Troyes, there is no sign that Henry allocated a specific estate for her maintenance but rather took revenues from whichever lands happened to be available to make up the required sum. Sometimes these were Duchy lands; at other times the dower lands of the Queen Dowager, Joan of Navarre, seem to have been used.[7] By July Henry was back in France, pursuing the Dauphin along the Loire, where he took Dreux on 8 August. By November Catherine had retreated into the customary seclusion at Windsor, and there on 6 December she was safely delivered of a son.[8] The child lived and flourished and the Queen had performed her most important and inescapable duty. There was an heir to both thrones.

Before Easter she had joined her husband, leaving their son in the safe care of his nursery and they spent the Whitsun time together in Paris, before Henry set off again on campaign. She was, presumably, served by her normal retinue of ladies, whom she would have paid, but for some unknown reason she was also on this occasion accompanied by several additional women whom the King rewarded. Lady Margaret Roos, Elizabeth Fitz Hugh, Catherine Chideock, Joanne Belknap, Joanna Troutbeck and Joanna Carey cost the exchequer an additional £140, but why they were employed is a mystery and their rewards are listed as 'extraordinary'. Perhaps the King owed their kindreds an obligation. More surprisingly, her confessor, John Boyers, was paid in the same way.[9] This time Henry had been summoned to relieve a Burgundian garrison at Cosne sur Loire but it soon transpired that the sickness that he had picked up at the fall of Meaux earlier in May was actually dysentery. By the time that he got to Corbeil he was too weak to continue and he had to be carried in a litter to Vincennes, where he died on 31 August. Catherine may or may not have been present (the sources do not agree) but if she were not, this should not be taken to suggest any kind of a rupture between them. Henry had in a sense died on active service, which his consort could not be expected to share. They had been married for a little over two years. The Queen's grief was palpable and we are told 'greatly edified the people'. She conducted his body back to England in a solemn and magnificent cortege, and erected a great tomb in his memory. It might have been expected that after the obsequies, Catherine would have returned to her own family because she was still only 21. However, her father died on 21 October and her brother was locked in combat with her son's Council for control of the kingdom of France. In the circumstances, home was where her son was, and she remained in England. Soon after the parliament confirmed her dower at the slightly reduced, but still substantial, figure of £6,000 a year, taken mostly from the Duchy of Lancaster and therefore presumably assessed on different lands. No more is heard of the 20,000 francs from France but the provision made was perfectly adequate for a Queen Dowager.

For the next few years, Catherine acted mainly as the mother of her young son. This was a personal, not a political role because, officially, the Earl of Warwick was the guardian of the King's person but the Queen Mother appeared regularly with the infant Henry. At the same time England was run by the Council, presided over by the King's uncle, Duke Humphrey of Gloucester, as protector. The French lands were similarly ruled by Humphrey's brother, John Duke of Bedford, who had his own council. Henry was moved around a good deal, partly for the sake of his health and partly to prove to the people that he was still alive and well. Catherine was, however, still only in her mid-twenties and was apparently highly sexed. As one chronicler put it (not too discreetly), she was 'unable fully to control her carnal passions'.[10] There were rumours of an affair with Edmund Beaufort, the nephew of the Cardinal Bishop of Winchester, accompanied inevitably by talk of a marriage, to which the Duke of Gloucester was adamantly opposed. It might have been as much because of this known weakness as because of the need to be near her son that Catherine went on living in the King's household until 1430. Henry VI was crowned in 1429 and this was presumably a rite of passage in more than one sense. He was now in the fullest sense a king but his education would also have moved on, into the hands of male tutors. He was no longer 'living among the women' and his mother was surplus to requirements. Despite the fact that the parliament of 1427–8 had decreed that the Queen Mother could only re-marry with the consent of the Council, Catherine seems to have celebrated her freedom by uniting herself with one of her sewers, a Welsh squire named Owain ap Maredudd ap Tudur.

Owain was the son of Maredudd ap Tudur ap Goronwy of Penmynydd in Anglesey and claimed descent on his mother's side from the princely house of Deheubarth. How he first encountered Catherine is something of a mystery. There are a number of unsubstantiated stories about his youth and upbringing and some of his kindred seem to have been involved in Glyn Dwr's revolt, although Owain himself would have been too young. Perhaps he had some connection with Henry as Prince of Wales although he would only have been about 13 when the latter became King. The first certain thing that is known about him is that he served in the retinue of Sir Walter Hungerford, the steward of the King's household, in France in May 1421. This would suggest that he held some position in that household, although what that might have been, and whether it was on the King's side or the Queen's is not known. Elis Gruffudd, the sixteenth-century Welsh chronicler, says that he was Catherine's 'sewer and servant' and that is probably correct although it cannot be substantiated. Most likely Owain was a handsome and well set-up young man and the sexually frustrated Catherine fancied him. There is a story that during a dance at court he fell into her lap while trying to execute a difficult pirouette but that would seem to be symbolic rather than factual! Under other circumstances she might have simply taken him as a lover but the risk of unattributable pregnancy was simply too great and at some time in 1529 or 1530 they were secretly married.

Her ladies apparently remonstrated with her for lowering herself in 'paying any attention to a person, who, although possessing some personal accomplishments … had no princely or even gentle alliance'. Worst of all, he was Welsh. Catherine apparently responded that, being a French woman, she did not understand that there were racial differences within Britain. He summoned some of his more respectable kindred to speak for him – but unfortunately they knew no language but Welsh.

Although after Catherine's death in 1537 he was disparagingly described in a council minute as 'Owen Tudor which dwelt with the said Catherine …' there is no reason to doubt the reality of their marriage. Although it was recorded that 'the high spirit of the Duke of Gloucester could not brook of her marriage', it was not openly challenged at the time. Aspersions of bastardy were subsequently cast on both her sons, but that was for transparently political reasons. It was probably when she realized that she was pregnant that Catherine withdrew from court and took up residence at Much Hadham in Hertfordshire, where at some point in 1430 their eldest son, Edmund, was born.

The Queen Mother was understandably concerned to make her position appear as respectable as possible. In 1431 she seems to have arranged for Owain's pedigree to be presented to the parliament, presumably emphasizing his connection with the quasi-royal house of Deheubarth and in 1432 he was granted letters of denizenship. These he needed, because although he was the King's subject, being a Welshman he was technically an alien in England and this was at a time when the Glyn Dwr revolt had left a number of anti-Welsh statutes on the record, making it (for example) illegal for a Welshman to hold land in England. By becoming a denizen, Owain became an honorary Englishman, although it is not clear that he ever held any significant property in England. Over the next five years Catherine must have been almost constantly pregnant because she bore Owain three more children: Jasper, who was born at another of her residences, Hatfield, at some time in 1432, David, who subsequently became a monk at Westminster and an unnamed daughter who seems to have died in infancy. Apart from motherhood, it is not clear how Catherine spent her time at this stage of her life. Her son, the King, seems to have regarded her with warm affection, and just a few days before her death, sent her a New Year's gift of 'a tablet of gold with a crucifix, garnished with saphire' and valued at £40.[11] She was also much prayed for, even during her lifetime, which suggests a charitable disposition and involvement in works of piety. Towards the end of her life, and probably after she was already ill, her children were assigned to the care of a sister of the Earl of Suffolk. This was undoubtedly intended as a snub to Owain and must have caused the ailing Queen Mother considerable distress but we have no direct evidence of her reaction. She seems to have retired to Bermondsey Abbey some months before her death and might have had some thoughts of taking the veil, but it was there, on 3 January 1437, that she died. Her will, which survives, is a very curious document. The king, who was still technically a minor, was made sole executor, her servants were to be paid, and masses said for her soul, but nothing was said either about her younger children or about her husband.[12] Perhaps some traces of her father's incapacity were afflicting Catherine towards the end of her life, or perhaps some rupture with her husband had put her in a state of denial. The fact that she was in Bermondsey Abbey at all suggests that something like that had happened. In any case she died as Queen Dowager and a princess of France – not as Mrs Owain Tudur.

Her death at first left her husband dangerously exposed. In July he was summoned before the Council but significantly declined to come without a safe conduct from the King that 'he should come and freely go'. This was granted, but honoured in the breach rather than the observance, for on his way home he was arrested and consigned to Newgate. Later in the year, as one chronicler disparagingly put it:

> One Owen, a man of neither birth nor livelihood, broke out of Newgate at searching time. The which Owen had wedded with Queen Katherine and had three or four children by her unknown to the common people until she was dead and buried ...

He was re-arrested and sent to Windsor Castle, where he might have remained had not his stepson intervened. In 1439 he was pardoned and his goods and lands (valued at £137 a year) were restored to him. Henry then awarded him an annuity of £40 a year 'by special grace' and, although he gave him no office or responsibility, Owain proved to be a loyal servant of the Lancastrian cause in the forthcoming civil strife. He was eventually captured and executed after the Yorkist victory at Mortimer's cross in 1461. He was buried in the Greyfriars church at Hereford, where his bastard son David (an afterthought born in 1459) subsequently erected a memorial.

His sons by Catherine, Edmund, who was aged about 7 at his mother's death, Jasper, who was 5, and the other David, who was about 3, do not seem to have been in their father's custody at any point. Whether their allocation to the care of the Earl of Suffolk's sister ever took effect we do not know but probably not because soon after Catherine's death they were placed with the Abbess of Barking and later with certain 'virtuous and holy priests'. The King assumed full responsibility for them and never attempted to deny that they were his kindred. They were educated in the royal household in a manner suitable to their status and Edmund was knighted on the 15 December 1449.[13] He was presumably brought up, at least in part, to be a soldier but it was in recognition of his royal blood rather than for service that he was created Earl of Richmond on 23 November 1452, with precedence over all other earls.[14] He was also recognized as the King's half brother at the Reading parliament of 1453. Because of that status he was granted in that year the wardship of the 10-year-old Margaret, the daughter of John Beaufort, Duke of Somerset, whom two years later he married. By 1456 he was fighting with the Lancastrian forces in Wales but was defeated by Sir William Herbert and died of the plague at Carmarthen in November of that year. His young bride gave birth to a posthumous son on 28 January 1457, who was subsequently to be King Henry VII.

As King, Henry demolished and rebuilt the chapel at Westminster Abbey where Catherine was buried. In referring to his intention to translate the remains of his uncle, King Henry VI, to the new chapel, he also mentioned 'the body of our Grand dam of right noble memory, Queen Katherine daughter of the King of France' as being interred in the same place. Unfortunately, when he himself came to be buried there his 'grand dam of right noble memory' was disinterred and not reburied. She seems to have remained above ground until the early nineteenth century, and in the seventeenth her body was something of a tourist attraction. After this ultimate indignity it is to be hoped that she rests in peace.

2

The Queen as Dominatrix: Margaret of Anjou

The circumstances of Henry VI's marriage to Margaret of Anjou could hardly have been more different from those of 1420. Then Henry V had been in control of the situation and had been able to bring his bride back to England as one of the spoils of victory. In 1444 the English were on the back foot, struggling to maintain their position in France and anxious to salvage the best peace that they could. For a few years after 1422 the young King's uncle, John, Duke of Bedford, had maintained a semblance of dominance but failure at Orleans and the subsequent crowning of the 'roi de Bourges' as King Charles VII of France had turned the political tide. The Burgundian alliance was already problematic as Duke Philip reassessed his priorities and after the death of his sister Anne, the Duchess of Bedford, in November 1432, it was effectively dead. In 1435 Bedford himself died, and Philip formally came to terms with Charles at Arras. Thereafter the English were clearly on the retreat, and this was a situation not helped by divided councils. The King's surviving uncle, Humphrey of Gloucester, was committed to the defence of the French lands, but although he held the formal precedence of Protector, his influence was in fact seriously challenged by Henry Beaufort the Cardinal Bishop of Winchester and large scale creditor of the Crown. Beaufort was not interested in the defence of France and as the King emerged from childhood into adolescence, he increasingly sympathized with the Cardinal's priorities. By the end of 1443 the English were concentrating their efforts on the defence of Calais and Normandy, and Francis I, the Duke of Brittany who had his own interests to protect against the resurgent power of Charles VII, was offering to mediate peace.

Charles, for his part, was willing to negotiate. His recent agreement with the Duke of Burgundy was already beginning to unravel and it seems that he was anxious to put the English war on hold while he dealt with Philip, in alliance with Duke Renée of Anjou. Renée was motivated by the desire to liquidate his obligation to pay Philip the balance of the enormous ransom that had been demanded on his release from Burgundian captivity in 1437. Although titular king of Naples, Sicily and Jerusalem and strongly connected at court, Renée was not in fact a particularly imposing ally but he was conveniently available – and he had a motive. Moreover Marie, Renée's sister, was Charles's queen. Since the King of England was unmarried, and of a marriageable age, it was natural for the King of France to seek that route to peace with England, and it seems that the original proposal came from the French side. Because Charles had no desire to give any pretext for a son of the marriage to renew his claims to the French throne, his own daughters were not on offer and the bride suggested was Margaret, the 14-year-old second daughter of his ally, Duke Renée. Margaret was suitable from the English point of view because she was of royal blood, the right age, and came of a proven breeding stock – she had several brothers as well as an older sister. She was appropriate from the French point of view precisely because she was not a great heiress and carried almost no political baggage. Although the military situation was not at that point particularly threatening, in January 1444 the English council decided to negotiate and at the beginning of February Henry sent the Earl of Suffolk to France to represent him. Suffolk was the King's personal choice and it was not a wise one as the Earl himself appreciated. He had been involved in Anglo-French peace feelers before and for that reason the French had specifically asked for him but the numerous French contacts that he had already established left him short of credibility in the eyes of Gloucester's supporters. They suspected that he would prove a 'soft touch' and he was worried lest a successful mission should be seen in that light.

It was already a concession on the English side to be discussing Margaret at all, not least because her dowry was likely to be negligible and any further concessions would seriously undermine the credibility of the whole exercise. Nevertheless, that is what happened. By 20 May it was clear that the English would be able to secure neither a full peace nor recognition of their existing position in France. Given his apprehensions of precisely such an outcome, Suffolk should probably have broken off the negotiation and come home. However, perhaps because he knew the King's mind, he settled for a two-year general truce in order to secure the marriage. His thinking seems to have been that once Margaret was in England as Queen, it would be relatively easy to turn the truce into a full peace. In any case, there had not even been a truce since Henry V's death, so that was an achievement of a kind. On 22 May a formal betrothal ceremony took place in St Martin's cathedral at Tours, presided over by the papal Legate, the Bishop of Brescia, and in the presence of Charles, Renée, their wives and a large concourse of French nobility. Suffolk acted as proxy for the King of England. The Earl and his entourage returned to England immediately after the ceremony, and were greeted by Henry with extravagant enthusiasm. It was not the least of that monarch's many misjudgements to have undervalued himself in such a fashion but Suffolk was generously rewarded and in September raised to a marquisate. Towards the end of the year the new marquis led a much larger and more formal mission back to France, including a number of noble ladies led by Jaquetta of Luxembourg, the dowager Duchess of Bedford, for the purpose of escorting Henry's bride to her new kingdom.[1] He was also charged to resume the peace negotiations, which had been suspended with the conclusion of the truce. It was to prove an expensive and protracted mission, which lasted until the following April, but the peace negotiations made no further progress and that was to prove an ominous failure.

Suffolk found the French Court at Nancy in December, from where Charles was busying himself about the siege of the Duke of Burgundy's stronghold at Metz. Both the French king and his ally may have been distracted by this circumstance, because it was February before Margaret finally put in an appearance. The delay caused rumours to circulate in England that the young queen was being withheld in order to extract further concessions from the pliable Suffolk. Specifically he was later accused of having promised to cede Henry's claims to Anjou and Maine to Duke Renée. There appears to have been no truth in these innuendoes, which were spread by Suffolk's political enemies, and relations continued to be friendly, but the long delay in Margaret's arrival inevitably aroused suspicions. Once she appeared, however, affairs proceeded with reasonable expedition. The wedding was celebrated at Nancy on 2 March, with Suffolk again standing in for Henry, and then the English set off for home.[2] The journey was slow and the bride tearful at the prospect of leaving her family and friends. The party reached Pontoise on 18 March and that was the last Valois held town on their route. There they were met by Henry's lieutenant and governor in France, the Duke of York and most of the French contingent said their farewells. A few, including of course several young women, were to accompany the Queen to England. Margaret may already have been suffering from homesickness, or possibly chagrin, and she did not appear either at Rouen or at Harfleur on the way, although state entries had been arranged at both. She was still suffering from some indeterminate ailment, which was probably made worse by seasickness, when she landed in England on 14 April.

It is claimed that Henry, in an unaccustomed gesture of chivalric enterprise, bore a letter to her disguised as a squire immediately after her landing. She did not, of course, recognize him (never having set eyes on the King of England) and he was apparently less than impressed.[3] Although one contemporary (admittedly French) declared that 'there was no princess in Christendom more accomplished than my lady Marguerite of Anjou [who] was already renowned in France for her beauty and her wit', most evidence does not confirm that she was a great beauty. Nevertheless, preparations for her second and final wedding proceeded apace, the precaution having already been taken to secure a dispensation for a marriage in Lent, and duly took place at Titchfield Abbey on 22 April. The celebrant was William Aincough, Bishop of Salisbury, and this time the King spoke for himself.[4] To mark the occasion the new Queen was apparently presented with a lion, which was promptly consigned to the menagerie at the Tower in the care of two grooms and at a cost of £2 5s 3d. As soon as the ceremony was over Henry headed back to Westminster to prepare for her entry into London and coronation, leaving Margaret in the care of Cardinal Beaufort, Suffolk's friend and a warm supporter of the peace with France. She proceeded to Eltham by comfortable stages and entered London on 28 May. Her reception had been carefully orchestrated as a celebration of peace and concord, with the Queen herself as the dove. She was crowned at Westminster two days later. As with Catherine, a quarter of a century earlier, the King did not appear, leaving his consort as the focus of all attention. Given that she was in a strange land and only 16 years old, she seems to have coped remarkably well.[5]

However, in using his bride in this way, the King was giving hostages to fortune. Supposing that the peace negotiations did not succeed? In that event there was a risk that his dove of peace would turn into a raven of discord. Even the Marquis of Suffolk was sceptical of success and took pains to warn the House of Commons on 2 June that a favourable outcome was by no means assured.[6] He was also anxious to refute the claims that were already being made, that he had offered unauthorized concessions. He had, he insisted, made no such offers but had confined himself strictly within the limits set out in the King's instructions. As a precaution, he insisted that his protestation be minuted, which was duly done (and is the reason why we know about it). At the same time, the feuding within the English Council was reflected in a public discourse that represented the Queen as symbol of surrender and mocked her father who, for all his extravagant pretensions, was unable to provide a suitable dowry for his daughter. As the duration of the truce ticked away the negotiations became increasingly urgent, but all that they achieved was an extension of the truce. The discussions were friendly enough but the negotiating positions on both sides were intractable. Militarily, the French had the upper hand and were not disposed to make any concessions; specifically they would not admit English claims to Normandy. The English, on the defensive, were caught between Henry's urgent desire for peace and the political storm that any further concessions would arouse. They could not yield ground either. The embassies came and went. A meeting between the Kings was promoted, agreed, postponed and postponed again. Meanwhile Margaret, whose personal investment in a successful outcome was considerable, was doing her best. Writing to her uncle in December 1445, she offered to 'employ herself effectually' in the cause of peace 'in such wise that you and all others, ought herein to be gratified'.[7] On 22 December, Henry proceeded to make the unilateral gesture that is usually attributed to Margaret's influence. He renounced his claim to the duchy of Maine in favour of Renée. This was not done through formal negotiation and undermined the position that his delegates were trying to sustain; moreover it brought peace no nearer and served merely to confirm the impression in England that the French were not interested in a settlement on any reasonable terms. Margaret was blamed for this surrender and those who had seen her arrival as symbolic of submission appeared to be justified.

As her arch critic, Thomas Gascoinge, wrote:

> this king of England, Henry VI, granted and gave Maine and Anjou at the request of his Queen, Margaret, daughter of the Duke of Lorraine who calls himself King of Sicily … and that aforesaid Queen of ours begged the King of England that [they] so be given to her father at the urging of William Pole, Duke of Suffolk and his wife who earlier had promised to request it.[8]

This was written well after the event and was a slander on Suffolk but it expresses a widely held view, both at the time and later. By the end of 1445, the Queen's traditional function as a mediatrix between her husband and her father's kindred had turned sour indeed. The harder she tried and the more successful her efforts, the more unpopular she was likely to become. Had she fulfilled her primary duty and started bearing Henry children the criticism might have been more muted but that did not happen. There does not appear to have been anything wrong with their relationship. Despite Henry's later mental problems and his reputation for extreme piety, at this stage his health and his sexual interest in his wife appear to have been entirely normal. It was just that she did not conceive – and this of course provoked the gossips no less than her peacemaking activities. There is little doubt that during the early days of her marriage, Margaret was a victim of Henry's political enemies, because apart from some ineffectual attempts to promote the peace negotiations, she had no public role. The surrender of Maine in return for an extension of the truce was critical in this respect. Not only was the Queen now represented as dominating her feeble husband but she was also using that control to diminish his honour rather than to enhance it. Shortly after it was being publicly said

> that the king was fitter for a cloister than a throne, and had in a manner deposed himself by leaving the affairs of his kingdom in the hands of a woman, who merely used his name to conceal her usurpation, since, in accordance with the laws of England, a queen consort hath no power, but title only …[9]

This was an opinion which was to be voiced with increasing insistence over the coming years and it was not good for the credibility of the regime.

By this time also the divisions within the Council and among the English nobility were assuming dangerous proportions. At the end of December 1446 the Duke of York was replaced as governor in France by Edmund Beaufort, Marquis of Dorset, the Cardinal's nephew, and the Duke of Gloucester was arrested and charged with treason at the parliament that was held at Bury St Edmunds in January 1447. The parliament had been carefully convened in a place far from Gloucester's main bases of support and he would almost certainly have been convicted but he spared them the embarrassment of a trial by dying (apparently of natural causes) on the 23 February.[10] All these developments were factional moves against the leading opponents of that conciliatory policy in France, which was fronted by the Marquis of Suffolk, but which was, it seems, really the policy of Henry VI and his queen. It may be significant that the English establishment in Normandy were strongly opposed to York's removal. At the same time the English officials in Maine were dragging their feet and at least two deadlines for the handover passed with nothing accomplished. Commissioners were appointed to accomplish the handover but even they prevaricated and Dorset, who had issued the formal instructions, seems to have been convinced that the surrender was a mistake. By March 1448 Charles was becoming exasperated, and deployed a show of force against Le Mans. This did the trick, and on 15 March Maine was finally ceded, amongst bitter recriminations on the English side.[11] This surrender did little to promote the still-flagging peace negotiations but it did enhance the careers of two of those who were now Henry's most trusted advisers. In March Edmund Beaufort was created Duke of Somerset, and in June William de la Pole was raised from the Marquisate of Suffolk to a Dukedom. With Richard of York having been shunted off to Ireland and Humphrey of Gloucester dead, the King's failure to maintain a balance within his council was becoming increasingly clear.

The ineptitude of English policy in France at this point beggars belief because the 'peace party', having secured its domination of the King's Council and surrendered any initiative in negotiation, attempted to recover its position by breaking the long standing truce. In March 1449 a mercenary captain in English service seized the town and fortress of Fougères on the Breton border. The story of this escapade is immensely complicated but de Surienne seems to have acted with the full complicity of the English governor, although the motivation for the attack remains obscure. It may have been intended to intimidate the Duke of Brittany or to inject some much-needed credibility into the English negotiating position. It seems to have been intended as little more than a gesture because, having carried out his attack, de Surienne was left to his own devices and the town was soon recaptured.[12] However, Charles understandably regarded it as unprovoked aggression and, picking up what he saw as a challenge, launched his armies against Normandy. On 10 November 1449 Rouen fell, and the English position in northern France collapsed completely. Attempts were made to send reinforcements, but these were frustrated by a shortage of munitions and a lack of money. With the fall of Caen in January 1450, the only English foothold left outside of Gascony was Calais.

The repercussions of this disaster were immediate. Unable to blame the King directly, the Duke of Suffolk became the scapegoat. The House of Commons seized upon the confession made *in extremis* by Adam Moleyns, the Keeper of the Privy Seal, who had been murdered at Portsmouth early in January, to frame a variety of charges against him, and he was impeached on the 7 February. A total of eight articles were framed, including responsibility for the surrender of Maine and Anjou, but his real crime was his failure to secure Normandy – in spite of the fact that he had never held the governorship, which had gone from the Duke of York to the Duke of Somerset some time before. The King tried to have the charges respited but the Commons were insistent and were strongly supported outside Parliament. Had Suffolk been tried, he would almost certainly have been found guilty; in order to prevent this, Henry stepped in and banished his friend for five years. He did this unilaterally, without any consultation or process of law. On his way into exile in May the Duke was seized at sea and summarily executed.[13] Before his elevation to the marquisate, William de la Pole had been Steward of the Household and he, together with Adam Moleyns, had come to symbolize that household dominance of the Council that was so bitterly and widely resented. Now both of them had died at the hands of assassins and when Jack Cade's men rose in rebellion in Kent later in 1450, household government was among their leading grievances, 'the law' they declared bitterly, 'serveth for nought else but to do wrong'.[14]

All this lightning was striking close to the Queen. She had been a friend of Suffolk's because he had so patiently negotiated for her marriage and Alice, his wife, was one of her ladies. The Duke of Somerset was also a friend who had performed many good offices for her. Her position made it inevitable that her closest associates would be those household officers who, in 1450, were being so much vilified. Cade's supporters had the Duchess of Suffolk and William Booth, Margaret's Chancellor, on their 'hit list', as well as the Duke of Somerset. Despite this and her reputation, her political role at this stage was in fact negligible. Her endowment of 10,000 marks (£6,600) a year made her a very rich woman and she was a generous patron, running a large household of her own. In 1447 she petitioned her husband for permission to found a new college in Cambridge on the grounds that the university had seen 'no college founded by any Queen of England hithertoward'. The foundation stone of Queens' college was laid on 15 April 1448. A sizeable collection of her letters show her working hard on behalf of clients – sometimes her own servants, sometimes others who had sought her intercession. She secured benefices for her chaplains and confessors, offices for lay petitioners and lucrative marriages for her ladies – or at least for those who were not already wed. The King in turn was generous to her. Realizing that the financial difficulties of the Crown had somewhat reduced her dower, in 1446 he settled on her for life an additional £2,000 worth of lands, drawn mainly from the Duchy of Lancaster and comprising the Honours of Tutbury, Leicester and Kenilworth.[15] This was also given precedence over all other Duchy grants, an additional security if times should become still harder. Margaret also received a number of rich wardships and other lucrative privileges and concessions. This did not make her popular with other disappointed petitioners, although it was hardly her fault. Cade did not directly attack her but many of his shots came close and almost her only known political intervention came in connection with that rebellion. Realizing (perhaps better than Henry) the seriousness of the threat that he represented and the importance of some kind of conciliation, she urged the general pardon that the King issued on 6 July 1450 – although whether she did it as a kneeling supplicant, with her hair unbound in the classical pose of the mediatrix, we do not know.

Although Henry and Margaret spent a great deal of time together and celebrated most of the major feasts in each other's company, the years passed without any sign of the longed-for pregnancy. Inevitably there were mutterings that 'she was none able to be queen of England … for because she beareth no child …'[16] but eventually, in the spring of 1453 and after nearly eight years of marriage, the feat was accomplished and Margaret conceived. There was great rejoicing, in which the King joined, but then, when she was about six-months' pregnant, disaster struck. Earlier in the year the King had appeared to be in good health and good spirits. At the end of April he had been intending to make an extended progress to pacify some of the discontents which were plainly visible but by the end of July news had been received of the crushing defeat at Castillon in Gascony and of the deaths of the English commanders, the Earl of Shrewsbury and his son. Nobody knows whether this news (which presaged the end of English Gascony) drove Henry over some hitherto unsuspected edge but within a few days he was in the grip of a mysterious condition, which it has been suggested may have been catatonic schizophrenia. Bereft of speech and of all understanding, he became a kind of vegetable. Nobody knew what to do, either medically or politically and for several weeks it was hoped that he would recover as quickly as he had succumbed. It was in these circumstances, on 13 October 1453 that Margaret was delivered of a son, who was promptly named Edward, after the Confessor whose translation feast it was. Archbishop Kemp, the Duke of Somerset and the Duchess of Buckingham stood as his godparents. We do not know whether the Queen might have taken a political stance in other circumstances. As it was the circumstances of her confinement and convalescence effectively took her out of the equation – for the time being.

Margaret's household accounts for this period survive among the records of the Duchy of Lancaster, and we know (for example) that her chancellor Lawrence Booth was paid £53 a year and that she was spending no more than £7 a day on feeding her servants and herself. One intriguing entry records that she gave the generous sum of £200 to one of her ladies on the occasion of her marriage. It has been speculated that this young lady was Elizabeth Woodville, who was one of her attendants and who married at about this time. Certainly 'Isabella, Lady Grey' (her married name) features among the Queen's attendants not long after. Because the birth of Edward so adversely affected the prospects of the Duke of York, it was to be expected that Yorkist rumours would surround her delivery. The child was not Henry's; alternatively the real child had been born dead and the King's supposed heir was a changeling. Margaret knew of these slanders and did not forget them but they made no difference to her political position.

Although nothing was said about the King's condition when Parliament reassembled in November, it was clear by then that some interim arrangement for the government of the realm was unavoidable. A Great Council was called on 12 November and, as soon as it assembled, it became clear that the Duke of Somerset, bereft of the King's support, was in deep trouble. The Duke of Norfolk accused him of treason with reference to the fiascos in France and he was arrested and conveyed to the Tower.[17] While Somerset was still in charge an attempt had been made to exclude the Duke of York from the Council but York was a prince of the blood, who had been Henry's putative heir and Norfolk favoured him. The suggestion was raised that he should be made protector of the realm for the duration of the King's illness, but this was immediately challenged by Margaret who in January 1454, with the full backing of Henry's household officers, put forward her own claim to the regency. As one observer wrote:

the Queen hath made a bill of five articles, desiring those articles to be granted: whereof the first is that she desireth to have the whole rule of this land; the second is that she may make the Chancellor, Treasurer, the Privy Seal and all other officers of this land ...[18]

Although she had her supporters outside the household, this was a demand of revolutionary implications and where the idea came from remains a mystery.

During the recent precedent of Henry's own minority, no one (least of all Catherine herself) had suggested the Queen Mother as Regent – nor had Isabella made any such claim during the frequent illnesses of Charles VII. It seems that motherhood had transformed a fairly conventional, not to say ornamental, consort, into a determined and ambitious player in the dangerous game of power politics. The unprecedented and unexpected nature of this bid played into the hands of the Duke of York, who was clearly determined to use the King's illness as a pretext to establish and secure his own position and those of his 'well willers'. He was nominated to open Parliament on the King's behalf on 14 February 1454 and that was a step in the desired direction, but the death of John Kempe, the Archbishop of Canterbury, on 22 March, forced the issue. A new appointment was urgent and only the King or his designated replacement could nominate. On 28 March a final attempt was made to get some sense out of Henry when Margaret brought in his infant son to receive his blessing. When that failed, on 3 April, York was appointed Protector on the same terms that Humphrey of Gloucester had enjoyed 32 years earlier. The Queen's bid appears to have been simply ignored. That, as it was to turn out, was a serious mistake.

The Duke of York went through the motions of reluctance to accept the appointment but in fact he was highly gratified and immediately secured the appointment of his brother-in-law, the Earl of Salisbury, to the vacant chancellorship. His position was not strong enough to enable him to remodel the Council and all the remaining officers continued in post, but Salisbury was a valuable ally. His other appointments were not numerous, or obviously partisan, and the translation of Thomas Bourgchier from Ely to Canterbury, which occurred at some time after 23 April, introduced a noticeably conciliatory voice. The most obvious focus of opposition was the royal household, now controlled by Margaret, but beyond a little trimming for financial reasons he was not strong enough to attack it. After all, the King might recover at any moment. Beside which, he had other priorities. Apart from Calais, English France was lost and the whole coastline in enemy hands because, despite the defeats, there was still no peace. Unpaid, the garrison of Calais mutinied and there were unresolved aristocratic faction fights going on all over England. In Ireland, too, York had difficulty in restoring the authority that he had formerly exercised there. This turbulent situation exposed the protector's limitations, and it has been fairly claimed that he acted less like a surrogate king, determined to impose impartial justice, and more like the leader of a magnate faction concerned to consolidate his position. Only in the north of England did he have any success in bringing peace and that was by supporting the Nevilles in their bid to destroy the Percies. In other words, it was a factional victory.

Then, at Christmas 1454, Henry recovered as suddenly as he had collapsed; or at least, he recovered sufficiently to resume his formal duties. He is reported to have been as a man awakening from a deep sleep, delighted to see his son (now 15 months old), and curious to know what had happened during his illness.[19] Whether he ever recovered fully is a moot point because, although he remained occasionally determined to assert himself, both his willpower and his judgement seem to have been permanently impaired. The immediate consequence was the release of the Duke of Somerset, although apparently strict conditions were applied, which should have kept him out of the political arena. At some time in February 1455 the Duke of York resigned his powers into the King's hands and, on 4 March, Somerset's sureties were discharged and the charges against him dismissed. The court party swiftly augmented its strength on the council, and the new chancellor was dismissed in favour of the Archbishop of Canterbury. By April the Duke of York and his friends had every reason to fear a regime of partisan revenge and when a Great Council was summoned to Leicester on 21 May, they abruptly withdrew from the court, fearing punitive measures against them. This was tantamount to an act of rebellion, and when the court was on its way to Leicester it was intercepted by York and Warwick with a retinue of some 4,000 armed men. On the court side, Buckingham and Somerset were also 'well accompanied' and the result was the first battle of St Albans on 22 May. The courtiers were routed and the Duke of Somerset was killed. Henry was present in person and, after the battle, was honourably conducted to the Abbey, where the Duke of York renewed his homage and fealty.[20] Where Margaret may have been is not apparent but after the battle she retreated to Greenwich. The Duke of York's supporters justified his action on the grounds that 'the government, as it was managed by the Queen, the Duke of Somerset and their friends, had been of late a great oppression and injustice to the people ...' but there are no contemporary complaints to that effect.[21]

It must have seemed that York's domination of the Council would now be secure, but the situation was not in fact so simple. Despite his undoubted feebleness, the King could not now be ignored, as he had been at the height of his illness. Nor was York in a position to displace those officers who had been appointed earlier in the year. Most important of all, the death of the Duke of Somerset had left the leadership of the court party in doubt. There was no favourite of sufficient status. In theory the King himself was the leader, but in practice it was now his strong-minded spouse. As Sir John Bocking wrote on 9 February 1456: 'The Queen is a great and strong laboured woman, for she spareth no pain to sue her things to an intent and conclusion to her power ...'

Consequently, although the Duke of York was again made protector in November 1455, he soon found himself in the impossible position of being confronted by a political adversary who had unique access to the monarch and who could not be removed by any means short of assassination. He resigned the protectorship on 25 February 1456 and Margaret embarked upon a three-year period of unofficial but very real power. As long as Henry was King she would be *alter rex*. Between the summer of 1456 and the summer of 1459 the court spent almost half its time within her power base in the West Midlands. It was at Coventry in October 1456 that Archbishop Bourgchier was dispossessed of the Great Seal in favour of William Wayneflete and Henry Viscount Bourgchier was replaced as Treasurer by the Earl of Salisbury.[22] At the same time Lawrence Booth became Keeper of the Privy Seal. Wayneflete was the King's confessor and Booth the Queen's Chancellor. Although Archbishop Bourgchier was not a party man, his displacement was a partisan move, as were the other appointments. The Great Council duly confirmed these officers, but Margaret's fingerprints are all over this. Members of the Council were expected to show the same deference to her as they did to the King and on formal occasions the King's sword was borne before her. When the royal couple entered Coventry (again) in September 1457 Henry was almost invisible behind the pomp that accompanied the Queen. There was no institutional basis and no theoretical justification for such pretensions. Margaret used Edward's Council as Prince of Wales and her own stake in the duchies of Cornwall and Lancaster but for the most part she relied upon sheer will power and strength of character. Although it was the basis of her power, no concept of the consort's position had ever envisaged such a situation. Only the accepted principle that it was the consort's duty to uphold the honour of her Lord lent any support to her position and that had always been understood in a quite different sense. Of course, she had allies and resources. Humphrey Stafford, Duke of Buckingham, John Talbot, Earl of Salisbury, and Thomas, Lord Stanley were all close associates. The overstrained Exchequer could be (to some extent) relieved by using the revenues assigned to Edward, by this time a child of about 5.

Margaret's implacable hostility to the Duke of York may have been partly personal, because both had abrasive personalities, but it may also have been dynastic. York was a Prince of the Blood, who had generally been recognized as Henry's heir before the birth of the Prince of Wales and would be so again if the Prince should meet with any kind of accident. There is no evidence that York had any designs on the Crown before 1457 but the Queen was sharply suspicious and defensive of her son's position – so defensive, indeed, that the Duke and his affinity decided eventually that the only solution to her intransigence was a complete change of regime. She was almost equally fierce against the Earl of

Warwick and that was to have serious implications in due course. Although some of Margaret's aggressive assertiveness has come to us through the medium of Yorkist propaganda, there is plenty of contemporary evidence of the perception that she was the real ruler of England; 'every lord in England at this time durst not disobey the Queen, for she ruled all that was done about the King, which was a good, simple and innocent man …'[23] Her advocacy of Lawrence Booth for the vacant see of Durham in 1457 was nothing if not preremptory. By comparison, Henry appears a man bemused, most notably in public for his passivity, and in private for an almost pathetic desire to reconcile the controversies with which he was surrounded. He was nothing like as hostile to York as Margaret but he seems to have been consistently overruled by her urgent representations. When the French attacked Sandwich in August 1457 (just to remind the English that there was still a war on), Henry did insist on the court returning to Westminster, but far too late for any effective countermeasures to be taken. His greatest effort to effect reconciliation was the so-called 'love day' of 25 March 1458, which succeeded to the extent of persuading Margaret and York to process hand in hand, but in the event solved nothing.

The partisan nature of the regime was by this time not only obvious but blatant. Neither the Duke of York nor his followers were either admitted to the Council or received any kind of favour. As one observer put it '… my lord of York hath been with the king, and is departed again in right good conceit with the King, but not in great conceit with the Queen …' And therein lay the rub. Henry continued in his ineffectual way to seek some sort of conciliation, but Margaret would have none of it, and she was by this time clearly the dominant partner in the relationship. So the situation continued to deteriorate until the court left again for Coventry in the spring of 1459. By this time someone had decided that the time had come to force an issue. It was not the King, and the suspicion naturally points to Margaret but she may, in this case, have been persuaded by some of her own more extreme supporters. Whoever was responsible, at the Great Council held in Coventry in June 1459, the Duke of York and his leading adherents were indicted for treason. This was, as it may have been intended to be, the signal for a full-scale military confrontation. The two sides were reasonably well matched both in terms of magnates and of the retinues of which both armies were comprised. On 23 September the Lancastrians were defeated at Bloreheath, but about three weeks later were victorious at Ludlow. As Agnes Strickland somewhat melodramatically put it, 'the martial blood of Charlemagne was flowing in [Margaret's] veins'. With the situation thus stalemated, a parliament was convened at Coventry on 20 November, which duly convicted the indicted lords, and on 11 December all those lords who were gathered at Coventry, which meant most of the court faction, swore a special oath, not only to the King, but also to the Queen and the Prince of Wales. Henry's crown was now clearly at stake.

York, meanwhile, had returned to Ireland, where his position was unaffected by his attainder. The Earl of Ormond and Wiltshire had been appointed in his place but the King's writ no longer ran in Ireland and the parliament there continued to support the Duke. His son, the Earl of March, with other Yorkist leaders, took refuge with the Earl of Warwick in Calais, where the King's writ did not run either. Plainly the realm was now falling apart. On 26 June 1460, March and his colleagues returned to England in force and, after some deliberation, they were welcomed into London. Bypassing the Tower, which was held against them, they set out to find the King at Northampton. There they defeated Henry's forces on 10 July, killing the Duke of Buckingham in the process, and brought the King back to London. Although he was helpless and virtually a prisoner, their intention seems to have been to renew their allegiance and merely to enforce the repeal of the attainders against them. However, his son's victory brought the Duke of York back from Ireland with a very different agenda. Parliament had been summoned to meet on 7 October, and on 10 October the Duke made a formal claim to the throne on the ground of lineage alone, without reference to Henry's incapacity.[24] To his evident surprise, the assembled Lords and Commons did not accept his claim, pointing out the oaths that had been taken to Henry – and to Prince Edward. However, there was no gainsaying the strength of his position, and on 31 October a compromise was agreed whereby Henry would retain the Crown for life, but York would be recognized as his heir in place of the Prince of Wales.[25] That the King accepted this was more a reflection of his weak understanding than of his weak position, because the attitude of the Lords, in particular, had indicated that a more robust defence might have produced a very different outcome. But why should anyone risk defending a position that the principal had already surrendered?

After Henry's capture at Northampton, Margaret and Edward escaped and fled to Denbigh in north Wales, and from there retreated into Scotland. Within a few months the Queen's worst fears were confirmed. Henry had (in a sense) defended his own position but had totally failed to defend his son's. Whatever respect Margaret might have had for her husband had by now disappeared. She had for some time been the real leader of the Lancastrian party and now she was that formidable animal – a mother in defence of her child. The Duke of York made the serious mistake of thinking that his cause was now won and underestimated both the Queen and her ability to inspire devoted service. He went to the north of England inadequately supported and was defeated and killed at Wakefield on 30 December by a Lancastrian army. Despite Shakespeare's dramatic presentation of the scene, Margaret was not present at Wakefield, and was responsible for Richard's death only in the most general sense.[26] She was, however, now in the ascendant, and returned to England at the head of a mixed army of Scots and the affinities of the northern lords. Marching south, she defeated the Earl of Warwick in a second battle at St Albans on 17 February 1461 and regained control of the King. This was symbolically important because she was still, of course, operating in his name but for all the input which he was now capable of making, she might just as well not have bothered. A stark choice had now been exposed. Did the English want to be ruled by a maverick Frenchwoman in the name of her 8-year-old son or by the Earl of March, the Duke of York's eldest son who had now inherited his claim?

It was the City of London that made the critical move. Alarmed at the thought of a northern invasion, and by reports of indiscipline in the Queen's army, the citizens refused to admit her.[27] Unable either to take the city or to sustain herself in the hostile environment of the home counties, Margaret withdrew northwards. This was the signal for the Yorkists to rally and many waverers seem to have joined them on the grounds that oaths taken to Henry were now meaningless because of his supine attitude. The Earl of March was proclaimed king as Edward IV in London on 4 March, amid general acclamations. At Towton, on 29 March, he caught up with Margaret's retreating army and totally defeated it. The Queen, taking Henry and Edward with her, escaped again into Scotland. The god of battles had now spoken to the satisfaction of enough of the lords of England to enable Edward to be crowned at Westminster on 28 June 1461.

This was not the end of the war and certainly not of Margaret's involvement but it did represent a critical turning point. From now on Henry's court, in so far as it existed, was a court in exile, dependent upon the hospitality of foreign rulers who might wish to use it for their own purposes. At the same time the Queen's substantial revenues disappeared almost overnight, leaving her similarly dependent. It was Margaret's misfortune that the supportive James II of Scotland had died in 1460, leaving his young son in the hands of his mother, Mary of Gueldres. Consequently, although the ex-Queen managed to arrange the handover of Berwick to the Scots in April 1461 and apparently promised Carlisle also in return for aid, nothing was forthcoming apart from some rather grudging hospitality. Margaret is alleged to have secured a betrothal between her 8-year-old son and the even younger sister of the new King of Scots but nothing came of it. At the same time Charles VII of France, who might have been willing to help, died on 22 July 1461 and his successor, Louis XI, was much more problematic to deal with. Nevertheless in April 1462, leaving Henry in Scotland, Margaret took

Edward to France with the aid of a sympathetic French merchant, and there she managed to extract 20,000 crowns from Louis in return for a pledge to surrender Calais, but nothing significant in the way of military assistance. By this time Lancastrian support within England was withering away. This was partly because Edward IV was doing quite a good job as king and partly because there seemed to be little point in maintaining an allegiance to so useless a creature as Henry VI, who was in any case run by his wife. A Scottish invasion did eventually take place in March 1463, which rallied enough enthusiasm among the northern lords to enable them to take Alnwick and Bamburgh, but they could not hold them and the invasion soon petered out once the enthusiasm for border plundering had been satisfied.

This appears to have convinced Margaret that nothing more was to be hoped for in the north and in August 1463 she returned to France, again taking Edward with her. Whether her relationship with Henry meant anything at all by this time is not known. They had spent a great deal of time apart over the previous three or four years and had probably had no sexual relationship for a decade. After the fall of Bamburgh at the end of 1463, he had fled into Lancashire, where he was betrayed and captured early in 1464. Although when she went to France on this occasion it was with the long-term objective of recovering power, it was with Prince Edward mainly in mind, and she seems to have had no scruples about leaving Henry behind. As it transpired they were never to meet again, although letters were exchanged as long as he was at Bamburgh. Once back in France, Margaret redoubled her diplomatic efforts. She was courteously received by the Duke of Burgundy but gained no assistance and, on 8 October Louis XI came to terms with Edward IV at Hesdin, one of the conditions of which was that he should not help the Lancastrians. She retreated to her father's court at Nancy. The ageing Renée, who was beset by problems of his own, nevertheless accepted a parental responsibility to provide for her. She was assigned the chateau of Koeur in the Duchy of Bar, with 6,000 crowns a year, and remained there until 1468. She still had with her a number of English servants, both male and female, and a hard core of loyal followers, including Sir John Fortescue. The size of her household has been variously estimated at between 50 and 200 and money was always tight. Nevertheless Edward, by this time 11 years old, was apparently given an education suitable to his status and prospects and seems to have grown into a rather warlike youth. Meanwhile Louis's relations with Edward IV had deteriorated again and the French king began to fish in troubled waters. Taking advantage of strains developing in the relationship of the English king with his erstwhile backer, the Earl of Warwick, Louis began to correspond with the latter as early as May 1467.[28] The intention, which was not yet clearly formed, was to detach Warwick and the King's brother the Duke of Clarence, with whom he was closely allied, from Edward's allegiance, and to use them to restore Henry VI. When the English King signed a new treaty with Philip of Burgundy in 1468, sealed by the marriage of Philip's heir to the King's sister, Louis' intentions hardened.

One obstacle in the way of his proposed intention was the implacable hostility of Margaret towards Warwick. It would be difficult to restore Henry without her collaboration but so well known were her feelings that she seems not even to have been appraised of the negotiation at this stage. That was probably just as well because when Warwick and Clarence raised a rebellion in England in 1469, surprising and capturing the King, their intentions remained opaque. It appears that Clarence may have been intending to press his own claim and nothing was said about Henry. The latter had been in the Tower since his capture at Waddington Hall and the defeat of the last of his armies at Hexham in 1464 and it may have been doubted whether he any longer had even residual credibility. In any case, his claim was not advanced and the rebellion collapsed in confusion, Edward being somewhat inclined to treat it as a bad joke. Baffled, but less defeated than the King believed, Warwick and Clarence retreated to Calais. Having learned from this frustrating experience, the former now made two decisions: first, that he would commit himself to Henry and, second, that he would come to terms with Margaret. Meeting with Louis, he agreed a plan of action, whereby he was to restore Henry with French military assistance and in return would enter into an alliance with Louis against Philip of Burgundy. Prince Edward would accompany him to England and would marry his daughter, Anne. Margaret, however, was not in a co-operative mood. She would at first not hear of the marriage arrangement and was not prepared to allow Edward to go with Warwick. With considerable difficulty, Louis managed to arrange a meeting between the two, at which a formal reconciliation took place – not without some self-abasement on Warwick's part. Anne and Edward were betrothed and actually married at Amboise in August 1470. It was agreed that the Prince would go to England, but only in his mother's company and after the real work had been done.

On 9 September 1470 the planned invasion took place. Submerged Lancastrian sentiment at once sprang to life and Warwick was able to recruit several noble retinues to his modest army. Meanwhile King Edward, quite inexcusably unprepared, was in Yorkshire. Warwick advanced on London, which received him, if not with joy, at least without hostility. The hapless Henry VI was taken out of the Tower and paraded at St Paul's as king. What he thought of the proceedings (if anything) is not known. Meanwhile Edward, caught by the treachery of Lord Montague, was left virtually defenceless against the Lancastrian advance.

Accompanied by his brother Richard and Lord Hastings, he fled to King's Lynn and crossed to Burgundy.[29] It appeared that Warwick's victory was complete and virtually bloodless. He began reshaping the government and addressed himself to the promised French alliance. Attainders were reversed at a parliament that convened on 26 November and new appointments were made. However, relations with the Duke of Clarence became strained as the latter received less than he considered to be his due, and a potentially serious rift began to open in the restored Lancastrian regime. Meanwhile Margaret hesitated, apparently unconvinced by the ease of Warwick's triumph and King Edward, with Burgundian support, planned his return. Philip knew perfectly well that if Henry became firmly re-established he would have a war with England on his hands, whereas if Edward were restored they would be friends. He also found his brother-in-law's presence in his territories an embarrassment. Consequently, he sent him on his way as soon as possible, with his blessing and a few troops. On 16 March Edward landed on the Yorkshire coast.

This time confusion and treachery favoured him because many Lancastrian lords were hostile to Warwick, and, although not prepared to fight against him, would not declare their allegiance until Margaret arrived to claim it. A game of blind man's buff ensued around Coventry, where news reached both sides that Clarence had abandoned Warwick and declared for his brother. In these circumstances the earl was not prepared to risk battle and Edward was allowed to proceed towards London unresisted. Nothing succeeds like success, and his forces were swelled by fresh retinues as they advanced. He reached the capital on 11 April and recovered the person of his ostensible rival, Henry. At the same time news reached Warwick that Louis had signed a three-month truce with the Burgundians. Just at the moment when he most needed them, neither of his main props were available. The French king had withdrawn and Margaret was still stuck at Harfleur. Until she arrived, neither the Duke of Somerset, nor the Earl of Devon nor the Earl of Pembroke would join him. Warwick had no option now but to risk battle, even on unfavourable terms, and advanced to Barnet where, on 13 April, he confronted Edward's forces coming from London. The result was an annihilating defeat and his own death. On the same day, Margaret, whose timely arrival might have saved the day, landed with Edward at Weymouth. Confronted with the news from Barnet, a lesser woman might well have re-embarked and returned to France but Margaret was made of sterner stuff. With the courage for which she had always been famous, she went to Exeter and marched north, recruiting men as she went, and this time the Duke of Somerset and the Earl of Devon were with her. Her intention seems to have been to cross into Wales to join forces with the Earl of Pembroke, but Edward, who was in hot pursuit, caught up with her forces at Tewkesbury on 4 May. The result was even more lethal than Barnet. Prince Edward, the Earl of Devon and numerous other lords and gentlemen died on the field of battle. Margaret and the Duke of Somerset were captured and the latter was executed on 6 May.[30] Edward re-entered his capital in triumph on 21 May, and that same night, ex-King Henry died in the Tower in mysterious circumstances but probably on Edward's orders.

Totally defeated, and with neither son nor husband left to her, Margaret remained in captivity in London until 1475, her plight only marginally alleviated by the efforts of her former waiting woman, Elizabeth, now Queen. When Edward signed the peace of Pequingy with Louis in the latter year, one of the conditions was that that the French King should take this unwanted dowager off his hands and she was ransomed for 50,000 crowns. Margaret renounced all claims in England and returned to France in January 1476. Her father, by now an old man, appears to have ceded his interests in Provence to Louis to secure her redemption and the King behaved decently towards his cousin. He made her renounce any possible claims that may have lingered from the days when she was theoretically queen of a large part of France and then made her an allowance of 6,000 crowns a year – the same that she had received before Henry's ill-fated readeption. By this time Margaret no longer had even the semblance of a court although a few die-hard Lancastrians still clung to her. Her entourage is alleged to have consisted of three ladies and seven gentlemen. Among these were some of the faithful women who had served her as Queen and when she came to make her will in August 1482, just a few days before her death, one of the witnesses was Margaret Vaux, who had been widowed at Tewkesbury, just a few days before her mistress. Even in her years of misfortune, Margaret still had the capacity to inspire devoted service.

Despite the fact that we know quite a lot about her political activities and over 80 of her letters survive, there are aspects of Margaret's personality that remain impenetrable. Her piety appears to have been conventional and the friendships that she formed mostly opportunist. Sex does not seem to have interested her. It took eight years of marriage to Henry before she conceived and after his collapse she seems to have lived a life of celibacy. The only scandal that ever touched her was a supposed liaison with the Duke of Suffolk in the 1440s and that was a mere slander aimed at Suffolk. She was quite unlike Catherine de Valois in that respect, being noted for her courage, cleverness and determination rather than for more typically feminine qualities. She was patroness of the Guild of Silkwomen, but did not, as far as we know, show any skill in that direction herself. She fitted out ships at her own expense to trade into the Mediterranean but that was not a particularly feminine accomplishment either. For a few years she wielded, by the sheer force of personality, real political power in a way she was not supposed to do as a mere consort, and she dominated the husband she was supposed to serve and revere. Edward IV is alleged to have said that 'he feared her more as a fugitive, and in want of the absolute necessities of life, than he did all the princes of the House of Lancaster combined'. As a consequence her historical reputation suffered severely, in England at least, and although George Chatellain's Burgundian chronicle praised her generously, in England she is best known through Shakespeare's plays. The chronicles from which the dramatist took his information were Yorkist and Tudor propaganda, where she appears as a termagent, cruel and cunning. In truth she was neither of these things, but circumstances did make a dominatrix, and as a mother she fought tooth and nail for the rights of her son. With a different husband and in other circumstances she might have been remembered more kindly but, as it is, she appears as an heroic and rather tragic figure, quite distinct from the other consorts of the period.

3

The Queen as Lover: Elizabeth Woodville

Edward IV's marriage to Elizabeth Grey (née Woodville) in 1464 created a highly unusual situation. Never before had a ruling king of England married one of his own subjects. The normal practice, both for rulers and potential rulers, had been to take a bride from one of the princely houses of western Europe, as had been the case with Margaret, Catherine, Anne of Bohemia or Philippa of Hainault. Henry Bolingbroke had married Mary Bohun long before there was any prospect of his becoming king and she had died by 1394. Edward the Black Prince had married Joan, daughter of the Earl of Kent, but he had never come to the throne at all. Consequently the normal protocols did not apply to Edward. There were no diplomatic hints, no cautious reactions and no complex negotiations. No dowry was in question and there were no foreign policy implications, except in a purely negative sense. The King of England had taken himself off the marriage market, so no alliance could be strengthened or peace mediated by that means. Neither Henry V nor Henry VI had seen the girls they were committed to until all the formalities had been completed and the nature of the relationship that followed had to be worked out step by step. Edward married Elizabeth because he wanted her and, if the rumours were true, had sought her as his mistress before he was constrained to marry her. In short their coming together was much more typical of the way in which ordinary young people met and fell in love than it was of a royal marriage – except in one very important respect. An ordinary bride was given away by her kinsfolk in a public ceremony, whereas in this case the marriage was kept so secret that it is not even certain that the bride's father knew what was happening. Edward was a notorious womanizer and the story that Elizabeth defended her honour with a dagger is credible, but if she traded her body for the status of queen they both did pretty well out of the deal. In a marriage that was to last for 19 years, she presented him with no fewer than ten children, which means that she must have been pregnant or convalescent well over half the time, a factor that needs to be borne in mind when the rest of her activities are assessed.

Elizabeth was the elder daughter of Sir Richard Woodville, a gentleman of limited means who had been a household knight and servant to John, Duke of Bedford, the younger brother of King Henry V, who had died in 1435. He was apparently a very handsome young man, and the Duchess, Jacquetta of Luxembourg, held him in high esteem. So high, indeed, that shortly after the Duke's death she married him. Jacquetta was the sister of the Count of St Pol, and came of the highest European nobility, so the marriage was a misalliance similar to that which Catherine de Valois had perpetrated in marrying Owain Tudur. There was, however, nothing morganatic about their union, which was publicly acknowledged, much to the rage of the Count and the rest of her family. She was, however, sufficiently close to the royal family to have needed the King's licence, and in March 1437 Sir Richard was fined the massive sum of £1,000 for having ignored that precaution and for livery of her dower, which was no doubt substantial enough to pay the fine.[1] By the time that happened Jacquetta must already have been pregnant with Elizabeth, who was born before the end of that year. The nature of her relationship with the duke is unknown but she had borne him no children and her need is plain. The fact that she proceeded to bear Sir Richard five sons and six daughters tells its own story.

Nothing very much is known about Elizabeth's upbringing but she presumably received the conventional education of a young gentlewoman, strong on piety and the domestic virtues but not conspicuous for 'book learning'. She was literate in English and probably in French, but not in Latin, which she only acquired partially and later. Despite her remarriage, her mother was still *persona grata* at court. She was one of the noble ladies sent to escort the young Queen Margaret to England in 1445 and shortly afterwards managed to attach young Elizabeth to the Queen's household as a *demoiselle d'honneur*. This would probably not have happened until she was of a marriageable age and can therefore be tentatively dated to 1449. She seems to have been a very attractive girl and was first sought in marriage by Sir Hugh Johns. Although Johns's suit was promoted by both the Duke of York and the Earl of Warwick, he found no favour. Elizabeth apparently did not fancy him and his backers came out of the wrong political stable to find any favour with Queen Margaret between 1450 and 1453, when this is alleged to have happened.

In fact she was not rushed into marriage at all but, in about 1456, at the relatively mature age of 19, she married John Grey, the son and heir of Edward, Lord Ferrers of Groby. This was a very suitable match for a young lady of her status and connections and argues the management of Sir Richard and his wife, although Elizabeth seems to have been sufficiently strong minded to veto the suggestion if the proposed groom had not appealed. Both Lord Ferrers and his son were good Lancastrians, and that mattered by 1456. Various manors in Northamptonshire and Essex were settled on the young couple and when Lord Ferrers died, on 18 December 1457, John inherited his title and with it the splendid estate of Bradgate in Leicestershire, where Elizabeth took up her residence. The new Lord Ferrers, however, was sufficiently committed to the King to be a fighting man, and on 17 February 1461 was severely injured at the second battle of St Albans. He died of his injuries on the 28 February, leaving Elizabeth as a young widow with two small sons. More importantly, she was on the wrong side of the tracks. St Albans had been a Lancastrian victory and Margaret had recovered control of her husband. This had virtually forced the young Earl of March into advancing his own claim and, because he swiftly secured control of London, it was there that he was proclaimed on 4 March. For about three weeks there were two kings in England but Edward's victory at Towton on 29 March proved decisive. The forces of Lancaster were reduced to a remnant, and Henry and Margaret became fugitives. Posthumously, Lord Ferrers became a traitor and his estate was forfeit. The Crown seized Bradgate, and Elizabeth and her family, in much reduced circumstances, were forced to retreat to her dower manor of Grafton. She was 24.

How much Edward may have known about Elizabeth at this point is not clear. He certainly knew Richard and Jacquetta and was on good terms with them in spite of the latter's Lancastrian connections. In the first year of his reign he made them a grant of £100 'by especial royal grace' for no known reason apart from general goodwill, so it is entirely likely that he had fallen for the charms of their young widowed daughter well before he famously encountered her in 1464. At that time he was 22 and one of the most eligible bachelors in Europe. He had also been on the marriage market almost from the day of his birth. In 1445 his father had tried to match him with Princess Madeleine of France (then aged 18 months) and in 1458 he had been dangled under the nose of Philip of Burgundy. Neither of these approaches had been successful but in 1461 the Burgundian proposal had been revived, the target in this case being specifically Philip's beautiful niece. That did not work either, but once Edward was on the throne the managerial Earl of Warwick tried to turn his unmarried status to political advantage, proposing first an improbable union with the Queen Mother of Scotland and then another French princess. As recently as February 1464 Henry of Castile had taken the initiative of proposing his own sister. It may have been that the King found these pressures intolerable and resented the presumption of the Earl of Warwick but, in April 1464, he decided to take his destiny into his own hands. On his way north to deal with the Lancastrians who were later to be defeated at Hexham he stopped at Stony Stratford and on 30 April he slipped away from his entourage and rode over to Grafton Regis, where Richard Woodville was presumably expecting him. Meanwhile Elizabeth was mired in lawsuits as she strove to recover some part of the Grey inheritance. The trouble was that John had been on the wrong side and it was only by a personal appeal to the King that she could hope to obtain redress. Apparently she had done a deal with Lord Hastings to obtain access to Edward but in the event he came to her instead.[2] According to romantically inclined chroniclers they met very early in the morning in Whittlebury Forest near Grafton, by chance as it would seem. The reality is likely to have been more prosaic and they probably met at Grafton at a more seasonable hour, perhaps by Richard's mediation but more likely by Jacquetta's. As a result, Thomas Grey, her elder son, was recognized as his father's heir, and Edward married Elizabeth in the presence of some half dozen people, including Jacquetta and the priest. Although the King's action bears all the marks of spontaneity, it is highly unlikely that his decision was as unpremeditated as it was made to appear. He knew enough of Elizabeth to know that he wanted her and she knew enough of his intentions to be prepared for them. Where Edward made his mistake was in keeping quiet about what had happened. He had (it would seem) nothing to be ashamed of – except that he had torn up the rule book insofar as it applied to royal marriages. It was not until September, four months later, when he was being pressed to marry Bona of Savoy, that he confessed what had happened.

Charles Ross described his marriage as 'the first major blunder of his political career' and pointed out that he had no need to marry 'this unsuitable widow' in order to assert his independence from the Earl of Warwick's control. If he had simply wanted to avoid the diplomatic entanglements of a foreign match, there were plenty of ladies available among the higher nobility. That, however, was not the point. He wanted Elizabeth and felt entitled to please himself.

'Now take heed what love may do' wrote the chronicler Gregory, 'for love will not nor may not cast no fault nor peril in no thing.'[3]

He knew perfectly well that if he had asked the advice of his council, they would have told him that the idea was unacceptable – so he did not ask them. This was unconventional but not in any sense unlawful. It may also have been in his mind that his realm was full of powerful affinities and if he had chosen his bride amongst the high aristocracy, he would inevitably have strengthened her kindred and offended others who felt equally deserving. There was a great deal to be said for looking right outside the system – and offending them all equally. Similar considerations applied to finding a bride abroad. If he had chosen within the Burgundian camp he could expect trouble from the French and if he had married a French wife the Duke of Burgundy would have been mortally offended. A Spanish or Italian princess might have resolved that issue but he did not want to look so far afield. There was a lot to be said for a queen whose kindred were unpretentious and could be used or not as the King might decide. As well as gratifying him sexually Elizabeth also provided him with a numerous family, which he could use or not as he chose, without having another powerful affinity breathing down his neck. Although Edward paid a price for his unusual behaviour there really was quite a lot to be said for Elizabeth.

However defensible the King's actions may have been, they attracted nothing but disapprobation at the time. In describing the Council's reaction to the news, Jean de Waurin wrote:

> ... they answered that she was not his match, however good and however fair she might be, and he must know well that she was no wife for a prince such as himself; for she was not the daughter of a Duke or an Earl, but her mother, the Duchess of Bedford had married a simple knight, so that although she was the child of a duchess and the niece of the Count of St.Pol, still she was no wife for him.[4]

Edward must have expected this reaction. The reason for his delay in making the news public was less embarrassment at having acted on impulse than a desire to give her time to acclimatize herself to the idea before being exposed to the role of royal consort. In other circumstances he might have waited a lot longer, but in the summer Louis XI started signalling that he wanted closer contacts with England. He began, not perhaps very wisely, to flatter the Earl of Warwick, seeing in him the real manager of English policy. It was through negotiations that were so initiated that the marriage offer of Bona of Savoy arose. Bona was not strictly a member of the royal family, being the daughter of the Duke of Savoy, but she was Louis' sister in law, and thus of his extended kindred. The offer was attractive to Warwick, who made positive signals, but he was not authorized to negotiate so important a matter on the King's behalf. The discussions were postponed, first to 8 June and then until the 1 October. During September, therefore, Edward had to declare himself, and either issue instructions for the marriage to be concluded – or not. The King met his Council about the middle of the month and revealed his true situation. On Michaelmas Day, 29 September, Elizabeth was formally presented to the court as Queen in Reading Abbey.[5]

Politically, the reaction was not as hostile as Edward might have feared. As Waurin makes clear, there was a great deal of 'tutting'. Both the Queen Mother and the Duke of Gloucester are supposed to have been offended but as the Duke was barely 12 years old at the time his opinion need not be taken too seriously. Both the Earl of Warwick and the Duke of Clarence took part in the Queen's 'coming out' and although Warwick is later supposed to have been seriously antagonized he did not show much sign of it at the time. The person who had the best reason to be upset was Louis XI, but he seems to have shrugged the whole affair off as diplomatic hitch and continued to pursue the idea of an alliance. It was 10 October before he finally learned that his conference was not going to resume but he was not unduly discouraged and kept up his contacts with Warwick. It is possible that both the King of France and the Earl began to look askance at the King of England at this time but their overt hostility came much later and in other political circumstances. Elizabeth was crowned with due pomp at Westminster on 26 May 1465, when Edward made the most conscientious efforts to elevate her in the public estimation. Not only were large sums spent on cloth of gold, and upon scarlet and gold uniforms for the heralds, but more than 40 new knights of the Bath were created (more than at Edward's own coronation) and the occasion was graced with the attendance of the Queen's uncle, Jacques de Luxembourg. Jacques played a prominent part in the coronation tournament but the real purpose of his presence was to emphasize Elizabeth's European status, via her mother.[6] She must have been in the early stages of pregnancy at the time of her crowning because the eldest child of her second marriage was born on 26 February 1466. The young Elizabeth's baptism was used as an occasion for a display of 'togetherness', perhaps aimed at a sceptical public. Her godmothers were her two grandmothers, Cecily Duchess of York and Jacquetta of Luxembourg, who were popularly supposed not to be on speaking terms, while the godfather was none other than the Earl of Warwick. The fact that she was a daughter may have caused a certain amount of headwagging because both of Elizabeth's children by her first marriage had been sons but the opportunity for a little family solidarity was not lost. However, two years into her marriage to the King, she had not yet presented him with an heir.

It has sometimes been suggested that Edward immediately set out to build up his wife's large family into a political faction, capable of balancing the Nevilles, or his own brothers, but there is little sign of that. What he did was to establish an aristocratic context for Elizabeth by securing marriages for her numerous unprovided sisters. Over the next few years Margaret was wedded to Thomas, Lord Maltravers, the heir to the Earl of Arundel; Anne to William, Viscount Bourchier, heir to the Earl of Essex, Jacquetta to John, Lord Strange of Knockin; Catherine to Henry Stafford, grandson and heir to the Duke of Buckingham; Mary to William Herbert (Lord Dunster), heir to Lord Herbert and Eleanor to Anthony, Lord Grey of Ruthin, heir to the Earl of Kent. Not all these unions were obtained without a certain amount of arm twisting and it was alleged that the Woodville girls had exhausted the pool of eligible young noblemen. However the kinship established through their wives did not in any sense pull these men together into a coherent party and apart from causing a certain amount of resentment among other noblemen with daughters to dispose of – notably the Earl of Warwick – its impact upon the political scene was negligible. No doubt it was more noticeable at court, but none of these ladies appear to have been the dominant parties in their several relationships. The Queen's involvement in brokering these deals varied but it was undoubtedly she who brought about the union between her 20-year-old brother, John, and the Dowager Duchess of Norfolk, who was about 65. Katherine de Mowbray (nee Neville) was extremely wealthy and had already survived three husbands. She was also the aunt of the Earl of Warwick and it may well have been this shameless piece of exploitation, which took place in January 1565, which turned Warwick against the Queen, rather than her marriage to Edward.[7] Elizabeth also seems to have been entirely responsible for a deal in October 1466 whereby she paid the King's sister Anne, Duchess of Exeter, 4000 marks to marry her daughter and heir (also Anne) to her own elder son, Thomas Grey. At the time Anne was already betrothed to Warwick's nephew, George Neville, the son and heir to the Earl of Northumberland.[8] The Earl of Warwick was not directly involved, but again the rather heavy-handed tactics that were employed argues a distinct lack of sensibility to Neville's interests – and honour – on the part of the Queen. At the same time, when the Earl sought to marry his eldest daughter to the Duke of Clarence, the King refused to give his consent – and so the tally of niggling grievances built up.

Apart from these matrimonial manipulations, Edward neither directly nor indirectly did much to favour the Woodville clan. Most obviously the Queen's father, Richard, was appointed to the lucrative office of Treasurer of England in March 1466 and created Earl Rivers in May. In August 1567 he succeeded the Earl of Worcester as Constable of England, and these offices together are calculated to have brought him an income of about £1,300 a year.[9] However he received no lands, and the increase in his wealth did not compare with the increments awarded to the Nevilles, or to Lord Hastings in the first year or two of the reign. Perhaps the King judged that the massive dower lands of the Duchess Jacquetta were more than sufficient to uphold the status of the King's father-in-law. Anthony, Richard's eldest son, was already married to Elizabeth, the heiress of Thomas Lord Scales and became Lord Scales in right of his wife when Thomas died. In November 1466 he was given the Lordship of the Isle of Wight and the Keepership of Carisbrooke castle but this was no more than a modest token of confidence. Anthony's younger brothers, Sir Edward and Sir Richard Woodville, seem to have gained nothing from their sister's elevation. The youngest member of the family, Lionel, was a priest who became dean of Exeter in 1478 at the age of 25 and Bishop of Salisbury four years later, both of which appointments he owed to the King's patronage.[10] Consequently, it cannot be fairly claimed that Edward either drained the resources of the Crown to provide for his wife's kindred, nor that he sought to create a party out of them to balance the Nevilles. In fact in 1465–6 he was still making far greater grants to the latter than ever came the way of the Woodvilles. No one had been starved of royal patronage to feed the Queen's relations.

Nor were the Queen's own revenues granted with a lavish or ill considered hand. After careful consultation with the Council, dower land to the value of £4,541 was settled on her, drawn mainly from the Duchy of Lancaster.[11] This was significantly less than the 10,000 marks (£6,600) that had been awarded to her predecessor, but it was secure revenue, and was several times adjusted upwards. With careful management Elizabeth was able to maintain her household on a lavish scale, and to dispense her own patronage generously. The main beneficiaries were her servants, to whom she remained conspicuously loyal, and the remoter members of her family – cousins usually – who did not come within the range of direct royal bounty. Apart from securing his marriage, and his rights of inheritance, there was not much at this time that she could do for Thomas, her elder son, who was only about 10 years old, and Richard, the younger, does not feature at all. Yet despite all this evidence of restraint and good management, Elizabeth undoubtedly remained very unpopular, and the question remains as to why this should have been so. Her direct political influence was very slight. She stood for no programme and had no agenda and yet the evidence of dislike is contemporary and does not depend upon later Yorkist and Tudor mythology. This was partly due to sheer snobbishness against her parvenue status. Despite all that Edward could do, and despite the fact that Richard had been created a baron by Henry VI in 1448, Elizabeth was seen and represented as the daughter of a 'mere knight'. It was also partly due to her own personality. In spite of her obvious sex appeal, she seems to have been a chilly and unamiable creature, very much wrapped up in her own affairs. Her patronage was always calculated to enhance her own position and the unattractive side of her good household management was a tight-fisted acquisitiveness. She was a generous patron of Queens' College, Cambridge and is seen as its co-founder, but that seems to have been occasioned less by an enthusiasm for education than from a desire to blot out the memory of her predecessor. With the possible exception of Lord Scales, the rest of her family showed similar characteristics, as the persecution of Sir Thomas Cook by Lord Rivers and his wife in 1468 appears to demonstrate. Cook, a former Lord Mayor of London, seems to have had Lancastrian sympathies, although in what ways these had been manifested is not clear. He was accused of treason at the instance of Lord Rivers and imprisoned. While he was in prison his house was ransacked by servants of Rivers and various property was stolen, apparently for the benefit of Lady Rivers. When he was brought to trial, Cook was acquitted, but found guilty of the lesser crime of misprision and fined £5,000. In response to his complaint, an independent commission was then appointed to assess the damage inflicted by Rivers and set it against his fine, but before this reported the Queen demanded the ancient (but largely forgotten) right of 'Queen's gold' to the tune of another £600, which he was compelled to pay. Not surprisingly, Cook became an even more enthusiastic Lancastrian and petitioned the readeption parliament in 1470 for losses of £14,666. The source of this story is Robert Fabyan's *Chronicle*, so it cannot be accepted entirely at face value.[12] However, Fabyan claims to have been Cook's apprentice at the time and as told it is full of circumstantial detail. The villain was clearly Rivers, but neither Edward nor Elizabeth emerge with any credit. It may not be irrelevant that the rebels executed the Earl in 1469 but there is no trace of the ill feeling that might have been expected to result between London and the King. What is most significant is that a story against the Queen's family, although almost certainly distorted and exaggerated, should have been relayed and accepted in such an authoritative way. It is probably fair to conclude that, although the King took no steps to convert the Woodville family into an aristocratic affinity, they nevertheless saw themselves in that light. There is some supporting evidence for that in the marriage agreements concluded on behalf of the Queen's sisters, which show Rivers trading favours on terms of equality with the great houses into which the young ladies were marrying. They may not have been particularly powerful in fact, but their pretensions grated and they did not carry their good fortune graciously.

When Edward was suddenly overwhelmed by rebellion in the summer of 1469, Elizabeth was safely ensconced in the Tower. The Earl of Warwick's objective seems to have been to recover control over the King, as though he had been no more *compos mentis* than Henry VI, but all he managed to achieve was the resolution of his private vendetta against the Woodvilles and their allies. On 25 July he had the better of a confused and sanguinary battle near Banbury, captured the King and executed (without any semblance of judicial process) the Earl of Devon, Earl Rivers, Sir John Woodville and Sir Thomas Herbert.[13] Warwick's more general political objectives are obscure. He endeavoured to call a parliament to York and may have been intending to depose Edward in favour of his brother the Duke of Clarence but he was not really in command of the situation and when Edward escaped from Middleham Castle in September, it seems that he decided to settle for a bargain. He had demonstrated that although he could obtain a temporary ascendancy, he could not obtain sufficient support to remove Edward – least of all in favour of Clarence. Moreover he had no appealing agenda. There were grievances out there to be exploited but he made no attempt to do so. His aims, as one scholar has observed, remained entirely and obviously selfish. On the other hand his lawless behaviour had earned him no punishment, because the King was bent on reconciliation.

[Edward] 'regarded nothing more than to win again the friendship of such noblemen as were now alienated from him, to confirm the goodwill of them that were hovering and inconstant, and to reduce the mind of the multitude ... unto their late obedience, affection and goodwill towards him.'[14]

So Warwick ended up more or less where he had started, a great nobleman and influential about the King but by no means enjoying the power that he coveted. The king was also now warned that he could not trust his erstwhile ally and the Queen, who had never had much affection for the Nevilles, was now bitterly alienated by the deaths of her father and uncle. Elizabeth does not appear very much in the discussions of these events but she was a good hater and she was spending time in her husband's company in February 1470 because that was when their next child was conceived.

Warwick undoubtedly realized that he had earned the bitter hostility of the Queen and may for that reason not entirely have trusted Edward's conciliatory pose. From his point of view he had merely scotched the Woodville snake and might in the process have made it even more dangerous. For whatever reason, when rebellion broke out in Lincolnshire, in March 1470, he decided to abandon his temporary reconciliation, and try again. Some of his and Clarence's retinues were already with the rebels when they were defeated near Stamford on 12 March. Warwick, however, had miscalculated badly. The rebellion was suppressed and no other major nobleman joined them in supporting it, so they had exposed themselves for nothing. On 24 March Edward issued a proclamation against them and they fled by devious routes to Calais. Refused entry there, but backed by a formidable fleet, Warwick and Clarence replenished their coffers with a little piracy and then, running out of other options, decided to seek the assistance of the King of France. Although it may have been forced upon them, this was a critical decision, because Louis was seeking a complete regime change in England in order to install a government sympathetic to himself and hostile to the Duke of Burgundy. This could only be accomplished if Clarence abandoned his claim, and the pair worked together for a restoration of Henry VI, then a prisoner in the Tower. As we have seen, a difficult negotiation with Margaret of Anjou successfully accomplished this change of allegiance and Warwick sailed from La Hogue with French and Lancastrian backing on 9 September, landing in Devon a couple of days later.[15] In the light of their two previous experiences, the result this time was truly astonishing. Three weeks later, on 2 October, after a series of misfortunes and miscalculations, Edward fled from King's Lynn to the Low Countries.

During the summer of 1470, as Edward was away in the north and her pregnancy steadily developed, Elizabeth remained ensconced in the royal apartments at the Tower, but when news of his precipitate flight reached her, she hastily transferred herself and her three young daughters to the safety of the sanctuary at Westminster. Although this misfortune might eventually cut off all her resources, for the time being she was well provided for, being accompanied by a large number of servants and several wagon loads of household goods. There, on 1 November, she gave birth to a son, who was promptly named Edward for his absent father. She was now the proud mother of an heir to the throne – if he eventually had any throne to inherit. The exiled king was speedily appraised of this happy event and indeed the exchange of letters between the royal couple seems not to have been greatly impeded by the circumstances of their separation. For the first time in her life, Elizabeth found herself popular. What has been called the 'feminine helplessness' of a newly delivered mother may have contributed to this but it was also the case that the restored government of Henry VI neither pleased nor impressed the Londoners, and expressing sympathy for Elizabeth was a low key way of dissenting. After her ordeal was over, several of her more prominent helpers were suitably rewarded. One Margaret Cobb (who may have been her midwife) was granted an annuity of £12; Dr Sergio, her physician received £40; a butcher named Gould who had kept her modest household supplied with meat, was allowed to lade a royal ship with tallow free of charge; and Abbot Thomas Milling, who had welcomed and protected her, was made Bishop of Hereford.

While his queen languished helplessly in sanctuary, Edward busied himself about the recovery of his kingdom. Duke Charles of Burgundy had been less than delighted to find his brother-in-law as a fugitive in his domain, and it was left to Louis of Bruges, within whose immediate jurisdiction the King had landed, to extend the hand of welcome. Although Charles was at war with France, and had every reason to fear the disposition of the new government in England, his first reaction was to conciliate Warwick rather than to help Edward. However, either by the persuasions of his wife, or by the logic of circumstance, his mind was changed. On 26 December 1470 he welcomed Edward to his court, and over the next few days a deal was done between them. Although he would not publicly make any statement in his support, nevertheless he would give him 50,000 florins (£20,000) and fit out three or four ships for him. Edward deployed his money to good effect, and on 11 March was able to leave Flushing with 36 ships and about 1,200 men, including several gunners.[16] He had also re-established contact with his brother and was reasonably confident that Clarence would support him once he had shown his hand. Meanwhile Warwick was expecting him, but having considerable difficulty in making defensive preparations. For a variety of reasons, his support was very limited and as he tried to mobilize against Edward that became abundantly clear. On 14 March the returning exile landed at Ravenspur on the Humber, in what should theoretically have been hostile territory. However the Earl of Northumberland, who was strong in the region, held his hand, and Edward was able to bluff his way into York. As other equivocators like Lord Montague continued to hold back, Edward moved south, and his support continued to grow. Most critically he was joined at Leicester by 3,000 men under Lord Hastings. On 2 April Clarence finally declared himself and, bypassing Warwick, who was then at Coventry, the King headed for London

The capital was divided, but Edward's supporters proved the stronger, and the Common Council resolved that 'as Edward late King of England was hastening towards the city with a powerful army, and as the inhabitants were not sufficiently versed in the use of arms to withstand so large a force, no attempt should be made to resist him ...'

Despite the equivocal use of 'late' in describing the King, this declaration was sufficient, and on 11 April 1471 Edward entered the city, securing in the process the person of his rival and several of the latter's more prominent supporters. He was also reunited with the wife, whom he had not seen for over a year, and introduced to his 6-month-old son. Elizabeth promptly moved out of the sanctuary, which had been her home for about eight months, and returned to the Tower. Although his supporters were now flocking to him, and his grip on London was secure, the Earl of Warwick remained unfought, and Margaret of Anjou still lurked in the wings. There was much to do. On 13 March Edward moved out of the city towards St Albans aware that Warwick was advancing. The following day, which was Easter Sunday, the two armies met at Barnet, and the Lancastrians were routed, both the Earl of Warwick and Lord Montague being killed on the field.[17] It was as decisive a victory as could well have been wished for and Edward had the bodies of his enemies displayed in St.Pauls. Two days later the news reached him that Margaret had landed at Weymouth and that the old Lancastrians were rallying to her. Instead of being able to enjoy his victory, he had now to pick up this fresh challenge. As Margaret and her son moved north from Exeter to Bristol, apparently well supported, and headed for the Severn to cross into Wales, Edward set off in hot pursuit, and after a number of false sightings finally caught up with her at Tewkesbury on 4 May. There he won an equally decisive victory, capturing Margaret and killing the Prince of Wales on the field.

It must have appeared at first that his victory was now total and secure but while he was occupied at Tewkesbury, fresh Lancastrian risings took place both in the north and in Kent. Thomas Neville, an illegitimate son of the Earl of Kent, known as the Bastard Faulconberg, had raised the county and was attacking London. The Queen, it was reported, was besieged in the Tower of London. In fact it did not quite come to that. Although the Bastard was supported by a number of armed ships, the Londoners feared a sack and resisted resolutely, until on 14 May Earl Rivers who was in command of the Tower, led a sortie which drove the attackers back. Reports that Edward himself was on his way with his victorious army finally demoralised the Kentishmen and they fled, the bastard himself escaping to Calais. On the same day, as he awaited reinforcements at Coventry, the news reached Edward that the northern rebellion had petered out. Partly because they had learned of the disaster at Tewkesbury and partly because the Earl of Northumberland remained loyal, it now appeared to the local leaders that they had neither a cause nor a captain and they laid down their arms and began to sue for pardon.[18] After this, there was only some tidying up to be done, like securing the submission of Calais, which was achieved during July. As Henry VI had died on the night of Edward's return to London from Coventry, his son had died at Tewkesbury, and Margaret was safely imprisoned, the Lancastrian challenge remained only in the obscure and fugitive figure of Henry of Richmond. For the next 12 years, England enjoyed an interval of peace.

In 1472 Louis of Bruges visited England at the King's invitation and was created Earl of Wiltshire as a gesture of gratitude for his help and support. In the journal of his visit, which was kept by a secretary, we get a number of glimpses of life at the English court. Elizabeth, as might be expected, features regularly in his account, but never doing anything of political significance. She attends lavish banquets, introduces the visitors to her children and is on one occasion surprised playing at marbles and ninepins with her ladies. Her second son, Richard, was born in August 1473, and she is noted to have offered with the King at the shrine of St. Edward at Westminster. Her mother, Jacquetta, died in 1472, causing her considerable distress, and she accompanied Edward on his visits to Oxford. There was, however, rather more to Elizabeth than this domestic routine might indicate. Her revenues were further, although not dramatically, augmented, and it was noted in 1475 that her influence in East Anglia was so great that she was 'regarded as one of the main instruments of royal policy'[19] in that area. In that year also, while the King was pursuing his brief and abortive war with France, which was ended at Picquigny on 29 August, Elizabeth was named as Governor of the Realm in his absence. She was probably a compromise candidate for this particular job, because Edward was not anxious to exalt any of his already powerful nobles to such a position. Nevertheless her appointment indicates a level of political involvement that would not be expected from the record of her activities. There was much resentment among the English military at the tame outcome of this confrontation but neither Elizabeth nor the King himself had to cope with any significant disturbances.

Meanwhile, the Queen went on bearing children. By the time that Edward returned from the wilderness she had produced three daughters and one son, all of them alive and well. In 1472 she bore another daughter, Margaret, who lived only a short while, and in 1473 (as we have seen) a second son, Richard. There then followed Anne (1475), George (1477), Catherine (1479) and Bridget (1480), of whom only George died young. It could be argued that Edward had found the ideal way to keep his wife out of political mischief and her fecundity made up for at least some of the qualities in which she may have been lacking. Meanwhile her frequent pregnancies gave her husband the opportunity to play the field, which he did apparently with enthusiasm and success. We do not know how many bastards Edward sired because he did not usually acknowledge them and only two appear in the records – Arthur, subsequently Viscount Lisle, and Grace, who was placed in Elizabeth's household, and was to be with her when she died. Grace may have been an unusually amiable child, or she may have been intended as a reminder to Elizabeth not to presume upon her connubial attractions. If Elizabeth ever resented these wanderings she was wise enough to say nothing and she certainly could not complain that her husband was neglecting her for other women.

The one political incident in which she is alleged to have been involved in these years was the second and fatal fall from grace of the King's brother the Duke of Clarence. Clarence was a surly, abrasive person, and although his return to allegiance in 1471 had been of great importance, Edward never really trusted him. His wife, Isobel, died on 22 December 1476, and there was soon talk of his re-marriage to his niece, Mary of Burgundy. Duke Charles was killed at Nancy in January 1477 and his widow Margaret was Clarence's sister. Margaret was desperate to preserve the integrity of the Burgundian inheritance, now in the hands of a mere girl, and saw a marriage within her own family as a means to enlist English support. Edward would not entertain the suggestion, for the good reason that if his brother ever disposed of the great power of Burgundy, he might well be tempted to try his luck again at home. For rather similar, if less potent reasons, he would also not countenance a union between Clarence and Margaret, the sister of the King of Scots, which was also suggested. The Duke sulked, publicly and offensively. He also, apparently, became tangentially involved in necromancy when some members of his household joined with a group that was trying to use the black arts to discover when Edward would die. This was the treasonable offence of 'compassing and imagining' the King's death. The group were convicted by a special commission on 19 May 1477, and two of them were put to death.[20] If, as seems likely, this was intended as a warning to Clarence, he paid no heed. Even before the verdict was delivered he had accused one of Duchess Isobel's former servants of having poisoned her. He had the unfortunate Ankarette Twynho seized and taken to Warwick by force, where she was convicted by an intimidated jury and hanged on 13 April.[21] The Duke had simply taken the law into his own hands in manifest contempt of his brother's authority and for that reason was arrested towards the end of June and committed to the Tower.

Elizabeth had no particular reason to sympathize with Ankarette Twynho but she did have good reason to fear and dislike Clarence. Not only did she not forget his pretensions in 1470, which had been made more threatening by the birth of his son in 1475, she also blamed him for the deaths of her father and uncle. Warwick, who shared that responsibility, was out of reach, but the Duke was now suddenly vulnerable to revenge. There is no direct evidence and the story may simply be a part of that 'black legend' that subsequently gathered around the Queen and her kindred but it is quite likely that Elizabeth urged her husband to deal with his troublesome brother once and for all. Something must account for his unprecedented behaviour because he appeared in person in the House of Lords in January 1478, and accused Clarence of Treason. Evidence of criminal misconduct was plentiful and genuine but that of treason was not. However, the King's word could not be gainsaid in his own Court and the Duke was duly convicted. There then followed a delay of ten days. This was common and was often allowed to the condemned to give them time to make their peace with God but, in this case, because of the peculiar circumstances, it was thought that Edward was struggling with his conscience – and that may well have been the case. The eventual outcome was as unprecedented as the trial because Clarence was neither pardoned nor publicly executed, but privately murdered – allegedly by being drowned in a butt of malmsey wine.[22] This detail is probably a picturesque fabrication, but of the private nature of his execution there can be no doubt. Later historians blamed both the Queen and the Duke of Gloucester for this bizarre outcome and, whereas Richard can certainly be exonerated, similar certainty cannot be deployed in support of Elizabeth. Even her worst enemies did not claim that she was directly responsible and the King himself must take the blame but in the private and unrecorded world of pillow talk the suspicion remains.

Elizabeth's piety appears to have been entirely conventional. She offered dutifully at various shrines and made pious donations of a modest nature. She is alleged to have had a particular devotion to the Virgin Mary as mediatrix but the evidence for any such enthusiasm is slight. She was chief Lady of the Garter but that reflected her status as queen rather than any particular devotion to chivalry. The only exception to this relative anonymity was her generosity to Queens' College in Cambridge but she never showed very much interest in the work of the college and was not a particular patron of scholars. Edward took a lively interest in the work of the new printing press established by William Caxton in 1576 but his main expenditure was not on books but on buildings. He virtually refounded the Order of the Garter and built the sumptuous chapel at Windsor as a setting for its ceremonial – but it was on the refurbishment of his own residences that he spent most of his money and time. His patronage of religion has been described as 'rather sparse' but did embrace the Carthusian monastery at Sheen, founded by Henry V, of which both Edward and his queen were generous supporters. In 1480 he was visited by his sister, the Dowager Duchess of Burgundy and, on her prompting, introduced the rigorous order of reformed, or Observant, Franciscans. Although he was also well known for the lavish equipment of his chapels this was probably his most significant contribution to the religious life of his kingdom. In literature both their tastes seem to have run to chronicles and French romances. Of humanist scholarship in the sense that that was understood in Italy, his Court appears to have been entirely innocent.

During the last six or seven years of his life, Edward's main diplomatic concern was the advantageous marriage of his own children and, although Elizabeth's hand in these negotiations must be assumed, it is often hard to trace. Her eldest son by her first marriage had already been provided for. As we have seen, he had been betrothed at first to Anne, daughter of the Duke of Exeter and, when Anne died young, married to Cecily the daughter and heir of Lord Bonville. He had been created Earl of Huntingdon in 1471, and Marquis of Dorset in 1475. By 1480 at the age of 25, he could consider himself well established in life. The diplomatic activity of 1475–81 was about Edward's own children. In 1476 the 6-year-old Edward was proposed as a match for the Infanta Isabella of Castile, then for a daughter of the Emperor Frederick III, and then for a daughter of the former Duke of Milan, but in every case '… the chief difficulty which they speak of will be owing to the great quantity of money which the king of England will want',[23] by way of dowry. In other words Edward was being greedy, and overpricing his son. More realistically, in 1481, an agreement was almost concluded with Duke Francis II of Brittany for a marriage with his daughter and heir Anne but this was abandoned at the last minute possibly because of the King's fears of the inevitable reaction from the King of France if the heir to one of his major fiefs were to wed the future King of England. Meanwhile Elizabeth (who was not, of course, the heir) had been betrothed to the Dauphin, and Cecily to the future James IV of Scotland, at the time boy of about 5. Of the older girls, only Mary was uncommitted and she may have been in poor health because she was to die in 1482 at the age of 15. Anne, Catherine and Bridget were too young and too far down the pecking order to have been considered in this context. Richard, although almost equally young, was conscripted because John Mowbray the fourth Duke of Norfolk had died in January 1476 leaving an infant daughter as his only heir. With an eye on securing the great Mowbray inheritance, Edward immediately hallmarked her for the young Duke of York and they were actually married at Westminster in January 1478.[24] In the event, she died in November 1481, long before the pair could have co-habited, but the King's objective had been secured because her inheritance lay vested in Duke Richard for the duration of his life, a situation confirmed by statute in January 1483.This was the sole extent of the King's success with all these negotiations, however, and when he died in April 1483 none of his surviving seven children was actually married. The whole job had, it appeared, been left for Elizabeth to do all over again.

The King's unexpected death left the Queen in no-mans land. Edward was a few days short of his 42nd birthday and had been ill for about a month. The cause of his death appears to have been overindulgence in wine, food and sex. In Shakespeare's words he had 'overmuch consumed his royal person' and either his liver, or his heart, or both, collapsed under the strain. Contemporary accounts show him as suitably penitent for his lifestyle when it was too late for amendment and concerned to reconcile the feuds that raged among the courtiers around him, particularly that between Lord Hastings and the Marquis of Dorset.[25] The story that he was exercised by a rivalry between Elizabeth and the Duke of Gloucester appears to be a later interpolation. The issue that he did not satisfactorily resolve, however, was who should hold the regency for his 12-year-old heir or what kind of office that should be. The last guidance in writing was a will drawn up at the time of his going to France in 1475. As we have seen, he had then left Elizabeth as Governor in his absence, so it was natural that she should have been named as Regent in the event of his demise. Apart from her family her power base at that time consisted of a *de facto* control over the council of the Prince of Wales, a position to which young Edward had been elevated within a year of his birth. For about three months the Queen appears to have presided at Council meetings, although her input into the discussions is not known. The King may have been dissatisfied with the results of this experiment because in the last week or so of his life he named his surviving brother, Richard of Gloucester, as Regent. There was no time to commit this formally to writing, but it was well enough known, and the Queen did not challenge it. Just as Edward appears to have transferred his sexual attentions to a new mistress – Jane Shore – in the last year of his life, so at the end he transferred his political trust to his brother. Elizabeth was left with her dower lands but with no political role.

However, the situation was not as straightforward as it appeared. Because Edward had not defined the regency that he conferred on his brother, it was open to interpretation. Although the realm was in 'quiet and prosperous estate' thanks to the late king's energetic and continuous judicial perambulations that was a fragile and personal achievement. Those who favoured Richard pointed to his proven track record and argued for a full Protectorate, which would include custody of the King's person, and would last until he achieved his majority at 18. Those most favourable to the Queen, on the other hand, tried to claim that the Protectorship should last only until the King was crowned – effectively a few weeks – after which the Queen Mother could be as much in control as she might chose. Alternatively, the Protectorate could be interpreted, not as the kind of full power that Humphrey of Gloucester had enjoyed, but as little more than a nominal presidency of the Council. Meanwhile Richard was still in the north, where he dutifully proclaimed Edward V at York as soon as news of the King's death reached him and wrote a suitable letter of condolence to the Queen. For all his apparent confidence and ruthlessness, however, Richard appears to have been of a nervous and suspicious disposition, and he undoubtedly knew of the efforts which Elizabeth and her friends were making in council to undermine his position. He had, apparently, no fixed hostility to the Woodville/Grey connection, but he was suspicious of their intentions, and particularly suspicious of the close relationship that existed between the young Prince of Wales and his maternal uncle, Earl Rivers. He was well aware that he hardly knew the boy himself, and might find it difficult to win his confidence. His suspicions were probably increased by the fact that the Marquis of Dorset was Constable of the Tower, Sir Edward Woodville commanded the fleet, and that a sizeable force had been assemble in the south-east in anticipation of another spat with France. In other words he feared a coup against himself, and seems to have been persuaded that not only his position but his life was in danger.

Meanwhile, plans were being made to bring the young king from Ludlow, where he had been discharging his princely functions, to London. He would be conducted by Earl Rivers, and Elizabeth, who seems to have had suspicions of her own, argued in council for a large force to escort him. The Council, however, was unwilling to entrust so substantial an army to Earl Rivers, and arguing that there was no need for such precautions, imposed a ceiling of 2,000 on the escort. Ironically Lord Hastings appears to he been the proposer of this limitation. Richard, who was simultaneously moving towards London with a much larger force, seized his opportunity, and intercepted the royal escort at Stony Stratford on the 30 April. Rivers and his nephew Richard Grey were arrested and the royal escort dismissed.[26] The Duke of Gloucester's intentions at this point are quite unclear because he proceeded towards London with his young charge as though nothing had happened and was welcomed by the Council as Protector.

Plans for Edward's coronation proceeded, and it seemed at first that Richard was simply claiming the full Protectorate as that had been proposed by his friends. The Queen, however, with what turned out to be a fully justified premonition of disaster, took refuge again in the Westminster sanctuary with her daughters and her younger son. If there had ever been a Woodville/Grey party bidding for power, it collapsed within a few days. The Marquis of Dorset joined his mother in the sanctuary and Sir Edward Woodville fled to Brittany. Richard of Gloucester reached London on 4 May, and the Council immediately confirmed his full powers. He immediately began to remodel the administration and conferred wide ranging powers upon his ally the Duke of Buckingham. However, he also fixed Edward's coronation for 22 June and called a parliament to meet on 25 June.[27]

At some point between the end of May and 12 June, Richard decided to seize the Crown. On the latter day he had Lord Hastings arrested at a Council meeting and summarily executed on the grounds that he had been intriguing with the Queen. This he justified on the grounds that '... the queen, her blood adherents and affinity ... have daily intended and doth intend to murder and destroy Us and our cousin the Duke of Buckingham.' This excuse reeks of paranoia, and seems not to have had the slightest justification. However, it did not in itself secure the Crown. That was achieved, partly by mustering large forces loyal to him from the north of England and partly by resurrecting a hoary old scandal that Edward's marriage to Elizabeth had been invalidated by a precontract.[28] Before he took this step, he had taken the precaution of extracting the young Richard of York from the sanctuary with smooth professions of loyalty and good faith, not unrelated to a discreet show of force. A charade of petition and acceptance having then been played out for the benefit of the citizens of London, Richard was proclaimed king as Richard III on 26 June and crowned with great pomp on 6 July. Anthony, Earl Rivers and Sir Richard Grey were summarily executed at Pontefract. Edward and his brother remained for some time in the Tower and then notoriously disappeared. By the autumn they were almost certainly dead.[29] Elizabeth had now become a political irrelevance. The parliament which convened in January 1484 obediently decreed that she had never been married to the late King Edward, and that all her children were consequently illegitimate. She was deprived of her dower lands and should theoretically have been reduced to penury. Having now no realistic option, and finding the Westminster sanctuary continually surrounded by the King's soldiers, in March 1484, Elizabeth came to terms. In spite of the carnage that he had wrought among her kindred, the kind of militant last-ditch option that might have appealed to Margaret of Anjou was not for her. She had every reason to suppose that her sons were dead, so there was no longer a political battle to be fought, moreover she had the interests of five daughters to protect as best she could. In return for surrendering all her claims Richard agreed to make a modest provision for her and to give her somewhere to live. On that understanding, she and her children quitted the sanctuary and the agreement was honoured on both sides. In the previous autumn Elizabeth had agreed to the betrothal of her eldest daughter to the Lancastrian pretender Henry of Richmond, but she now withdrew from that position and the younger Elizabeth, now 17, instead was welcomed at King Richard's court. After the death of his wife Anne Neville in March 1485, there were rumours that he intended to marry her but they appear to have been unsubstantiated and Elizabeth was no party to them.

The events of August 1485 did not immediately rescue her from poverty and obscurity, but when the new king, Henry VII, decided to honour his three-year-old pledge to marry her eldest daughter, her fortunes were revived. Having withdrawn her consent for this union as part of her understanding with Richard she was now constrained to renew it and the wedding duly took place in January 1486. Elizabeth was now again a member of the royal family. Her dower lands were restored on 5 March 1486 and when Arthur was born in September, she stood as godmother. In July, when a three-year truce was signed with the Scots, a multiple marriage package was discussed which would have matched the Queen Dowager (then about 50) with the 34-year-old (and widowed) King of Scots and two of her daughters with two of his sons, but nothing came of the negotiation. Henry may not have been very fond of his mother-in-law – hence his willingness to despatch her to Scotland – but the idea that he suspected her of involvement in the Lambert Simnel fiasco is a pure fabrication. Had Elizabeth really been convinced that Simnel was her missing son, she might have been sorely tempted but she had good reason to believe that he had died four years earlier, and there is no contemporary evidence to support the charge. What did happen, however, was that her endowment was transferred in February 1487 to her daughter and that then, or shortly after, she retired to Bermondsey Abbey. This arrangement seems to have been voluntary rather than punitive and when Henry made her a gift of 200 marks in March 1488, he described her as the 'right dear and right well beloved Queen Elizabeth, late wife unto the noble prince of famous memory King Edward IV, and mother unto our dearest wife the Queen …'[30]

The king gave her an annuity of £400 in 1490, and several other presents over the next few years, as well as arranging honourable marriages for three of her four remaining daughters.[31] The fourth and youngest, Bridget, took the veil. By the terms of his own hereditary claim to the throne (such as it was) Henry should have described Edward IV as a usurper, but he never did so, reserving that epithet for Richard III. This was straightforward pragmatism because if Edward had been a lawful king, and properly married to Elizabeth, then Edward V had also been a lawful king and his own wife was legitimate. This placed all the odium on Richard and made Henry the reconciler of the feud between York and Lancaster.

Elizabeth lived in retirement at Bermondsey for about five years, dying in April 1492. Her will survives but in truth she had little to leave but her blessing because she had been entirely supported by the King and Queen during the last few years of her life and seems to have surrendered her moveable possessions to the Abbey. She was 55 and had lived a normal span for her generation. Like Margaret, she has had a bad posthumous press, being represented as greedy, cold and unscrupulous and the contemporary evidence is not entirely supportive. However her political ambition is largely unproven. It was Edward who decided to promote her kindred and he was able to do that at little cost to himself. Nor did he turn them into a powerful faction in the process; they were not a very amiable bunch, but they were no threat to anyone. Her supposed political interventions – for instance against the Duke of Clarence – are uncorroborated and for the most part her influence was entirely domestic and was confined to patronage. How real a threat the Woodville/Grey connection was to Richard in 1483 is very hard to determine but when it came to the point, they did not put up much of a fight. Nor was Elizabeth in any real sense the leader of such a party. She had some influence in the council after Edward's death and was certainly a symbolic figurehead but she did not have the spirit or intelligence to be a real leader – and in that she differed from Margaret. Elizabeth was the King's lover, who also happened to be married to him, and the rest of her image is largely constructed on that basis.

S. Harding Del. & Sculp.

QUEEN KATHARINE.

Henry V.

From a Curious Limning in a (MS) Prayer Book, in the Possession of

Mr. Edwards Bookseller Pall Mall.

London Pub: Sepr. 1. 1792. by E & S Harding Pall Mall.

1. Catherine de Valois by Sylvester Harding; after Unknown artist (National Portrait Gallery, London)

Barrett sculp.

Marriage of Henry the 6.th

2. The Marriage of Henry VI to Margaret of Anjou by Barrett (National Portrait Gallery, London)

3. Elizabeth Woodville Queen of Edward IV by Johann Gottlieb Facius; or by Georg Siegmund Facius; after Thomas Kerrich (National Portrait Gallery, London)

ELIZABETHA · VXOR
HENRICI · VII ·

4. Elizabeth of York by Unknown artist (National Portrait Gallery, London)

5. Catherine of Aragon by Unknown artist (National Portrait Gallery, London)

6. Anne of Cleves by Hans Holbein the Younger

The Queen as Helpmate: Elizabeth of York

With the marriage of Henry VII to Elizabeth of York in January 1486, we come upon yet another different type of Queen. Like her mother, Elizabeth was home bred and reared but, unlike her, she was of royal blood. Indeed, given the absence of any Salic Law in England, she had a far better claim to the throne than her husband. Richard's attempt to impugn her mother's marriage had been effective in the summer of 1483, and remained orthodox as long as the King lived, but it was not emphasized when he came to terms with the older Elizabeth in March 1484. The younger Elizabeth returned to court, was friendly with the Queen and her illegitimacy was simply taken for granted. In a later age, Elizabeth and Henry might have reigned together, like Mary and William, but England was not yet ready for such an experiment. There had not been a ruling Queen since the Norman conquest and Henry, despite his dubious pedigree, had the advantages of being male and of unchallenged legitimacy.[1] He also, more critically, had led the army that had defeated and killed the childless Richard at Bosworth. Richard, by moving against Edward V, had split the Yorkist party right down the middle but, although his opponents continued to regard Elizabeth as Edward's legitimate daughter, in the circumstances of August 1485 nobody was pressing her claims as his heir. Nevertheless when she and Henry married both her supporters and the Lancastrian party came together to celebrate the union of the red rose and the white and the healing of the long and bloody feud that they represented.[2]

Elizabeth was Edward's first-born child and, as we have seen, her baptism in February 1466 had been an occasion for a display of family solidarity. From then until the birth of Edward junior in 1470, she was her father's heir and had immediately been deployed on the marriage market. This was in the interest of trying to heal his feud with the Nevilles following the fiasco of 1469. She was betrothed to George, the son of John Neville, Marquis Montague. However John blotted his copybook by betraying Edward in the summer of 1470 and then died fighting against him at Barnet in 1471. So the betrothal disappeared and was heard of no more. George, who must have been almost as young as his intended bride, was still a minor in 1480, and died unmarried in 1483. Apart from that, Elizabeth's public role was minimal. When the King had his father's remains transferred from Pontefract to Fotheringhay in 1466, she was present as a very small child. Her uncle, Richard of Gloucester, then 14, was the chief mourner on that occasion. At about the same time Edward settled on her for life the manor of Great Lynford in Buckinghamshire. The reason for this rather curious gesture is unclear, but it may have been some compensation for the fact that she had no title. If she had been a boy she would have been created Duke of Cornwall at birth and enjoyed the revenues of the Duchy. As it was, presumably the profits of Great Lynford went towards paying some of her nursery expenses but the point of such an allocation is elusive. During the crisis of 1470–1 Elizabeth was with her mother and her sister Mary in sanctuary but presumably spent most of her time with a faithful nurse or nurses because the Queen was busy giving birth to her first-born son.

When Edward went off to France in 1475, he left behind his will, naming the Queen as Governor of the Realm and allocating 10,000 crowns for the marriage portion of his elder daughter. There does not seem to have been any bridegroom in prospect at that time so she was still an available asset to be deployed diplomatically and that is just what Edward did at Pecquingy a few months later. When this treaty was signed in August 1475 one of the clauses was for a marriage between Elizabeth and Louis's young son, Charles, the Dauphin. The King of France was to provide a jointure of £60,000, and Mary was to cover as substitute in the event of anything untoward happening to the older child, who was then about 9. Apparently Elizabeth was known thereafter at the English court as Madame la Dauphine and was taught to speak and to write both French and Spanish in preparation for her future role. Contemporary reports relate that she was already a precocious reader and writer in English and she seems to have been generally a highly intelligent and teachable child, although there is no record of who was responsible for these accomplishments. Mary was to be taken out of her treaty commitment in 1481 by betrothal to the King of Denmark but died still well short of her majority, in the following year. In December 1482 Louis came to terms with Maximilian, the husband of Mary of Burgundy at Arras and effectively abandoned the Pecquingy agreement, which deprived Elizabeth of her expected dignity and her father of his peace of mind. The French action on this occasion was (allegedly) one of the causes for Edward's premature demise in the following April.

We do not know how Elizabeth reacted to her father's unexpected death. She was 17 and must have been well aware of the political tensions that this situation created. At first the prognosis was good. All the talk was of her brother's coronation and of his arrival from the Marches of Wales. Then, quite suddenly, there was panic. Her uncle Anthony had been arrested and Edward was coming under the escort of another uncle, Richard, whom the Princess can hardly have known. At the news, her mother took fright, and bundled her and her siblings back into the Westminster sanctuary, which must have carried uncomfortable memories from her early childhood. At first this panic must have seemed rather unnecessary, as preparations for the coronation continued as though nothing had happened. Perhaps lulled into a sense of false security, or perhaps just not able to muster the willpower to resist, the Queen Dowager was persuaded to let her younger son join his brother.[3] Then there were rumours – Richard was plotting to take the Crown himself – and disaster struck. A preacher put up by the Protector denounced the Dowager's marriage as false and all her children as bastards. The older Elizabeth may (or may not) have been in touch with Lord Hastings via his mistress, Jane Shore, in an attempt to check this headlong progress. Jane had been Edward's last mistress and Elizabeth would almost certainly have known her. Within a few days, Hastings had paid for this alleged treason with his head, Richard was proclaimed king and rumours started arriving that Anthony and his brother had been executed in the north. On 6 July Richard was crowned and, shortly after, his two young nephews disappeared in the Tower. The distress of the women in sanctuary can only be imagined. Years later Bernard Andreas was to say of the young Elizabeth 'the love she bore her brothers and sisters was unheard of and almost incredible'. Even allowing for poetic licence that is strong testimony. From later evidence she seems to have had a loving and gentle disposition, which may have made her unfit for government, but was considered a great commendation in a consort. Unfortunately no contemporary commented upon how she endured the loss of her brothers, whose death was generally accepted long before she was allowed to emerge from the sanctuary.

Richard had no desire to make more enemies by storming Westminster so he sat down patiently to besiege it, using his household troops for the purpose. The intention was not to starve the occupants out but to intimidate them. The siege lasted for nine months before the Dowager finally came to terms and it must have been a very bleak autumn and winter for the girls, who were accustomed not only to their comforts but also to flattering attentions. Now they were simply Edward's illegitimate offspring. In March 1484, as we have seen, the Dowager surrendered. In return for giving up all her pretensions and eschewing political activity, she was provided with a modest competence and houses to live in, 'honest places of good name and fame', while Richard undertook to marry her daughters to 'gentlemen born' with a small portion of 200 marks each. Presumably these were the best terms Elizabeth could get. Soon after there was talk of marrying Elizabeth to William Stillington, the illegitimate son of Robert, Bishop of Bath and Wells. Presumably an Episcopal bastard was deemed to be gentleman enough for a royal one. However, neither the Dowager not her daughter would have anything to do with such a suggestion and the idea (if it was ever seriously proposed) was dropped. Meanwhile a much more momentous development had taken place at Rennes, although it is unlikely that it appeared that way at the time. By December 1483, Henry of Richmond, the Lancastrian pretender, had realized that Richard's actions in the summer had seriously alienated many Yorkist supporters. Although he had not been able to take advantage of the Duke of Buckingham's rebellion in the autumn, it had benefited him in several ways. Most importantly the dissident Yorkists, convinced that Edward V and his brother were dead, were now looking to him to unseat the usurper. To strengthen that alliance it was suggested to Henry that he should undertake to marry Elizabeth, now the senior Yorkist claimant. This can hardly have been done without the permission of the Queen Dowager and the story is that her Welsh physician, a man named Lewis, carried her letters to Henry undertaking to support his claim in return for the marriage.[4] Towards the end of December, therefore, in Rennes Cathedral, Henry of Richmond solemnly swore that, when the opportunity presented itself, he would marry Elizabeth of York. The Princess herself was probably aware that this action had been taken, but her reaction is not known. It must have seemed a good deal less realistic than her erstwhile marriage to the Dauphin and when she came to terms with Richard, the Dowager had perforce to drop the whole idea. Romantic stories allege that the Princess kept up a clandestine correspondence with Henry despite her mother's withdrawal and even sent him a ring of betrothal but no evidence substantiates them. For about a year after her emergence from sanctuary, the young Elizabeth was at court, probably as some kind of attendant upon the Queen, Anne Neville, with whom she is said to have been friendly. It seems likely that Richard, who had not lost his suspicious nature, wanted to keep her where he could see her. When Anne died in March 1485 there were rumours that Richard would marry her himself. These rumours were so persistent that the King issued a formal denial – and indeed a bastard niece would hardly have been a suitable bride.[5] Instead, Elizabeth was packed off to Sheriff Hutton in Yorkshire, where she remained throughout the summer.

The circumstances of Henry's landing and of his advance to Bosworth, are well known. He won his decisive victory on 22 August less by the strength of his own forces (which numbered barely 5,000) than by the dubious tactics of Lord Stanley and the Earl of Northumberland. The latter, having ostensibly brought his power to support Richard, did absolutely nothing. The former joined Henry just as the battle was turning in his favour. The victory in itself would probably have settled nothing if Richard had survived, but in fact he died on the field of battle and his crown was symbolically transferred to Henry on the spot. Richard's failure to rally committed support is something of a mystery and there was much talk at the time of divine judgement. Henry acted as king from the moment of his victory and even dated his reign from the day before the battle. Before he left Leicester for London, he sent Sir Robert Willoughby to Sheriff Hutton to secure the persons of Edward, Earl of Warwick, the 10-year-old son of the Duke of Clarence, and of Elizabeth, each of whom presented a potential threat to his claim. Warwick was immediately consigned to the Tower but Elizabeth was temporarily returned to the custody of her mother and accommodation was provided for them at Westminster. In September he appointed a new Chancellor and a new Lord Privy Seal, while Lord Dynham, the Treasurer, continued in his post. On 15 September he also summoned a parliament, which duly convened on 7 November. This assembly dutifully endorsed the King's title (thereby annulling his previous attainder), annulled the attainders of those who had been supporting him since 1483 and replaced them with some of his recent enemies. It also petitioned him to honour his two-year-old pledge to marry Elizabeth 'Daughter of King Edward IV'.[6] Nothing was said about her being Edward's heir, but as Giovanni de Giglis reported to the Pope, everyone considered this to be for the advantage of the kingdom.[7] Edward had been Duke of York as well as king, and that title had descended to his younger son. If Richard was dead, as was generally assumed, it was at the King's discretion whether to recognize Elizabeth as Duchess in her own right, and it is possible that he did so in November or December, although no instrument confirms that. If it did happen, then she would have enjoyed the revenues of that Duchy for about a month before her wedding.

Henry responded positively to the parliamentary petition, and even offered excuses for his delay: there had been plague in the capital, it was necessary to gather money, and so on. The ceremony eventually took place on 18 January 1486, with the Archbishop of Canterbury, Cardinal Bourchier, officiating. In fact the couple were sufficiently near in kin to need a papal dispensation but so well disposed was Pope Innocent VIII that his Legate was able to give that verbally early in January in order not to hold up the ceremony.[8] It is probable, indeed, that Elizabeth was already pregnant, given the fact that Arthur was born just eight months later, and the Legate may have had good cause to suspect that. Innocent certainly seem to have seen this wedding as the ideal way to end the feud which had so disrupted England, because when the written dispensation finally arrived in March, it addressed the King as 'Henry of Lancaster' and the Queen as 'Elizabeth of York', referring specifically to the healing of the dynastic breach. The people of London seem to have felt the same because we are told that they greeted the occasion with 'bonfires, dancing, songs and banquets' in the streets. It should be noted, however, that when Parliament recognized Henry's title in November, it made no reference to Elizabeth and the King never allowed the slightest suggestion that his wife reinforced his position.

The wedding was not immediately followed by a coronation. This was probably because Henry had more urgent things to attend to, although it might be because she was soon realised to be pregnant. It is also possible that the King had no desire to emphasize his consort's royal credentials at this stage, having, to his mind, done that quite sufficiently in the wedding. Instead, the King took off on what was likely to be a difficult and even dangerous progress to the north, to the heartlands of Richard's support, while the Queen retreated to Winchester, where she, her mother and her sisters appear to have been the guests of the Queen Mother, Margaret Beaufort. The role of this formidable matriarch has been carefully studied and she seems to have performed many of the functions that might otherwise have fallen to the consort. She was extremely well endowed financially, had a large affinity of dependents, dispensed much patronage and seems to have lived virtually independently from her third husband, the Earl of Derby. Relations with the Queen Dowager may well have been difficult (the two women were much of an age) and it may well have been that tension rather than any political suspicion that caused the older Elizabeth to retreat to Bermondsey in 1487. Margaret seems to have assumed a propriatorial interest in the young Elizabeth, which her mother may well have resented, although the Queen herself seems to have been completely relaxed about it, as she was about most things.

Arthur was born on 19 September 1486 at Winchester and Elizabeth, who seems to have had a difficult labour, went down with a fever immediately afterwards. This was not apparently thought to be life threatening but it did mean that she had to be carried to her churching. Her mother stood as godmother at the christening but we know little else about the ceremony apart from the fact that it was nearly wrecked by the late arrival of the Earl of Oxford, one of the godfathers. Like her mother, Elizabeth was destined to become a baby factory. In a married life of seventeen years she bore her husband at least six children who are recorded, and several others who are not recorded and may have been still births – including the daughter whom she died giving birth to. Her fertility equalled that of her mother, but she was less fortunate with survivals. When the Queen Dowager died in 1492, five of her seven daughters were still alive and of her three sons only one had died a natural death. When the Queen died in 1503 she left two daughters and one son and, although it was Henry's survival that saved the dynasty, his mother had in other respects been unfortunate. Henry's critics later claimed that the King's relationship with his wife was lacking in warmth or affection but her frequent pregnances and the devastating effect that her death had on him point to a quite different conclusion. He is rumoured to have been enamoured of Katherine Herbert, a daughter of the Earl of Pembroke, with whom he was brought up for some years, but that was before his betrothal to Elizabeth. The Princess was warned about Katherine in the autumn of 1485 but seems not to have taken her rivalry seriously – and in that she was fully justified. Unlike his father in law, Henry was a man of great continence and although he obviously made full use of his wife he seems never to have strayed after other women, a characteristic in which he resembled his pious namesake and predecessor.

Financial provision for the Queen is something of a mystery because the evidence is not entirely consistent. Apart from the problem over the Duchy of York there are suggestions that she was deemed to have inherited the lands of the Earldom of March because she appears to have been holding property belonging to that patrimony in Herefordshire in September 1486, long before she had received any formal grant. Parliament also authorized her to 'sue in her own name … all manner of rents etc. due to her …', which would have been pointless if she had not been holding property. Later, in 1494, certain lands of the earldom in Ireland were described as being 'in the king's hands in the right of Elizabeth the Queen Consort', which points in the same direction.[9] However, it was not until 26 November 1487, following her coronation, that any formal grant was made directly to her – a long list of lands and other properties being conferred for life. These seem to have been the same as those that had been granted to her mother in March 1486, and confirm other references to the transfer of that patrimony.[10] In March 1488 she was granted certain royalties and other rents and both these grants were confirmed on 1 February 1492, about three months before her mother died, when she was also granted the reversion of some of her grandmother's property.[11] Consequently, unlike any of her predecessors, and because the grants were made in this piecemeal fashion, it is not possible to say what Elizabeth's properties as consort were actually worth In 1495 she was granted the castle and lordship of Fotheringhay in Northamptonshire but in the same year was noted to be so deeply in debt that she was forced to pawn £500 worth of plate, and to borrow £2,000 from her husband to satisfy her creditors. The suggestion is that this was rather due to excessive generosity than to inadequate income. It is probably safe to conclude that Henry would have wanted to make suitable provision for his Queen, and that would have meant committing between £4,000 and £5,000 of annual revenue but it is impossible to say just how that endowment was put together.

During the summer of 1487 Henry was much preoccupied with the rebellion that came to an end at Stoke on 16 June. After that he had to try to stabilize the situation in Ireland, where there had been much support for Lambert Simnel's imposture; it was not until November that he got around to crowning his Queen. When it came, it was worth the wait. Elizabeth set out by barge from Greenwich on 24 June and the King welcomed her at the Tower, where they spent the night. The following day she processed on her own through the City to Westminster, her train being borne by her sister Cecily. The earls of Oxford, Derby and Nottingham acted as Stewards for the occasion and the ceremony was performed by the new Archbishop, John Morton. Henry watched the proceedings from 'a closed lattice box between the altar and the pulpit' and, as was customary, the Queen presided at the following banquet. Her mother, apparently, was not present although whether this was by the King's orders or not is unclear. However her stepbrother the Marquis of Dorset, who had been under arrest for his suspected part in the Simnel rising, was specially released to attend.

Thereafter the Queen can only be occasionally observed going about her business. She was in a way a model consort, never overstepping the traditional limitations, so comments upon her activities are comparatively rare. Her accounts show her both giving and receiving gifts, not only from the humble, who brought her cherries and apples, but also from the powerful and well connected. Her goodwill was obviously worth cultivating.[12] Her household provided a refuge for several of Richard's former servants; Edward Chaderton, his Treasurer of the Chamber, for example became her Chancellor. There was nothing particularly surprising about that as both Margaret Beaufort and the King himself had strong Yorkist contingents in their households but they were rather less welcoming to those with close connections to the previous regime. Although there are a number of contemporary testimonies to her intelligence and, as we have seen, she had several languages, she was not to any great extent a patron of scholars and even Bernard Andrée did not credit her with such a function. When she appears as a patron of letters it is usually in association with Margaret Beaufort, who is much better known for that sort of patronage. They both, for example, sponsored Caxton's edition of the *Fifteen Oes* in 1491, and jointly gave a copy of Wykyn de Worde's edition of Walter Hilton's *Scala Perfectionis* to her Lady Margery Roos in 1494. The two ladies were also associated occasionally in pious benefactions and were, along with the King and the royal children, the subjects of the prayers of many endowed chantries. They were together created Ladies of the Garter in 1488, and when Elizabeth became Chief Lady in 1495 no jealousy seems to have resulted. Margaret was 53 in that year and Elizabeth 29, but despite this difference relations seem to have remained entirely harmonious. In this, as in so many other matters, Elizabeth seems to have remained true to her motto, 'humble and reverent'. After a chequered childhood and a turbulent adolescence, her married life was singularly peaceful. Insofar as she features as an independent patron, it was in the most peaceful of arts. She loved the revels – minstelsy and disguisings – paying both William Cornish and Richard Fayrfax for what must have been specially commissioned pieces. She kept a pack of greyhounds, which were intended for hare coursing, but was not otherwise known for any keenness on hunting. There is also a hint that she had some skill in draftmanship and a knowledge of architecture because when Robert Vertue rebuilt the palace at Greenwich for King Henry he worked from plans that had been drawn up by the Queen. There seems to have been more to this self-effacing woman than meets the eye.

Elizabeth's independent political role is equally obscure. On one occasion she was appealed to by one of her tenants in Wales against some arbitrary action by the King's uncle, Jasper Duke of Bedford. Instead of referring this complaint to the King, as might have been expected, the Queen dealt with it herself, and wrote a sharp letter to Jasper, which seems to have had the desired effect.[13] The queen could never be ignored, especially when it came to promotions within the household, but her normal tactics seem to have been subtle and 'feminine' and thus escaped the attentions of the commentators. Her part in planning the education of her children is typical in this respect. Both Arthur and Henry were given a first-class grounding in classical humanism and this is normally attributed to the influence of Margaret Beaufort over her son, but their first steps in learning would have been taken 'among the women' and would have been directed by Elizabeth. Arthur was subsequently taught by the poet Bernard Andrée, who later declared that he had made him familiar with the works of Homer, Vergil, Ovid, Terence, Thucidides, Livy and several others, while Henry was entrusted to the care of John Skelton. The latter also claimed full credit for the young Prince's accomplishments:

> … I gave him drink of the sugared well
> Of Helicon's waters crystalline,
> Acquainting him with the muses nine.[14]

Both these tutors were appointed by the King, as was Skelton's successor, William Hone, who also taught Princess Mary. Hone may well not have come on the scene until after Elizabeth's death, but both Skelton and Andrée were functioning in the 1490s. Skelton and Hone were Cambridge men, and it has been deduced that Margaret found them after consultations with her friend John Fisher but the evidence for this is purely circumstantial. Given Elizabeth's known fondness for music and the excellence of the musical training that both Henry and Margaret certainly had, it is easy to conclude that the Queen's hand was behind at least some of their education.

Somewhat more visible is her involvement in the matrimonial fortunes of her siblings and children. Her sister Cecily, the closest to her in age, was married at some date between 25 November 1487 (when she bore the Queen's train) and 1 June 1488, to John, Viscount Welles, who was the King's uncle of the half blood (he was an illegitimate brother of Jasper Tudor, the King's full uncle). John had been involved in Buckingham's rebellion in 1483, and had escaped to join Henry in Britanny. He was recognized as Baron Welles when his attainder was reversed in 1485 and he was created Viscount in the summer of 1487. He received several substantial grants from the Crown and his marriage to Cecily was obviously part of his general build up. He died on 9 February 1498 leaving only a daughter, Ann, who died shortly after her father. Cecily remarried in 1503, after her sister was dead. Anne, her next surviving sister, was married on 4 February 1495 to Thomas Howard junior, son and heir of the Earl of Surrey. Thomas was to be a great man under Henry VIII, succeeding his father as Duke of Norfolk in 1524, but Anne did not live to be Duchess of Norfolk, dying in 1511. They had no children who survived. Catherine, the next eldest, was married in October of the same year to Sir William Courtenay, who was to be created Earl of Devon in 1511 and who died about a month later. Their son, Henry, created Marquis of Exeter in 1525, eventually paid for his Plantagenant blood with his head, being executed by Henry VIII in 1538. Catherine died in 1517. Elizabeth's youngest sibling, Bridget, took the veil at Dartford at some time before 1500 but whether this was by choice or because the Queen failed to find a suitable husband for her is not clear. All these marriages were officially provided by the King, and in the case of Viscount Welles that was obviously so, but it would have been normal practice for the Queen to act as broker, particularly in obtaining the consent of her sisters to whom, as we have seen, she was very close. There are a few hints and suggestions in the records that this was the case, although specific evidence is scarce.

Only one of her own children was married in her lifetime and for that little more than her consent was required. Almost from the moment of his accession, Henry had been keen on the idea of an alliance with Ferdinand and Isabella of Spain, not least because he foresaw trouble with France over the Duchy of Britanny. Duke Francis II died on 9 September 1488, leaving his young daughter Anne as his heir and at the mercy of Charles VIII of France. On 10 February 1489 Henry signed the Treaty of Redon with Anne's council in an attempt to safeguard the independence of the Duchy.[15] However, distracted by the appearance of Perkin Warbeck in Ireland, he was unable to prevent Charles from divorcing his existing wife in order to marry Anne. That wedding took place on 6 December 1491. Meanwhile Henry had been seeking his remedies. A marriage between the 2-year-old Prince Arthur and the 3-year-old Catherine, Ferdinand's youngest daughter, had been the subject of diplomatic exchanges since 1488, and the Treaty of Medina del Campo on the 28 March 1489 affected a formal agreement.[16] This has to be seen as part of the same strategy as the Treaty of Redon but it did not work against Charles, who simply shrugged off the threat. Eventually Henry made a gesture of war with France, and allowed himself to be bought off at Etaples in November 1492 without doing anything for the Bretons, but in securing the marriage agreement he had achieved the other of his two main objectives. The Trastamara were one of the most ancient and prestigious ruling houses in Europe and it was a great coup for Henry that they should be prepared to commit one of their daughters to his heir. Nevertheless for the time being nothing happened. This was partly because of the youth of both parties, and partly because of the trouble caused by Perkin Warbeck, who was active from 1492 until 1497. Ferdinand was understandably reluctant to commit his daughter to a realm that was threatened by a pretender. The marriage treaty was confirmed on 1 October 1496, but still nothing happened. It was later alleged that Ferdinand made any formal ceremony conditional upon the execution of the Earl of Warwick, who appeared to be the catalyst for most of the trouble, but no contemporary evidence confirms that. Instead the first proxy marriage between Catherine and Arthur took place in May 1499, and the Treaty of Alliance was confirmed two months later.[17] By that time Warbeck was in custody and the threat had all but disappeared. A further proxy ceremony took place in November 1500, by which time both Warwick and Warbeck had been executed. Catherine finally arrived in England in October 1501. Her dowry had been fixed at 200,000 Spanish escudos (about £60,000), half of which was paid on her arrival. The other half was due at the time of her marriage but was never paid and remained as a bone of contention.

The celebrations that attended the final and personal nuptials between Arthur and Catherine were protracted and elaborate. The City of London provided a costly allegorical spectacle – a series of pageants in six separate scenes – the first of which, representing St Katherine and St Ursula, was set upon London Bridge. It is not known who devised these pageants, but knowing Elizabeth's fondness for this kind of display it is probable that she played a part. The fifth pageant represented the Temple of God, and was set at the Standard in Cheapside. It was there that the King and Queen took their stands, and witnessed the near blasphemous representation of Henry VII as God the Father and Arthur as God the Son. This noble King, says Prelacy (the presenter), has now ordained a marriage between his son and Katheryn, 'the kyngys dowgthyr of Spayn'.[18] Flattery could hardly go further. The sequel, however, was tragic rather than romantic. Whether the marriage was ever consummated was later to be the subject of fierce debate and the memories of those who had been close to the couple varied. The principal evidence for consummation came from Father Geraldini, her confessor. Arthur was 15 and she 17, so it is perfectly possible, but he seems to have been a feeble youth physically so Catherine's later denials carry conviction. The hopeful couple were despatched to Ludlow in the Welsh Marches, the centre of Arthur's jurisdiction as Prince of Wales, and there, on 2 April 1502, Arthur died. Both his parents were devastated; Henry by the loss of his heir and Elizabeth by the loss of her son. Edmund, their third son, had lived for only two weeks in the summer of 1500, so the dynasty now hung by the slender thread of Henry's life. We are told that Elizabeth went, as her duty required, to comfort her husband in his loss but was so overcome by emotion that he had to comfort her.[19] The news, as Leland put it, had 'smote her sorrowful to the heart'. Apparently she reassured him that she was still young enough to repair the loss and that turned out to be a fatal mistake.

Edmund's short life had not been a good omen, but the couple decided to try again, and by the autumn of the same year, Elizabeth was pregnant once more. On 2 February 1503 the Queen was delivered of a daughter in the Royal lodgings at the Tower. The child was named Catherine, after the widowed Princess of Wales, but she lived only a few days. Then, just over a week later, Elizabeth herself succumbed to puerperal fever and died on her 37th birthday. As Polydore Vergil wrote: 'the queen herself died in childbirth. She was a woman of such character that it would have been hard to judge whether she displayed more of majesty and dignity in her life than of wisdom and moderation ...'[20]

There had been a great and perhaps unusual level of affection between the couple and Henry 'privily departed into a solitary place and would no man should resort to him'.[21] Astrologers had assured him that she would live to be at least 80, but then astrologers had assured her mother before her birth that she would be a boy. The star gazers did not have a good success rate with Elizabeth. In due course her body was conveyed to Westminster and interred in the still-incomplete chapel, which was to be named after her husband. Her funeral was formal and elaborate as became her status and cost the princely sum of £2,800. Alone among the queens we have so far considered, Elizabeth died in her husband's lifetime, and was thus accorded the full honours due to the sovereign's consort. Just over six years later Henry joined her in the same tomb, which was finally completed by his son, with the magnificent memorial by Torrigiano that still marks the spot.

Although Elizabeth did not live to see them completed, negotiations were already far advanced for the marriage of her elder daughter Margaret at the time of her death. Relations with Scotland had been slowly improving since James III's abortive invasion of 1487. James had died in 1488 and his young heir was anxious to come to terms. A commission was issued in June 1495 to negotiate a marriage between James IV and Margaret, then aged six. Elizabeth had acquiesced in this, but is alleged to have begged her husband not to surrender custody of the child until she had reached the minimum age for cohabitation, which was 12.[22] As it turned out, she need not have worried because James changed his mind and received the pretender Perkin Warbeck in November of the same year, with royal honours. It was only when James became disillusioned with Warbeck and abandoned him in July 1496 that the threads could be picked up again. Progress was again slow and it was not until July 1497 that fresh instructions were issued to Richard Fox, Lord Privy Seal and Bishop of Durham, who was Henry's most experienced negotiator. The result was a series of short truces, culminating in the indefinite Truce of Ayton in February 1498, but there was no renewal of the marriage negotiation at that stage. It was not until Warbeck had been executed in 1499, and a reassuring mission had gone from Spain to Scotland, that that subject could be raised again. A full peace treaty and marriage agreement was finally concluded on 24 January 1502, by which time Margaret was already 12.[23] The deaths, first of Arthur and then of the Queen herself, put all these arrangements on hold, and it was not until August 1503 that the Princess finally travelled north to meet her future husband. If Elizabeth had entertained doubts about entrusting her eldest daughter to so remote a land, she was spared the need to see it happening.

Meanwhile, Catherine was left in England without a husband and Henry without a wife. When the news of Arthur's death reached him, Ferdinand immediately demanded the return of his daughter and the refund of the part of her dowry that he had already paid. This, it soon transpired, was a negotiating position and by September of the same year an agreement had been drafted to maintain the alliance by transferring the hand of the 17-year-old Catherine to the 11-year-old Henry junior. This new treaty was finally ratified on 30 September 1503.[24] It was realized that a papal dispensation would be necessary because of the degree of consanguinity created by Catherine's first marriage but no difficulty seems to have been anticipated. The marriage was to be celebrated as soon as Henry reached his fourteenth birthday, that is on or after 28 June 1505. The papal bureaucracy finally ground out a dispensation at some point during the spring of that year, but by then Henry had changed his mind and caused his son to repudiate the agreement as soon as he had passed 14. By then circumstances had changed in Spain too, because Isabella of Castile died on 26 November 1504. Not only had Isabella been keener on Catherine's second marriage than Ferdinand, she had also been Queen of Castile in her own right and although in her will she attempted to make Ferdinand Governor of the realm, her heir was not her husband but her elder daughter Joanna. Joanna was married to the Archduke Philip of the Netherlands and the mother of two promising sons, but many Castilian nobles did not fancy the alien Philip as King Consort, preferring the terms of Isabella's will. A sharp political struggle then ensued, during which Philip and Joanna went to Spain and successfully asserted their rights. However in 1506 Philip died and Joanna (it was conveniently alleged) became deranged. This enabled Ferdinand to reassert himself as Regent, but it also meant that, if Joanna was deemed disqualified the next heir to the throne was Catherine. She thus became one complication too many for her father who was quite happy for her to remain in England, marriage or no marriage. Poor Catherine, now aged 20, was thus left in limbo as Dowager Princess of Wales, without a role and with inadequate financial support. Her endowment of one-third of the revenues of Wales had come to an end with Arthur's death and Henry cancelled the replacement allowance of £1,200 a year when her betrothal to the new Prince of Wales was cancelled. Thereafter he made her only spasmodic payments, apparently as the spirit moved him.[25]

Meanwhile, both the widowed kings were on the look out for new partners. Ferdinand took the opportunity to end his long-running feud with France and signed the treaty of Blois with Louis XII in October 1505, one of the conditions of which was that he should marry Louis's niece, Germaine de Foix, and that wedding duly took place on 18 March 1506. This not only strengthened Ferdinand's hand in Spain; it also distanced him from the King of England. There was never any question of hostilities, but relations cooled. Henry was less successful, and perhaps less determined. His first target seems to have been the widowed Queen Joan of Naples, who was Ferdinand's niece, and his envoys sent a very precise physical description of the lady from Valencia in June 1505.[26] Ferdinand declared himself in favour of the proposal but nothing eventually came of it. However attractive Joan may have been, she would, it appears, have been no substitute for Elizabeth. Neighbouring princes were also keen to take advantage of the King's availability. The Archduke Philip offered his sister Margaret, the widowed Duchess of Savoy, and a treaty was actually signed to effect that in 1506. Louis XII proffered his niece, Margaret of Angouleme. In the event it was the ladies themselves who declined the prospect but Henry's pursuit was dutiful rather than enthusiastic. He was clearly more interested in using the negotiations for diplomatic purposes than he was in actually getting married again. It may have been a factor that his own health was in slow decline. The main purpose of marrying again would have been to strengthen his dynasty by begetting more children and it may well be that by about 1505 Henry was beginning to feel that that feat was beyond him. For whatever reason, he did not marry again and when he died in April 1509 he left an adult son (just) and a widowed daughter-in-law, both ready to start again. The rumours that he had at one time designs on Catherine himself appear to be without foundation and, knowing the King's scrupulosity, are intrinsically improbable. His last matrimonial move was on behalf of his younger daughter, Mary, then aged 11. On 1 October 1508 he completed a treaty with Margaret of Savoy, his erstwhile intended and by then governor of the Netherlands, to wed her to Margaret's eight-year-old charge, the Archduke Charles – later the Emperor Charles V – but once again the treaty proved abortive.[27]

Of all the women we have so far considered, Elizabeth of York appears to have been the most gentle and the most conventional of queens. Despite the intrinsic strength of her political position, she never seems to have made the slightest attempt to exploit it and although her position as the heir of York is constantly alluded to there is never any suggestion that it threatened the King's position. Her influence was nearly all behind the scenes. It should not be discounted for that reason but is extraordinarily difficult to assess. After her death one commentator described her as 'one of the most gracious and best beloved princesses of the world'[28], while the Venetian ambassador called her 'a very handsome woman, and in conduct very able'. She was an ideal helpmate, and also discharged her parental duty with notable success. In spite of the bitter disappointments of Edmund's and Arthur's deaths, she left two children who were to dominate the succeeding centuries: Henry VIII, the father of Mary and Elizabeth, and Margaret, the grandmother of Mary of Scotland and great grandmother of James VI and I.

5

The Queen as Foreign Ally: Catherine of Aragon and Anne of Cleves

Catherine had come to England in 1501 as the pledge of an alliance between Henry VII and her father, Ferdinand of Aragon. The marriage that had sealed that alliance had lasted only a few months and, at the age of 17, Catherine had been left a widow. In order to maintain the alliance, and avoid repaying that part of her dowry that he had already received, Henry had then proposed and Ferdinand had agreed to betroth her to Arthur's younger brother, Henry, a step for which a dispensation from consanguinity was required. At first it had been suspected that Arthur had left his widow pregnant, but by the time that the dispensation was issued it was clear that that was not the case. It was, however, assumed that the union had been consummated, in spite of the protestations of her *duenna*, Donna Elvira, and of Catherine herself, because it was the consummation rather than the ceremony of marriage that created the consanguinity.[1] The second marriage, however, had not taken place. The kings drifted apart and in June 1505, when the younger Henry reached his fourteenth birthday, his father caused him to repudiate the agreement. This should have been the signal for Catherine to go home but political circumstances in Castile made her presence in Spain unwelcome to her father, as we have seen, so she remained in England as the Dowager Princess of Wales. In 1507, when she was 22 and still unmarried, her father had accredited her as his ambassador in England, thus giving her a unique formal recognition.[2] It had been common in the past for royal consorts to act as *de facto* representatives of their families in England – but Catherine was not such a consort, and there was no precedent for an unmarried woman to act as an ambassador. Her role proved to be complex and exacting because Ferdinand's remarriage had left him in alliance with France, a move that Henry had sought to counter by closer ties to the Habsburgs. It was for that reason that she found herself involved in a negotiation with Maximilian for a marriage between the King of England and her own sister Juana, the widow of King Phillip. The fact that Juana was alleged to be insane does not appear to have deterred either of the negotiators. It is not surprising that Catherine soon called for reinforcements. She did not trust her nominal colleague in the embassy, the long serving but by now somewhat ineffectual Dr De Puebla, and asked her father to send a suitable nobleman as her colleague.[3] As his interests would be directly threatened by the proposed marriage, he responded swiftly and Don Guitierre Gomez de Fuensalida reached England on 22 February 1508. Fuensalida was inexperienced and inept, but he was disposed to listen to Catherine, who in turn had learned from the much-despised De Puebla.[4] It was probably as much the result of Henry's deteriorating health as of the diplomatic efforts of the Spaniards, but the marriage never happened, and when the King died on 21 April 1509, she found herself facing a completely different situation.

During the lean years between 1502 and 1507, when she had had nothing to do and very little money, and while her remaining Spanish servants drifted away or got married, Catherine had consoled herself with pious exercises. She had also convinced herself that it was the will of God that she should marry Prince Henry. This conviction reconciled her to staying in England and survived his formal repudiation of the agreement in 1505. Indeed the latter was a diplomatic chess move and the young Prince's true feelings are unknown. The very next year he was referring to her as his 'most dear and well beloved consort, the princess my wife ...' but that may also have been a diplomatic move intended to press Maximilian. When Henry VIII came to the throne his relations with his sister-in-law can only be deduced. They must have known each other well by sight and that may have been sufficient to establish a mutual attraction. At almost 18, Henry was a magnificent specimen, with his maternal grandfather's imposing physique – already head and shoulders taller than most of his servants. At this stage of her life Catherine was apparently slender and petite, auburn haired and pretty – if Michael Sittow's portrait is to be trusted. Whether, however, they had had any opportunity to become familiar with each other, we do not know. According to Fuensalida (who was not the sharpest of observers) the young Prince had been carefully chaperoned right up to the moment of his accession and kept busy with his books and physical exercises. At the same time Catherine lived at court after her allocation of Durham House was withdrawn in November 1505 and her ambassadorial duties required frequent attendance. It is certainly true that Henry's father gave him no formal duties or responsibilities, beyond his purely notional responsibilities as Prince of Wales, but his virtual seclusion is unlikely. Unlike his brother at a similar age, he seems never to have visited the Marches, let alone lived there.[5]

Nevertheless the speed and effectiveness with which he seized the reins of government in May 1509 appears to give the lie to Fuensalida's description of a boy brought up 'almost like a young damsel'. Years later, and in very different circumstances, the chronicler Edward Hall attributed his actions to the initiative of the council that he had inherited from his father, and whereas that may have been true in respect of his rapid moves against the unpopular Richard Empson and Edmund Dudley, it is unlikely to have been true of his marriage. Hall wrote: '... the king was moved by some of his council that it should be honourable and profitable to his realm to take to wife the Lady Katherine, late wife to his brother Prince Arthur deceased ...'[6]

In fact his council seems to have been taken by surprise. Henry himself later claimed that he had been piously acting in accordance with his father's dying wish, but on 27 April, five days after the old king's death, the Council was unaware of any such instruction. On that day they assured Fuensalida that their master was completely uncommitted, and even added that he would be unlikely to consider his sister-in-law because of scruples over the dispensation.[7] Then, a few days later, the ambassador was summoned back, and began his interview with a defensive speech, retailing all the difficulties in Anglo-Spanish relations. Ferdinand had delayed giving his consent to the proposed marriage between his grandson Charles and the King's sister Mary and he had dallied interminably about paying the balance of Catherine's original dowry. At that point Henry, who had been waiting impatiently in an adjoining room, interrupted the proceedings with a message. What he wanted, he declared, was a triple alliance between himself, the Emperor and Ferdinand to curb the ambitions of France, and to that end he intended to marry Catherine forthwith.[8] All the wearying difficulties about the dowry, about Mary's betrothal and about Catherine's status, were simply swept aside. Fuensalida's erstwhile colleague was about to become Queen and his main duty now was to facilitate that as quickly as possible. The Princess was understandably jubilant. Through all the slights to which she had been subjected and all the difficulties of being a female ambassador linked to a man who turned out to be an arrogant and foolish colleague, her faith in ultimate success had never wavered. Only at the very end, in March 1509, had she apparently given way to a brief fit of despair. Now she was vindicated and being the pious soul that she was she attributed the entire astonishing reversal to God. He had heard and answered her pleas as only He could do, turning the King's heart, which (like that of all princes and governors) was in His hand alone. The events of these dramatic days between April and June of 1509 made an indelible impression upon her mind.

Henry and Catherine were married on 11 June in the Franciscan church at Greenwich and crowned together at Westminster on midsummer's day.[9] This was unprecedented. Richard II, Henry V, Henry VI, Edward IV and Henry VII had all been unmarried at the time of their accessions but Richard and Henry VI had succeeded as minors and all their respective Queens had been crowned separately. Only in the case of Henry VIII did marriage intervene between accession and coronation in a way that made this unique event possible. Despite the fact that the King's Council remained largely unchanged, the atmosphere of the court was transformed. Archbishop Warham remained as Chancellor, Richard Fox, Bishop of Winchester, remained Lord Privy Seal and the Earl of Surrey remained Treasurer, but there was a new king and that was what mattered. The fact that Henry was lavishly praised by humanist scholars on the look out for patronage is less important than the general contemporary evidence of how full of life and joy the royal couple were at this point. Their coronation was celebrated with a magnificent tournament, featuring the Knights of Pallas and the Knights of Diana, who symbolized that odd mixture of Italian humanism and Burgundian chivalry that was Henry's distinctive trademark. There had been no such tournament in England since the high days of Edward IV. Although he had had no enthusiasm for these sports himself, Henry VII had made sure that his son had been instructed by the very best masters-at-arms and, at the time of his accession, Henry VIII had the reputation of being the finest jouster in the land. This may not have been entirely deserved, but he was certainly very proficient, and for the next twenty years his enthusiasm for the sport was inexhaustible. On many subsequent occasions he was to enter the lists in person, but not this time. Jousting was a dangerous sport, even for the most accomplished and he was probably persuaded that the last thing England needed at such an auspicious juncture was for any misfortune to befall him. Instead he did honour to his mistress with 'noble triumphs and goodly shows', which featured the Queen's symbol of the pomegranate 'gilded with fine gold' in every conceivable place. The joy of these days was somewhat tempered by the death at the end of June of the King's grandmother, Margaret Beaufort, 'a woman of singular wisdom and policy, and also of most virtuous life' as the chronicler put it.[10] She had, however, died full of years and honours and although her obsequies were fully observed there is no sign that the King mourned unduly. He was too full of the opportunities of his own sunrise. Catherine was equally happy. 'These kingdoms ... are in great peace, and entertain much love to the king my lord and to me. Our time is spent in continual festival', she wrote to her father, who was as surprised and gratified as anyone by what had happened.

For the time being Henry was behaving like the overgrown schoolboy that he was. He would burst in on Catherine and her ladies at unseasonable hours and in all sorts of elaborate disguises, expecting her to be endlessly diverted and amused. She responded to this exuberance with tolerance and good humour and all the evidence suggests that at this time their relationship was both warm and loving.

They had, after all, much in common. Their intellectual tastes and educational background were very similar, allowing for the gender differences of the time. Both loved finery and display, both rode well and hunted with enthusiasm. Catherine took great pains with her physical appearance and was punctiliously deferential to her Lord in public – and probably in private too. He was, after all, worthy of her respect. He was not only an effective and conscientious king, he was also an intelligent man, with a splendid body. What more could any girl want? It is probable that her piety was both deeper and more heartfelt than his – he was always inclined to be rather intellectual in his faith – but the deep flaws of personality that the strains of life were subsequently to make only too clear were not obvious in the Henry of 1509. Meanwhile, Catherine was far more than a bedfellow. Her credentials as an ambassador had, of course, come to an end with the old king's death and had not been renewed in the new circumstances but her function continued. It is unlikely that Henry needed any prompting in the direction of alliance with Ferdinand, or war with France, but if he did, Catherine provided it. Her political experience was far greater than his and her intelligence just as sharp. Added to which the King was at ease in her company – far more so than with leading councillors such as William Warham or Sir Henry Marney. How much Catherine may have known of the domestic affairs of England is uncertain. Her knowledge of the language had come on by leaps and bounds since she was accredited as ambassador and now as Queen she was no longer inclined to seek the companionship of Spanish-speaking familiars. Instead she showed an unobtrusive but effective capacity for friendship and quietly rebuilt the good will of some aristocratic families, which the old king had treated with indifference or hostility – the Duke of Clarence's widowed daughter, Margaret Pole being a good case in point.

The nature of her sexual relationship with her husband can only be deduced from circumstantial evidence. The chances are that both were virgins when they married and although that would not be surprising in the case of a well brought-up royal princess – even if she was 24 – it would have been unusual for such a vigorous specimen of young manhood as Henry. However his name had never been linked with any woman, even in the most salacious gossip, and it seems that in that respect at least, Fuensalida was right. When it came to the test, it seems likely that Henry's sexual performance never had the stallion-like qualities that he liked to pretend and that it was left to his equally inexperienced but perhaps more worldly wise wife to coax him into action. If that was the case, she succeeded very well, because she conceived within weeks of her wedding – a circumstance that seems to have given her husband rather more confidence than he deserved. Catherine's pregnancy was part of the general euphoria of the court in the autumn of 1509. There were further jousts and this time Henry wore her favour in the lists and laid his trophies at her feet. Then there was a hitch, which looks more ominous with hindsight than it did at the time. In January 1510 the Queen was delivered of a child – only instead of the healthy son that her mother-in-law had managed in similar circumstances, this child was a girl, born prematurely and dead. In Spain, Ferdinand heard the news at the same time that he learned that his daughter's other great project – the Anglo-Spanish treaty of alliance, was signed and sealed.[11]

The royal couple shrugged off the misfortune of the still-birth. These things happened. They were both young and, more importantly, had proved their fertility. Within a few weeks, as the diplomatic preliminaries to war with France continued to build, Catherine conceived again. For the time being, at least, there was nothing wrong with their sexual relationship – and the Queen was certainly a trier. This time her pregnancy ran its full course and on New Year's day, 1511, she was delivered of a son. The whole country exploded with joy. The prince was named Henry, and baptized with great magnificence. The King, with what everyone thought was a proper sense of priorities, made a pilgrimage to Walsingham to give thanks for the birth of his heir, before turning his attention to more secular festivities. When celebrating, the King's mind was nothing if not conventional. A great tournament and feast was decreed, and Henry appeared in the guise of 'Coeur loyale' to win the chief prize (of course) and lay it at Catherine's feet.[12] It is to be hoped that she, recently convalescent and newly churched, was suitably impressed. Their joy, however, and that of the country, was shortlived, because on 22 February the young Prince died in his magnificent cradle at Richmond. We have no idea what killed him. There was no recorded birth defect and the modern suspicion would be an infection of some kind but at the time it was seen as a judgement of God. Modern research suggests that something like 40 per cent of aristocratic children who were born alive failed to survive their first year but without the benefit of such knowledge, Henry and Catherine were devastated. If it was a judgement – who was being judged?[13] In the event of a miscarriage or still birth it was customary to blame the woman but this was neither and the Queen's life was conspicuously blameless. Could it be Henry himself who was under the cross and, if so, why? Catherine spent agonized hours in prayer, seeking for a solution. The King, more resilient or less introspective, after a brief agony of self-pity, turned his attention to other things. In May he sent an expeditionary force of 1,000 archers under Lord Darcy to assist Ferdinand against the Moors. The result was a fiasco because the King of Spain changed his mind and sent them home again. Henry would probably have been a good deal more chagrined than he was if he had not been at the same time engaged in joining the Holy League, with Ferdinand and the Pope, which gave him the perfect pretext for the war that he was seeking against France. He shrugged off his disappointment over Darcy's dismissal and began to prepare for a much larger expedition in 1512, which was to form part of an Anglo-Spanish attack on Aquitaine, designed (in Henry's eyes at least) to recover England's 'ancient right' to Gascony, which had been lost 60 years before.[14]

So Henry had got his war but success continued to elude him. The Marquis of Dorset duly arrived at Fuentarrabia in June 1512 to find none of the support services promised by Ferdinand in place and he was stranded without supplies and with no agreed plan of campaign. Meanwhile the Spaniards used his presence as a cover for the seizure of Navarre. After several weeks of inaction, the English force became mutinous and taking advantage of an illness that had laid low their commander the officers hired ships and returned to England. Henry was furious and Ferdinand self-righteous. 'The King of Aragon was sore discontent with their departing, for they spent much money and substance in his country, and said openly that if they had tarried he would have invaded Guienne ...'[15]

Whether there was any truth in this protestation we do not know but the King of England certainly felt betrayed. He was too deeply committed to the war to back out but he lost his appetite for combined operations in the south. Instead he turned his attentions to Picardy and his target for the campaign of 1513 became the city and fortress of Tournai. Whether his suspicious relationship with Ferdinand had any affect upon his marriage is hard to tell. According to rumours picked up by Don Luis Caroz, now the Spanish ambassador in London, Henry was casting lustful eyes upon Anne Hastings and Elizabeth Ratcliffe, two married sisters of the Duke of Buckingham. From the same source we learn that this led to a furious spat with the Duke and to the dismissal of Elizabeth from the Queen's service. As the lady was a favourite of Catherine's, this in turn led to a domestic quarrel of some ferocity.[16] Caroz, however, was not particularly close to the Court and the Queen kept him at an arms length. She might no longer be officially ambassador but no one was going to usurp her position when it came to mediating between her father and her husband.

The rumours probably arose not from any actual infidelity on Henry's part but from his enthusiasm for a kind of charade known as 'courtly love'. This was a game played by bored courtiers wherein a man would chose a 'mistress' from among the available ladies, would bombard her with trivial gifts and amorous verses and profess his undying devotion. She would then respond as the mood took her, with coy encouragement or furious disdain – usually the latter. This game could go through several rounds, and the 'winners' were those who kept up the pretence longest and most convincingly – particularly the ones who produced the most elegant verses or songs. Real relationships were not supposed to be in question but, human nature being what it is, they sometimes were. The King himself was much in demand as a partner in such games and, after two or three years of playing exclusively with his wife, had probably decided to broaden his field a little. Beyond the inevitable tiffs and sulks, there is no reason to suppose at this stage that his relationship with Catherine was under any sort of real stress. When he went campaigning in France in June 1513 he named her as Governor of the Realm and Captain General in his absence. This was supposed to be a largely honorific position and there is plenty of evidence that the King's council continued to govern from his camp, wherever that might be, but it turned out to be rather more real than either of them had anticipated. On 11 August a Scottish herald turned up at Henry's camp and issued a formal declaration of war.[17] In spite of being married to the King's sister, James IV was unable to resist the temptation to resurrect the 'auld alliance' and to seize an opportunity while Henry was distracted. This turned out to be a big mistake because Catherine, with exemplary speed and efficiency, raised an army and despatched it north under the command of the Earl of Surrey. More than that, she also raised a back-up force, which she commanded in person. On 9 September Surrey annihilated the Scots at Flodden, and James fell on the field of battle. When the news reached Catherine as she advanced to Leicester, she disbanded her army and went home – as well she might. When Henry took first Therouanne and then Tournai, and won the somewhat notional battle of the Spurs, he sent his trophies home to his Queen but she already had the bloodstained coat that James had worn at Flodden. There is an unsubstantiated report from James Banisius, an Imperial agent in London, that Catherine was in an advanced state of pregnancy at the time of the Scottish invasion and gave birth soon after to a live son, who lived for a few days. However, there is no conclusive proof of this, which would have been surprising had it been a fact, and her personal command of the reserve army suggests that she was in no such condition.

There is more than a suggestion that the Queen sided with her husband when his relations with her father became strained, and her communications with the latter became perfunctory. When Ferdinand contracted out of the Holy League in February 1514, they virtually ceased. This time Henry had every right to feel betrayed, but the rumours that he was thinking of taking this resentment out on his wife by divorcing her appear to be later rationalizations. Caroz complained that Catherine was forgetting Spain in order to court the favour of the English and this time he seems to have been right. By September 1514 she was pregnant again and this time her condition is sufficiently authenticated, because in January 1515 she was delivered of a stillborn son 'of eight months'. There was grief and lamentation – not as sharp as in 1511, but just as heartfelt. Time was no longer on the Queen's side. She was 30 and beginning to run to fat. Her physical beauty was fading, she had endured three, or possibly four pregnancies and still there was no child. At the same time, her role as a 'pillow councillor' was diminishing. For several years after his accession, Henry had continued to rely on his father's councillors, but by 1514 he had a man of his own. That man was Thomas Wolsey, originally his father's chaplain, whom he had appointed almoner a few months after his accession. This in itself was not a great promotion but it did give opportunities for contact with the King, which Wolsey was quick to exploit. In 1511 he was entrusted with the logistics of Lord Darcy's abortive mission and its failure was no reflection on his efficiency. He became a member of the Council, again not a matter of great significance but a sign of growing confidence. Then in 1512 he managed, not only Dorset's campaign but also the more successful naval operations that took place around Brest.[18] In February 1514 he became Bishop of Lincoln and in September was translated to York. Finally, in December 1515, he succeeded Warham as Chancellor. By 1515 Wolsey was unquestionably the King's chief minister and adviser and in the process put the Queen's nose badly out of joint. Although there was a reconciliation between Henry and Ferdinand early in 1515, Catherine did not recover her mediating position and her political influence dwindled. Her connections with Spain also became more tenuous in other ways. Her Spanish confessor, Fray Diego, was notoriously indiscreet and by the end of 1515 had been compelled to go home. At the same time the last of Catherine's devoted band of Spanish ladies, Maria de Salinas, left her to become Lady Willoughby. She still had Spanish servants but they no longer had their former intimacy. Then in January 1516, her father died, and her relations with her 16-year-old nephew, Charles, who succeeded him, were for the time being distant. There are no signs that the Queen was particularly distressed by these changes. Apart from a passing qualm just before Henry VII's death, she had never expressed any desire to return to Spain and was fully committed to her husband's realm.

In the autumn of 1515, she was again pregnant, and in February 1516 – at long last – was delivered of a healthy child. The rejoicings were genuine but muted, for the child was a girl. A fit piece to play on the diplomatic chess board but not a suitable heir. Henry was determinedly upbeat, 'by God's grace' he is alleged to have said, 'the sons will follow'. We do not know Catherine's reaction.[19] No doubt she was relieved to have done at least part of her primary duty but she knew better than her husband that her time was now getting short. It was not so much her age that was a problem but physical wear and tear. Henry did not give up and there is no suggestion that his pastimes kept him from her bed but it was early in 1518 before she conceived again. On 9 November she was delivered of a still born girl. The old curse had struck again and although the King persevered, at least fitfully, for another four or five years, Catherine did not conceive again. She was only 33 and probably did not reach the menopause for another six or seven years but she was worn out and her childbearing years were over. Meanwhile, Henry had at last taken a genuine mistress. Just when he started taking a serious interest in Elizabeth Blount is not certain and it is possible that the King was not sure himself. Bessy had been born in about 1500, and on the payroll of the court from 1512. She was a pretty and vivacious blond, not over blessed with brains but accomplished in the courtly arts. It is quite probable that Henry started playing courtly love with her at some time during 1516. By 1518 they were sharing a bed and late in 1518, ironically at about the same time that Catherine had her last still birth, she was found to be pregnant. At some unknown date in 1519, she was delivered of a healthy son, who was immediately acknowledged and named Henry Fitzroy. Thomas Wolsey, by now Cardinal, stood as his godfather. The birth of young Henry affected Catherine profoundly. In the first place it was incontrovertible proof that she was at least sharing her husband's affections with another woman. This was a situation with which Elizabeth Woodville had become very familiar but not any of the other queens we have been considering, as far as we know. More importantly, it appeared to demonstrate that her gynaecological misfortunes were her own fault. It was in any case conventional wisdom to blame the woman for still births and miscarriages but this demonstrated that, with another woman, Henry was perfectly capable of getting a healthy son. The agonizing implications of this hit the Queen hard, and may well have actually inhibited any further conception on her part. She increased her religious devotions, searching for some way of appeasing a God who was only too obviously displeased with her.

Like every other queen, she had been given a jointure on her marriage: lands to the value of about £3,000, which, if not generous by the standards of the recent past, at least gave her considerable freedom of action. Just how much of this was dispensed by her almoner or the stewards of her various manors in the form of charity we do not know but it was enough to gain her the reputation of a Lady Bountiful. This was not a social policy, or a hint to her husband that he had better do something about poor relief. It was a Christian duty and combined with the fact that she was a member of the Franciscan tertiaries, and was alleged to wear a hair shirt under her royal robes, served to give her a reputation for exemplary piety. In other words, Catherine began to be cast as a female role model and, although this was to become profoundly irritating to Henry in due course, it had its advantages. She was an ideal intermediary for all sorts of petitions, particularly from humble clergy and widows and orphans and, although she almost certainly did intercede for the Evil May Day rioters in 1517, it was a part carefully choreographed for her by Wolsey, even to the kneeling posture and the unbound hair.[20] All this was woman's work, as her contemporaries noted with satisfaction – just as the Virgin Mary in heaven, so Queen Catherine in England. As 1520 came and went, and the Queen began to approach her fortieth birthday, she was compensating as hard as she possibly could for failing in her primary duty. There was not, and probably would not now be, a male heir.

Henry was not rushing his fences, but he had to consider his options. His older sister, Margaret, had married in Scotland and was Queen Mother to the young King, James V. The fact that she was married a second time (to the Earl of Angus) and had produced a daughter was a mere distraction. James was an alien born and the king of a foreign realm. Could he be considered as the heir of England? His younger sister, Mary, betrothed as a child to the Archduke Charles, had eventually been traded for peace with France and had married the ageing Louis XII in 1514. She had, it was alleged, danced him to death in a few months and then, being a wilful wench, had forced herself on the (more or less willing) Duke of Suffolk, sent to bring her home. It was just as well that Louis had been too debilitated to leave her pregnant, because there could have been doubts about the paternity of any child born within a reasonable time after her marriage to Brandon. As it was, they had later produced only daughters, who did not count in this context. The real issue in the early 1520s concerned Henry's own daughter, Mary, and her bastard half brother. Fitzroy would only have been a factor if he could have been legitimated and there was no prospect of that. The only recognized method of legitimating bastards was if the parents subsequently married and that was ruled out. Not only had the King's relationship with Elizabeth Blount come to an end, perhaps even before the child was born, but by 1522, having withdrawn from the Court, she was married to Gilbert Tailboys, son and heir of Lord Tailboys of Kyme. The King may have toyed with the idea of getting some kind of special dispensation from the Pope but it was not pursued. His main attention focused on Mary. A daughter's main use, as we have seen in other connections, was as a matrimonial bait, and Mary was first used in that way when Wolsey was angling for the treaty of universal peace, which is known as the treaty of London in 1518. After Louis death, the 1514 treaty with France had rather fallen apart. His cousin and successor, Francis of Angouleme, was not particularly hostile but he was too like Henry, both in age and ambition, for their relations to be easy. Given that the King of Spain was the 18-year-old Charles of Ghent, who was having problems establishing himself in the south, the possibility of settling international relations for some time to come seemed to be too good to miss. By taking the initiative in these negotiations, Wolsey obviously hoped to please the Pope (who was always on the look out for peace settlements) but also to enhance his master's and his own prestige. Part of the bait was a marriage between the 2-year-old Mary, and Francis's even younger son, the Dauphin and, when the treaty was completed, that was one of the agreements. There could have been no more complete demonstration of the eclipse of Catherine's political influence than the betrothal of her cherished only child in France, a country that she had devoted most of her life to opposing.

She dutifully accompanied Henry to the Field of Cloth of Gold in 1520, but appears to have played a purely passive role in those festivities. However, she may have been gratified to notice that, far from sealing any friendship with the King of France, this meeting rather encouraged their rivalry. Within a few months Henry had abandoned Wolsey's balancing act, and gone back to the Imperial alliance which had been embodied in the Holy League.[21] One reason for this may have been suspicion of Francis but mainly it was a consequence of the death of the Emperor Maximilian in 1519. The Holy Roman Empire was elective and three candidates entered the field – Charles of Spain, Francis of France, and Henry himself. Nobody (except Henry) took the latter's chances seriously at all and Charles had both hereditary influence and the Fuggers on his side, so he was duly elected.[22] This new alignment spelled the end for the optimistic treaty of London because France now had Habsburg territory on its three main landward frontiers, which meant that a renewal of the wars in northern Italy was almost certain – and Henry was in the strategic position of controlling the 'fourth front' – the Channel. If the King of England had really been keen on maintaining the balance of power he would have sided with France at this point but Henry was only interested in securing the maximum advantage for himself. So, partly to maintain good relations with the Low Countries (where Antwerp was London's main trading partner), and partly hoping again to grab a bit of northern France, he sided with the Emperor. Charles visited England in 1521 and signed a new treaty of alliance, plainly aimed against France. He also met his aunt for the first time, and allowed himself to be betrothed to his host's 5-year-old daughter. The little girl danced for his pleasure and remembered their brief encounter for the rest of her life. Whether this about turn in English policy owed anything to Catherine's influence is not clear but probably not. Henry had sufficient reasons for his action and no particular need to gratify his Queen. However, she was certainly pleased by the turn of events and would very much sooner have had her own nephew as a prospective son-in-law than the Dauphin of France. It is probable that no one took the betrothal very seriously, because it was unlikely that the 21-year-old Emperor would wait for his child bride to grow up but it was a recognized way of sealing an alliance. More importantly, Catherine established a friendly relationship with Charles, which was to prove of great significance when the hostile winds began to blow.

Meanwhile, the King had taken another mistress. This time no marital pregnancy provided an excuse for infidelity, but Catherine in her late thirties was no longer the pretty girl he had married. 'Rather ugly than otherwise' sniffed the Venetian ambassador and no longer an exciting partner to a husband seven years her junior. Mary Boleyn was the daughter of Sir Thomas, an experienced courtier and diplomat, who had succeed in infiltrating his elder daughter into the entourage that had accompanied the King's sister Mary to France in 1514. On Mary's return (as Duchess of Suffolk), her servant had remained at court. Mary Boleyn appears to have been physically attractive, but rather bland as a person. She replaced Elizabeth Blount in the King's bed at some time in 1519 or 1520, a relationship that again grew out of the cavortings of courtly love. In 1521 she was married to William Carey, a gentleman of the Privy Chamber, presumably as a precaution, but seems not to have slept with him until the King had finished with her. She did not become pregnant by Henry but immediately conceived as soon as she began cohabiting with her husband, which suggests that the King was no longer as potent as he had been in the early days of his marriage, because it was never suggested that there was anything platonic about his relationship with Mary. Catherine must have known about all this but she held her tongue as a dutiful royal wife was bound to do and concentrated on the education of their child, and her manifold pieties.

The year 1525 was eventful. Henry's attempt to wage war against France had stuttered badly in 1523, and relations with his ally the Emperor had become increasingly strained. Consequently when, early in 1525, Charles won a great victory over Francis at Pavia, and captured him, he treated Henry's plans for the exploitation of his victory with disdain. If the King of England wanted a piece of France, let him earn it for himself. Henry, hamstrung by the failure of Wolsey's attempt to raise more money through the so called Amicable Grant in the spring of 1525, decided instead to settle with the French, and did so at the treaty of the More in August.[23] This effectively spelt the end of the Imperial alliance and the end of Mary's betrothal to Charles. He married the more suitably aged Isabella of Portugal in 1526. Meanwhile, Henry had the succession very much on his mind. He had by this time given up on Catherine and accepted the fact that she would never bear him the legitimate son that he so desperately needed. On 18 June he created his bastard son Duke of Richmond and the choice of this royal title may have been significant. He probably was not seriously considering trying to legitimate him but was rather sending out a signal that his options were still open.

The following month Princess Mary was sent off to the Marches of Wales with a lavish entourage, but was not given the formal title that would have acknowledged her right to succeed.[24] If we exclude the possibility of legitimating Henry Fitzroy, the King had only three options. The first was simply to acknowledge Mary as his heir and try to make sure that she eventually married someone who would be acceptable as King Consort. Given the general aversion of the English to the prospect of foreign rule this would not be easy. The second was a variation, whereby Mary would be married as quickly as possible in the hope that she would bear a son to whom the Crown could pass direct. This was to gamble not only on the King's longevity but also on Mary's acquiescence in allowing herself to be so passed over. The third option was to repudiate Catherine and start again. At some time during 1525, Henry decided to go for the third option.

For the time being, nothing happened. Catherine fretted about her daughter's health and about her Latin, engaging her countryman Juan Luis Vives to write two works for her instruction, *De Institutione Foeminae Christianae* in 1523 and *De Ratione Studia Puerilis* in 1524. When she went to Wales she was accompanied by Dr Richard Featherstone as schoolmaster and the most elaborate instructions for her life and deportment were drawn up under Catherine's eye.[25] It is quite possible that Henry's decision to send his daughter so far away at the age of nine had something to do with lessening her mother's influence but if that was his thinking it did not work. The King, meanwhile, was coming to a resolution of his problem. There had been doubts about the lawfulness of his marriage before it had ever happened, hence the dispensation, but in his enthusiasm at the time, Henry had simply swept them aside. Perhaps he had been wrong to do so. Henry was Bible learned and knew that the Book of Leviticus prohibited a man from marrying his brother's wife, and pronounced that the couple would be childless. Perhaps that was the Law of God, and could not be dispensed? He became convinced. The facts that he had married his brother's widow, not his wife, and that he and Catherine were not childless were eased away by linguistic scholarship. The Hebrew had really said 'they shall be without sons', which fitted his situation exactly.[26] By the end of 1526 Henry had convinced himself that his marriage had broken a Divine Law and that he was being punished. It was no true marriage and the woman with whom he had slept for six or seven years and who had endured half a dozen pregnancies at his hands was not really his wife.

Catherine seems to have been quite unaware of these thought processes but she was also becoming a liability for more than strictly dynastic reasons. Henry had fallen out with the Emperor to the extent of being theoretically at war with him and Catherine symbolized, even if she no longer represented, the Imperial alliance. Towards the end of 1526 the Imperial ambassador Mendoza wrote that 'the principal cause of [her] misfortune is that she identifies herself entirely with the Emperor's interests ...' and early in 1527 he repeated the sentiment, 'she will do her best to restore the old alliance between Spain and England, but though her will is good, her means are small ...' Small indeed; but by 1527 there was more than one reason why Catherine had become an embarrassment. Later there were many stories about how the King's marriage first came to be called in question. It was alleged (by Catherine, who could not stand him) that Wolsey had planted the seeds of doubt. Another candidate (according to George Cavendish) was the Bishop of Tarbes, who was sent by Francis I to negotiate a possible marriage between Mary and the Duc d'Orleans; but he did not arrive until April, by which time the first moves had already been planned.[27] There is little doubt that the 'scruple' came from the King himself or that it antedated any serious involvement with Anne Boleyn, Mary's sister, whom Henry was pursuing by the later part of 1527.

The chronology of that affair has been much debated, largely because there were always rumours flying around the court that Henry was 'enamoured' of this or that unnamed damsel and it is difficult to know when these stories begin to focus on Anne. Probably a standard courtly flirtation began to become serious at some time during 1526. By the end of that year the King had almost certainly propositioned her and been rejected. Anne was, by all accounts, no great beauty, but she had been trained at Mechelen at the court of Margaret of Austria and was accomplished in all the wiles of seduction. These were probably second nature to her and it came as something of a surprise when the King was snared. In the light of what happened subsequently her reaction looks calculated but it was probably no such thing at the time. Henry, however, was not inclined to give up, and the sudden weakening of Catherine's position in the summer of 1527 created a new and exciting possibility.

Proceedings commenced with a secret court convened by Wolsey at Westminster, wherein the King was charged with having co-habited for 18 years with a woman who was not his wife. Several sessions were held in the latter part of May, but no conclusion was reached. Henry then, overcome by his conscience (or possibly by desire for Anne), took matters into his own hands, and on 22 June confronted Catherine with the news that they were not, and never had been, married. The Queen appears to have had no inkling of what was afoot and was totally astounded.[28] Not only had she never entertained a moment's doubt about the lawfulness of her marriage but she was, as we have seen, quite convinced that God had decreed it. Her reaction was highly emotional but also extremely pragmatic. Realizing that her husband would have to resort to Rome for a decision, she immediately despatched her steward, a Spaniard named Francisco Felipez, with a message to her nephew the Emperor in Valladolid, warning him what was afoot and soliciting his immediate aid. Charles, goaded by this insult to his family honour, reacted immediately. He wrote to Catherine, pledging his full support, to Henry, begging him to desist from so dishonourable a course, and to the Pope to forestall any resulting proceedings in the Curia. Clement, meanwhile, had been terrorized and imprisoned by a mutinous army operating under the Emperor's banner, but without his knowledge, who in May 1527 had sacked the Imperial City and confined the Pope to the Castel de St Angelo. By the time that Charles's message arrived the siege had been lifted but Clement was in no position to refuse any request that the Emperor might make, irrespective of its justice. Henry had therefore lost his case in the one place where it mattered, even before it had begun.[29]

Thereafter it was a case of irresistible force and immoveable matter, because the belligerent positions taken up in the summer of 1527 did not change significantly for the next five-and-a-half years. It used to be argued that Henry's position was purely selfish, whereas Catherine's was one of principle – 'the king wanted to change his woman' as Robert Bolt put it, paraphrasing some contemporary opinions. However, in terms of moral altitude, there was nothing to chose between them. By the autumn of that year the King knew that he wanted Anne Boleyn – no doubt for personal gratification but also because the country needed a legitimate male heir. It is usually believed that Anne held out on him, demanding marriage as the price of complaisance, but that is not necessarily what happened. He could have taken her by force without risk of serious consequences and she must have known that. On the other hand, another bastard would be no use to him. He needed a son born in recognized wedlock and that could not happen unless or until he managed to get rid of Catherine. So it is more likely that he was the one holding back from intercourse. The Queen, on the other hand, knew perfectly well that she would never be able to give Henry the son that he needed. She seems to have believed, perhaps from the example of her own mother, that there was no reason why a woman should not rule a kingdom but that was to fly in the face of English opinion, which was not reconciled to such an eventuality. Moreover there was a possibility of escape, which perhaps a loving and dutiful wife should have grasped. If she had taken the veil, her marriage would automatically have been dissolved without impugning either its original legitimacy or the status of their daughter. This option was offered to her on at least two occasions and rejected with scorn. However, given the circumstances and her almost obsessive piety, it was a perfectly reasonable suggestion to make. Two factors contributed to the actual impasse. The first was Henry's incredible clumsiness. Had he approached her gently, explaining the problem (if it needed explaining) and appealed to her good nature or sense of duty, she might have agreed to withdraw gracefully. She would, after all, have had relatively little to lose and quite a lot to gain. However, that did not happen and his method of broaching the matter aroused all her fighting instincts. The second was the fact that Catherine came to realize that she had been supplanted in her husband's affections by one of her own women – and a mere gentlewoman into the bargain. Once she had grasped this fact, it is not surprising that surrender was not an option. Both Henry and Catherine were being selfish – and very human – but the one incontrovertible fact is that Henry needed a lawful son and in that respect the interests of the kingdom were at stake.

At first it seems that no one understood the full nature of the King's intentions. Wolsey was still thinking of a French princess to replace Catherine while he dealt with Henry's scruple. When he discovered the truth in 1528, he was not happy but had no option but to continue pressing the King's case at Rome. He got nowhere, and nor did the numerous special missions that Henry sent between 1527 and 1532. Clement shifted and prevaricated but would not budge. This intransigence had two main causes. One was obviously the political pressure of the Emperor, but the other was his extreme reluctance to admit that Julius II's dispensation might have been *ultra vires*, in pretending to dispense with a Divine Law which was not amenable to such treatment.[30] Henry's case was not strong in canon law, and would have needed skill and good luck to have prevailed, but it was much better than it was made to appear, both at the time and since. The nearest the King came to success was the Legatine Court, which assembled at Blackfriars in July 1529, but that was little better than a sham. Catherine duly appeared and (as had no doubt been expected) immediately appealed her cause to Rome. The Court was adjourned and the appeal stood. By this time the Queen had very strong support. In England Bishop John Fisher led a powerful legal and canonical team, which conducted her defence, and she enjoyed the strong (if surreptitious) backing of all those aristocratic families who hated and feared the rise of the Boleyns. Her image as a 'wronged woman' appealed to other women up and down the land. Abroad, her nephew continued to promote her cause in Rome and his newly arrived ambassador in England, Eustace Chapuys, immediately constituted himself as her prime champion and protector. Henry only tolerated his blatant interference because he had no desire to sever diplomatic relations with the Emperor, being uncertain of the friendship of the French.

Wolsey fell from favour in the autumn of 1529, having failed to give the King what he both wanted and needed. He died in November 1530 facing charges of treason but his disappearance did nothing to resolve what was by that time known as 'the King's great matter'. Meanwhile, Catherine remained at Court, in a kind of *ménage a trois* with Anne Boleyn, discharging her formal duties and still recognized as Queen, but clearly out of the King's bed and favour. Finally, in an attempt to break the deadlock and perhaps in an effort to stave off the radical action that he was then contemplating, on 31 July 1531 the King caused a delegation of about 30 councillors and peers to wait upon the Queen at Greenwich and plead with her in the name of the King and kingdom. They were wasting their time and breath. Catherine merely reaffirmed her position and her willingness to abide by the papal decision, which she knew perfectly well would be in her favour. Exasperated, Henry left the court, taking Anne with him, and a few days later, on 14 August, went to Woodstock, ordering the Queen to remain at Windsor. With a kind of heroic innocence, Catherine complained that this was no way for Henry to treat his wife, whereupon he exploded with wrath, declaring that he would receive no more messages from her – and never wished to see her again. That was the end of the *ménage a trois*, and also of any talk of a reconciliation. Anne had, in a sense, seen off her rival, but legally nothing had changed. Whether he chose to acknowledge the fact or not, he was still married to Catherine, and Anne had, and could have, no status.

Over the previous two years Henry had tried numerous ways to extract a favourable decision from Rome. He had tried browbeating his own Church with charges of praemunire; he had tried claiming that papal jurisdiction did not extend to matrimony; he had tried pleading the ancient rights of England. Nothing worked, and all that he achieved was the interminable delay in the delivery of the papal sentence, which was driving Catherine and her supporters mad.[31] After the summer of 1531, the emphasis changed. Catherine now kept her own court, separate from that of the King, Chapuys visited her regularly and she became increasingly a focus for opposition, not only to the Boleyn ascendancy but also to the King. By the Christmas of 1531 the political nation was becoming increasingly divided and Henry rejected Catherine's proffered New Year gift. The King later alleged that his strong-minded wife could have raised a rebellion against him, such was her support, and waged a war 'as fierce as any her mother Isabella had waged in Spain'.[32] That may or may not have been true but the Queen had no such intention. Her sole purpose was to force Henry to drop his annulment petition. The King was now on his metal and by the beginning of 1532 had become convinced (or had convinced himself) that the Pope was claiming jurisdiction to which he had no right. In other words that the papacy was merely a human institution that was usurping upon the authority of kings. Although he would never have admitted it, this was dangerously close to the heretical position taken up by Martin Luther and his followers a few years earlier. By March 1532 his new chief adviser, the self-taught lawyer Thomas Cromwell, had worked out a way to turn this conviction into law by using the ancient and reputable instrument of Parliament. Taking advantage of anti-clerical sentiment in the House of Commons stimulated by a row over mortuary fees, on 18 March he introduced into the House 'A supplication against the Ordinaries'.

Catherine's defences remained impregnable, but she was now being outflanked. By the autumn of 1532 the King had determined to ignore the Pope and seek a solution using the legislative resources available within England. In August Archbishop Warham died and he had the opportunity to appoint a new prelate who would co-operate in his scheme. Meanwhile he created Anne Marquis of Pembroke and took her off to France to meet Francis, whose friendship, or at least acquiescence, was essential now he was set on a course that was bound to leave the Emperor even more alienated. The French king tactfully avoided meeting Anne but in other respects was supportive because his quarrels with the Emperor were never ending. At some time during their stay in Calais, Henry and Anne at last slept together. In January 1533 the amenable Thomas Cranmer became the new Archbishop of Canterbury and Anne was discovered to be pregnant. The climax swiftly followed. Henry and Anne were secretly married and Cranmer's court at Dunstable declared his first marriage null and void. Catherine, of course, refused to recognize either the court or its decision, but her position was now extremely precarious.[33] On the basis of Cranmer's decision, Henry declared that she was no longer Queen, but Dowager Princess of Wales and that their daughter, Mary, was illegitimate. Neither woman (Mary was by now 17) would accept this judgement, which was embodied in a proclamation issued on 5 July.[34] A proclamation was not a law and the penalty decreed for disobedience was as yet only 'extreme displeasure' but it put the Queen's supporters on the spot. Chapuys was full of righteous indignation and her household servants, who had a low political profile, ignored it. However, her more prominent political sympathizers began to draw in their horns. Offending the King was a risky business and those with careers to consider, like the King's former secretary Stephen Gardiner, changed sides. Catherine was by no means abandoned but by the time that Elizabeth was born in September 1533, her position was becoming increasingly beleaguered.

This was, in a sense, her own choice. The King's proclamation had concluded: '... nevertheless the King's most gracious pleasure is that the said Lady Catherine shall be well used, obeyed and entreated according to her honour and noble parentage, by the name, style and title of Princess Dowager.'

And he was as good as his word. Although he reduced her establishment in accordance with his own perception of her status, it was still costing him nearly £3,000 a year – very far from the poverty to which Chapuys complained that she had been reduced.[35] Catherine could simply have accepted the *fait accompli*, which had left her in a kind of honourable retirement or she could have taken the veil, even at this late stage, or she could have demanded to go back to Spain. Instead she remained obdurate, thus making her own life far more wretched than it need have been and the lives of all her servants and wellwishers extremely difficult. Almost the only satisfaction that the autumn of 1533 brought to her and her friends was that Anne's child, for which so much had been sacrificed, turned out to be a girl. Henry did not know what to do about her. He moved her from Ampthill in July 1533 to Buckden in Huntingdonshire, a manor of the Bishop of Ely, where she complained of the proximity of the fens. Finally, perhaps in response to these pleas, or perhaps for reasons of his own, in May 1534 he moved her again, this time to Kimbolton, which was smaller than Buckden, but more salubrious. At that time he again reduced her household, but not by very much and she still retained a core of Spanish servants, including her physician and apothecary. Chapuys made an endless nuisance of himself with protests against her dishonourable treatment and more seriously intrigued vigorously with disaffected nobles on her behalf. Cromwell kept a careful eye on his behaviour and probably knew that, whereas Charles was not disposed to curb his activities, he was paying absolutely no heed to his pleas for intervention. Catherine might be his aunt and he had no intention of abandoning her but at the same time he had no intention either of getting embroiled in England's domestic affairs. He would confine himself to preventing any reconciliation between Henry and the Pope, who in the autumn of 1533 had ordered the King of England to take his wife back, under pain of excommunication.[36] Only in one respect did Henry behave vindictively towards his ex-wife. He refused to allow any personal contact between Catherine and Mary. Messages, sometime apparently written in Spanish, passed to and fro, borne by trusty messengers, but even when her daughter was ill, the Queen was not allowed to visit her. By 1535 the King was aware that the daughter was potentially more dangerous than the mother. For all her obstinacy, Catherine would never countenance any armed opposition to the King's will – but Mary was much less experienced and more suggestible. If rebellion was to stir as the King moved definitively to end Papal authority in England, it was only too likely that she would become its figurehead. She was just as recalcitrant as Catherine and unless or until he had a legitimate son there would be many who would continue to regard her as his lawful heir. In 1534 Henry's first Succession Act made it high treason to deny Elizabeth's legitimacy, or to affirm the validity of his first marriage. An oath was imposed on all subjects to that effect but it was not administered to Mary and her mother. The King knew their minds well enough but had no desire to cut their heads off.[37]

Towards the end of 1535 Catherine became ill and in January of the following year she died at Kimbolton, insisting to the last that she was the Queen of England.

Mary (to her great grief) was not allowed to come to her but her passing was exemplary in its piety and she was laid to rest with all the honours due a Dowager Princess, in Peterborough Cathedral. There were, inevitably, rumours of poison and Catherine had herself apparently feared no less. However, they were only rumours. If Henry had been willing to yield to the temptation to do away with her he would have done so long before. It would appear that the former Queen succumbed to a series of heart attacks. She was 51. Even if we accept the validity of Cranmer's sentence, she had still been accepted as Henry's wife for almost 24 years – far longer than any of her successors. She was a highly intelligent and well-educated woman, who had been in her time a great patron of scholars and the recipient of many dedications. Vives is only the best known example. In her youth she had been not only attractive but light hearted and good humoured. Unfortunately neither her good looks nor her good humour survived advancing years and misfortune. Her strong-mindedness became the most inflexible and self destructive obstinacy and her piety, from being gracious, became obsessive. There is no doubt that in the last years of her life she courted a kind of virtual martyrdom and took a grim satisfaction from the fact that, in 1533, her daughter was similarly afflicted for her sake. For the first ten years of her marriage she had devoted all her considerable influence to maintaining the alliance between her husband and her homeland but lost that battle eventually because of her father's death and the rise of Thomas Wolsey. Paradoxically, it was the King's attempts to get rid of her that revived that relationship in a different and even more potent form. Without really intending to be so, she became her nephew's bridgehead into English politics and a pressure point that the Emperor found of great value in his dealings with the King of England. Despite spending more than 35 years in England and enduring both good and bad fortune, Catherine never forgot that she was of the royal blood of Spain. How dare a mere Tudor treat her so disrespectfully!

If Catherine could be dubbed 'the wife who never was', the same title might be applied more realistically to Anne of Cleves. Henry had married Catherine because he wanted her and because she represented a long-standing alliance that corresponded with his present strategic needs. He married Anne because she represented a short-term solution to a pressing problem. When the problem disappeared, the marriage came down to a question of personal chemistry, which was soon found to be non-existent. The year 1539 was, or appeared to be, a dangerous time for England. The King had declared his independence of the Pope five years before and stood excommunicate, which was standing invitation for any neighbouring prince to attack him in the name of the Church.[38] As long as the Emperor and the King of France were at daggers drawn there was small

chance of that happening but on 12 January 1539 they came to terms in the
Treaty of Toledo and each agreed not to come to any understanding with England
without the consent of the other. There was talk of withdrawing their diplomatic
representatives and the threat seemed to be real. Henry reacted in three ways. First
he ordered musters up and down the country, mobilized his fleet and commenced
a series of fortifications along the south coast.[39] This had the desired, if not
intended, effect of uniting the country behind its king. However unhappy some
Englishmen might be with the drift of the King's recent policies, they were not
prepared to contemplate some foreigner interfering to put things right. Secondly
he caused the Act of Six Articles to be passed. This was a reaffirmation of Catholic
orthodoxy on certain key theological issues, particularly the sacrament of the
mass. Henry might have repudiated the Pope, dissolved the monasteries and
authorized a vernacular Bible, but he had no desire to be thought a heretic and
chose this method of distancing himself from the creeping evangelicalism that
Cromwell and Cranmer had been promoting over the previous five years. This
apparently pulled the rug from under his third objective, which was to seek an
alliance with the only European power that seemed reliably anti-papal – the
Schmalkaldic League of Germany. Faced with the Treaty of Toledo, England was
dangerously isolated and the League appeared to offer the only realistic option.
The Leaguers, however, were insistent that Henry subscribe to the Lutheran
Augsburg confession before they would enter into any formal agreement and that
Henry was determined not to do. The Act of Six Articles reaffirmed that refusal,
and negotiations with the League broke down. Cleves-Julich, however, was not
a member of the League. Its Duke was a Catholic of reforming tendencies who
was perennially at odds with the Emperor. Cleves-Julich was not a major power
but the Duke had his own allies and contacts among the anti-Habsburg German
princes. Moreover, he had a sister available for marriage.

Henry had been without a partner since the tragic death of Jane Seymour
in October 1537, and a considerable number of options had been considered,
including several French princesses before the Treaty of Toledo appeared to cut
off that line of advance. For some time his preferred choice had been Christina
of Denmark but that lady had eventually declined the honour, allegedly declaring
that she would prefer to keep her head on her shoulders.[40] A negotiation with
Cleves had been suggested as early as June 1538, but it was only after the death
of the old Duke in February 1539 and the succession of his son William, that
official feelers were put out. The original proposal had been for a match between
the young Duke and Mary, now back in favour in England, but still illegitimate
but this was quickly superseded by a negotiation for the King himself to marry
William's unassigned sister, Anne, then aged 24. The summer advanced and the

Franco-Imperial threat failed to materialize but Thomas Cromwell was keen to see the King wedded again and pressed on with the negotiation. One son was not sufficient for dynastic security although Edward, Jane Seymour's son, appeared to be a robust child just entering his third year. Hans Holbein was sent across to draw the lady's portrait and his effort (which still survives) was sufficient to convince the King of Anne's charms. There was some discussion of a possible pre-contract but that had been disposed of by the end of September and the treaty was finally signed on 4 October 1539.[41] What nobody disclosed, and the English envoys probably did not have the chance to observe, was that Anne was in many respects an extremely unsuitable consort. She was, admittedly, not a Lutheran, and was passably handsome, but she was almost completely uneducated, having been brought up in the domestic seclusion of the family castle. Whereas both Catherine and Anne Boleyn had been sophisticated young ladies, fluent in several languages and accomplished in the courtly arts, and Jane Seymour had received a respectable renaissance education, Anne was a bumpkin. She spoke no language but German, was ignorant of music and knew only the dances of her native land. For a man whose needs were not only physical but intellectual and who expected his consort to shine at court and to be a patron of the arts she was a disaster waiting to happen.

For his part, Henry was compliant rather than enthusiastic. He professed himself satisfied with the arrangements, and prepared to greet his new bride, but this was unknown territory to him. In each of his first three marriages he had known that he wanted the woman concerned, but in this case he had only a portrait to go on and knew that the match was primarily diplomatic. He was hopeful and confident that Thomas Cromwell had done his best, but no more. Anne set off on her journey to England – with what trepidation we do not know – at the end of October. She was honourably accompanied but no member of her own family came with her even part of the way. In the light of what happened subsequently it might be that domestic relations at home were not all that cordial and her brother may even have been glad to see the back of her. An unmarried sister of 24 could be an embarrassment. She came via Calais, the sea route from Antwerp being deemed too hazardous in the winter, and Lord Lisle received her there on 11 December. Bad weather then stayed her journey until 27 December, forcing Henry to keep Christmas on his own. So far, despite her leisurely progress, all seemed well. She made a very good impression on the Lisles. In spite of language difficulties, she seemed gracious and sweet tempered, and passed her enforced stay in Calais by endeavouring to learn something of the English Court. Finally, on 27 December the wind changed and she was able to make a swift passage to England in one of the splendid ships that the King had sent to escort her. Never having seen an ocean-going ship before she was more than a little awed.

Henry meanwhile, his curiosity at last stimulated, decided on a quixotic gesture. He would intercept her in disguise on her journey through Kent. On 1 January 1540 an anonymous group of English gentlemen invaded the Princess's apartments in the bishop's palace at Rochester, claiming to bear a New Year gift from the King. Anne had not the slightest idea what to do. She spoke no English, or French, and probably feared that she was about to be abducted. Henry, who was one of the group, was profoundly disappointed. He had probably expected the kind of witty improvization that he would have got from Anne Boleyn, or the young Catherine and not this lumpish bewilderment. Realizing his mistake, the King withdrew and returned in his own proper person, with his companions abasing themselves in case any misunderstanding should persist. This time Anne could not fail to realize who he was, and somewhat numbly 'humbled herself'. They embraced and Henry withdrew but the damage had been done. Anne had appeared as a plain and rather stupid young woman, quite unable to rise to the unexpected. Henry returned to Greenwich, observing curtly 'I like her not'.[42] From this low point it was downhill all the way. Anne was received with formal splendour at Shooter's Hill, presented with magnificent jewels and royal robes, and married to the King at Greenwich on Twelfth Night, 6 January, but none of this persuaded Henry to find her acceptable. Since he had first set eyes on her he had not ceased to complain, he was putting his head into a yoke, he had not been 'well handled' by his advisers and so on. A last minute attempt was made to find a loophole in the agreement, but there was none. For the sake of public honesty the marriage had to go ahead, even although the Cleves alliance was by this time irrelevant.

Poor Anne could do nothing right. The Germans were 'beggarly knaves' – she was a heretic who would lead the King astray (which was not true), and she did not look the part. Cromwell did his best to soothe his master's anxieties, and hoped for the best. However (not surprisingly) the wedding night was a fiasco. Anne was so innocent that she had not the faintest idea what was supposed to happen, and was not at all disconcerted when Henry failed to perform. 'At this rate', one of her English ladies observed, 'it will be a long time before we have a Duke of York'.[43] Henry, typically, blamed his impotence upon her lack of physical attractiveness – her breasts were the wrong shape, and so on. He even doubted that she was a virgin, which in the circumstances was ridiculous. Anne must have been aware of the chill that surrounded her splendour, but seems to have had no inkling of the reason for it. For the time being the public life of the court proceeded without disruption. The King and Queen proceeded by barge from

Greenwich to Westminster on 4 February, and a thousand rounds of ordnance were fired from the Tower in greeting. The Queen's household numbered nearly 130 men and women, including a number of German ladies and aristocratic English girls, one of whom was Catherine Howard. In April the parliament confirmed the Queen's dower lands. Anne was not crowned but that would not have been expected immediately in any case and superficially all appeared to be well. However, below the surface, there was furious paddling. Most of this concerns the fall of Thomas Cromwell and need not concern us here, except insofar as one of the charges brought against him was that he had manoeuvred the King into the Cleves marriage against his will, which was plausible but untrue. Henry had known perfectly well what he was doing even if he had come to dislike it. More relevantly, attempts were made to get the King off the hook by resurrecting the matter of Anne's pre-contract, but that proved to be impossible. Finally it was decided to proceed on the grounds of non-consummation, which was undeniable if humiliating. The archbishop's court secretly pronounced on this issue towards the end of June – a decision of which Anne seems to have been completely unaware. On 24 June the Queen went to Richmond, and there, on the following day, she was visited by the King's commissioners who informed her that her marriage to Henry was invalid.

The message was carefully delivered through an interpreter and was received with extraordinary composure. Anne may not have known what non-consummation meant, but she seems to have been hugely relieved at being discharged of a responsibility that she had found to be beyond her. She declared herself to be content with whatever the King might decide and signed her letter of submission 'Anna, daughter of Cleves'. If Anne had decided to fight in the manner of Catherine, she could have made life very difficult for the King. She could have rejected the verdict of a schismatical ecclesiastical Court and insisted upon her contractual rights but she chose to do none of these things. Instead she accepted a generous settlement of lands worth about £3,000 a year – some three-quarters of her jointure – and decided to stay in England. The Duke her brother may have been chagrined at her rejection but in fact he had lost nothing and it may be significant that he made no attempt to insist on her return to Cleves. Anne never married but she remained on the fringes of the Court, becoming friendly with both Mary and Elizabeth, although she appears to have been upset by Catherine Parr's evangelical associations. After Henry's death she made a rather half-hearted attempt to have her marriage annulment overturned in order to claim the full jointure of a Queen Dowager but did not persist when Edward's council proved to be unsympathetic. In her later years she turned her household into a kind of miniature Rhenish court and her German servants occasionally caused problems. She had no sympathy with Edward's Protestant regime but (unlike Mary) it treated her with kid gloves. She returned to court at the beginning of Mary's reign, and died after a long illness at Chelsea Manor on 16 July 1557, at the age of 42.[44] As a Queen, Anne had been a non-event, and as a person she seems to have been better known for her good nature and charm than for any particular intelligence, wit, or talent. In the reign of Henry VIII, she was a diplomatic footnote, and is remembered best for her quite spectacular ignorance of matters sexual. The only remarkable thing about her encounter with Henry is that, in spite of his extensive experience with at least half a dozen women, he seems not to have known whether she was a virgin or not.

The Domestic Queens: Anne Boleyn, Jane Seymour and Catherine Parr

Apart from the brief and disastrous experiment with Anne of Cleves, after 1527 Henry VIII found all his wives in England. They were chosen for different reasons at different stages of his career but each was his own subject and therefore did not have to be bargained for with any neighbouring dynasty. This did not usually correspond with the advice of his Council, which was conventionally inclined to marry the King for diplomatic reasons, but Henry knew his own mind in such matters, and (Anne of Cleves again excepted), always pleased himself. Anne Boleyn was by far the most significant politically because the campaign needed to secure her forced the King into radical ecclesiastical courses and her fall shook the establishment to its foundations. Jane was significant for quite a different reason, because she was the mother of his son, and perhaps the best loved of all his consorts. By the time that he married the second Catherine in 1543, Henry was physically a spent force, and the erstwhile Lady Latimer is best known as the nurse who coped with an increasingly irritable and irascible husband and gave him what little peace his divided and self-interested court could afford.

Anne was born in about 1501, and was the younger daughter of Sir Thomas Boleyn and his wife Elizabeth Howard, the sister of Thomas Earl of Surrey and subsequently Duke of Norfolk. Sir Thomas was a knight of good lineage and his wife came from one of the best noble houses in England.[1] He was also a diplomat and a courtier of influence who, in 1513, managed to secure for his younger daughter a coveted position at the Court of Margaret of Austria, the Regent of the Low Countries. That he chose to give Anne such a training rather than her older sibling Mary is significant. The following year Mary was to accompany the Princess her namesake when the latter was offered to Louis XII on the altar of matrimony, but Anne was clearly the brighter, and considered to be the more teachable. Margaret was choosy about who she would accept and her willingness to receive Anne is similarly a great complement to the child. The language of the court at Mechelen was French, and Margaret was meticulous, both in chaperoning her young charges and in providing them with a sophisticated education. Anne remained in that stimulating environment for over a year, before joining her sister in Paris by 5 November 1514, the date on which Mary was crowned Queen of France. When Louis died, the older Boleyn girl returned, as we have seen, to England, but Anne remained in France, transferring her service to the new queen, Claude, who was a girl not much older than herself. While Mary Boleyn was catching the King's eye and sharing his bed, her younger sister remained in France, acting, it would appear, as an interpreter for the numerous English missions that visited the French Court at this time, including one led by her own father. Queen Claude was of a retiring nature and was almost constantly pregnant, so not very much is known of Anne's exposure to the King's household, which travelled around with him, but she is thought to have met and been influenced by the King's sister, Margaret of Angouleme. She attended Queen Claude to the Field of Cloth of Gold in 1520 – which was something of a Boleyn family reunion – and became an accomplished dancer and musician. When eventually in November 1521 Anglo-French relations had deteriorated to such an extent that war was in prospect, Sir Thomas brought his younger daughter home. By then she was 20 and, as one contemporary put it, 'more French than English'. She was also a poised and self-assured courtier – and an accomplished flirt in the best Gallic tradition.

As might be expected, her marriage had been under discussion in England without reference to her own wishes. Both Wolsey and the Earl of Surrey were keen to marry her to James Butler, who was about three years her junior, as a means of resolving an ongoing dispute between the Butlers and the Boleyns over the Earldom of Ormond. James was living in Wolsey's household at the time, as something between a guest and a hostage, and as late as October 1521 the Cardinal, then in Calais, wrote to the King: 'I shall, at my return to your presence, devise with your Grace how the marriage betwixt him and Sir Thomas Boleyn's daughter may be brought to pass ... for the perfecting of which marriage I shall endeavour myself at my return, with all effect.'[2]

The marriage never took place, probably for reasons which had more to do with Irish politics than with anything that happened in England, but it is also possible that someone asked Anne, who proved less than enthusiastic. It seems that for some time after her return to England she was thought of as being betrothed in some sense to James Butler, but no formal engagement was ever made. She was, of course, much sought after but, rather surprisingly, there seem to have been no real negotiations. The story of her entanglement with Lord Henry Percy, the son of the Earl of Northumberland, is both late and problematic. It is told by George Cavendish, who dates it to a time after the King had become seriously interested, which would be some time in 1527. However, the fifth Earl, who features prominently in the story, died in May of that year; so it is possible that the events narrated occurred in 1526, or that Cavendish's elderly memory was at fault in some other way. The fact is that for all her obvious allure, she was still available at the age of 25 or 26, when her game of courtly love with Henry started to become real. It looks as though Sir Thomas, already the father of one royal mistress, was well aware of the King's increasingly vulnerable state of mind over his marriage, and was plotting the eventual outcome. However, there is not a shred of evidence that anything so purposeful was going on.

When Anne returned to England, it was to a position in the Privy Chamber of the Queen. By the beginning of 1522, Catherine's days of power were long since passed, but for an appointment of this kind her decision would still have been required, so it is reasonable to suppose that she had no idea that she was setting up a rival for herself. However, the appointment did mean that Anne was in regular attendance at the Court, and available to take part in its festivities. The first recorded occasion upon which she did that was when she appeared in the character of Perseverance in the defence of the Chateau Verte on 1 March. This involved elaborate dressing up, and a mimic battle in the best Burgundian tradition. Henry led the assault on the chateau, which symbolized female coyness or reluctance, and (of course) won a great victory, which was symbolized by an elaborate dance.[3] Anne's appearance at this stage of her career was described or recollected later by many writers, who differ according to whether they regarded her with favour or not, but in certain respects they are in agreement. She was no dazzling beauty but had an electrifying sexuality: 'Very eloquent and gracious, and reasonably good looking' one contemporary who knew her well wrote, although he was a priest who would hardly have commented upon her allure. Probably the fairest description comes from a Venetian diplomat who was at the English court at the time: 'Not one of the handsomest women in the world, she is of middling stature, swarthy complexion, long neck, wide mouth, a bosom not much raised, and eyes which are black and beautiful ...'[4] It was not, however, her appearance that attracted men; in the words of Eric Ives, 'she radiated sex'[5], and Henry was not the only male to be captivated. Apart from young Henry Percy, who bitterly rued his father's hostile intervention, Sir Thomas Wyatt equally found her almost irresistible, and had to be warned off by an infatuated monarch.[6]

Part of Anne's fascination was her accomplishments. She danced excellently in several different modes, played a number of musical instruments and was an accomplished and witty conversationalist, both in English and French. She was also both feisty and independent – and while both these characteristics attracted the King they may have put off other suitors. If she had been seriously intending to marry during the early 1520s then she had not done very well. Men were fascinated but wary because they did not necessarily want a woman with her own agenda – at least not as a wife. The King's attentions, therefore, although they may have been unexpected and even unwelcome at first, nevertheless soon created a dazzling possibility that no girl in Anne's position could have resisted. As we have seen, the chronology of this relationship is not straightforward. That Henry bombarded her with passionate love letters and wanted to make her his mistress, and also that she refused, is well attested and can probably be dated to late in 1526. By April 1527 Henry had decided that he wanted to rid himself of Catherine because that is when the first secret meetings to effect that were held, and by August he had decided that he wanted Anne as her replacement. In that month he applied to Rome for a dispensation to marry a woman although she was related to him in the 'first degree of affinity ... from ... forbidden wedlock'.[7] Anne was not named, but the consanguinity alluded to was clearly that created by his liaison with her sister. When Wolsey went off to France on 22 June, he knew all about the King's intentions with regards to Catherine but did not know about Anne. So the chances are that Henry applied for his dispensation almost immediately after she had signalled her willingness to be a party to his plan – that is at sometime during July 1527. At that stage neither of them was thinking long term; they expected to be married within a matter of months.

What then transpired had nothing to do with Anne. It was the result of Catherine's recalcitrance and of the political support that she enjoyed, both within England and in Rome. At first Henry expected that his good standing with the Pope would guarantee success in what was, after all, not an unprecedented quest.[8] Only gradually did it become clear, both to the King and to Wolsey, that they were beating their heads against a brick wall. Meanwhile, Anne's influence grew. She lived most of the year at court, had frequent access to Henry and excited in him a fury of frustration. There was more to Anne, however, than sexual torment; she quickly revealed herself to be a politician of skill and resource. Thomas Wolsey was the first to perceive this. His own favour had been uncertain since he had taken the blame for the failure of the Amicable Grant in 1525 and it is significant that Henry never discussed Anne's position with his chancellor until it was public knowledge. During 1528 she was becoming an alternative source of encouragement and advice. Wolsey was far too canny to resent this openly, and he played to his strength. Because of his unique position as a minister of the Crown and a prince of the Church, the King was bound to rely on him to untangle the Gordian knots in the Curia. Anne knew this perfectly well, and as delays and difficulties built up, increasingly looked to him for a solution. She may not have trusted him, or even liked him, but for the time being there seemed to be no realistic alternative.[9]

This phase of the royal quest came to a dramatic end in the summer of 1529. The Legatine Court, which Clement had ostensibly conceded, was nothing more than a sham because Cardinal Lorenzo Campeggio, the Protector of England, who was the specific papal representative, was under secret orders to deliver no verdict. Neither Wolsey (the other Legate) nor the King was aware of this deception, and Henry certainly expected the court to declare in his favour. It duly convened at Blackfriars on 18 June, and on 21 June both Henry and Catherine appeared. The Queen then withdrew on the ground that her case should only be heard in Rome and was declared contumacious. So far so good for the King but that was the limit of his success. Over the next month the Court became bogged down in technicalities, perhaps intentionally, and Wolsey wrote to Clement, urging him to order expedition. Nothing could have been further from Clement's intention. On 13 July he revoked the case to the Rota, and on 27 July (in ignorance of that decision) Campeggio adjourned the court for the vacation.[10] Henry exploded with rage and Wolsey stood directly in the path of his wrath. What was the use of a Cardinal Legate who could not even deliver a routine annulment? On 18 October he was relieved of the Great Seal and rusticated to his diocese. There is no reason to suppose that Anne was in any way responsible for this outcome, despite later stories to the contrary; nevertheless the cardinal's fall left her in a position of unchallenged influence. On 8 December her father was created Earl of Wiltshire and Ormond and her brother, now Viscount Rochford and a member of the Privy Chamber, was sent on a mission to France.[11] It is hard to say whether there had been any such thing as a 'Boleyn party' at court before October 1529 but afterwards there certainly was and it was in the ascendant.

Politically, therefore, Wolsey's fall was a major breakthrough for Anne, but in terms of her conflict with Catherine it led her nowhere. Henry's affection seemed genuine enough and was ardently expressed but the previous year, when Anne had been forced to withdraw to Hever by an outbreak of the sweating sickness in her household, he had for a while appeared regularly with his wife. Despite the *ménage a trois* that the King had established by the autumn of 1529, the Queen showed no sign of either budging or being budged. From time to time Anne became frustrated and we are told that on one occasion, probably in November of that year, she had lashed out at her royal lover:

> Did I not tell you that when you disputed with the Queen, she was sure to have the upper hand? I see that some fine morning you will succumb to her reasoning, and that you will cast me off. I have been waiting long and might in the meantime have contracted some advantageous marriage … But alas! Farewell to my time and youth spent to no purpose at all.[12]

Rather surprisingly, Henry seems to have found such outbursts stimulating and they certainly did no harm to their relationship but, on the other hand, they solved nothing either. By the beginning of 1530 a new post-Wolsey regime was in place, with Sir Thomas More as Chancellor and the Duke of Norfolk who was Anne's uncle, as President of the Council. When her father had been raised to the peerage his allies, George Hastings and Robert Ratcliffe, had also been created respectively Earls of Huntingdon and Sussex. Between them they dominated the council and, as the French ambassador Jean du Bellay wrote, '... above everyone, Mademoiselle Anne'.[13] Politically, Catherine was now heavily outgunned but unless the Boleyn armament could be brought to bear on its target it would make little difference. So preoccupied had Wolsey and the King been in August 1529 that England was almost left out of the Peace of Cambrai altogether. Some rapid last-minute footwork avoided that, but her interests received no consideration. For the time being, Europe was at peace, which meant that Henry had even less leverage in Rome than before and the King could not afford to indulge in such absent-mindedness in the future. Now that there was no Wolsey to take the blame, or credit, he had to concentrate harder, which was not easy when his matrimonial affairs were in such a terminal mess.

As we have seen, in the summer of 1531 he made a decision of sorts. He broke up the *ménage a trois* and dismissed Catherine from the court. This left Anne in sole possession – but possession of what? Her ascendancy depended entirely upon her sexuality and upon Henry's willingness to be impressed by it. She had no kind of legal security at all and the next year must have been a radical test of nerve. In that situation the ultimate victory may not have been won by Anne at all but rather by Thomas Cromwell, who had succeeded in transferring himself from Wolsey's service to the King's and, having quickly assessed the politics of the court, made haste to align himself with the Boleyn party. It was almost certainly Cromwell rather than Anne who finally persuaded Henry that he could use the ancient and honourable device of statute law to sever the bond that tied him to his wife. The Act for the conditional restraint of Annates in 1532 was probably a final attempt at blackmail and, when that did not work, the King decided to pursue his unilateral course anyway, relying on statute to tidy up as he went. On 22 August William Warham died, and on 1 September Anne was created Marquis of Pembroke. In one sense this creation was merely a temporary expedient, designed to give her some official status ahead of Henry's planned meeting with Francis of France in the autumn, but in another sense it was a recognition of her real status. Anne did not sit at the Council Board but she was far more really a councillor than many who did. She was knowledgeable, opinionated, and a leader of men – not just in the obvious way of a woman, but in a real political sense. She did not eventually meet Francis, who had only one use for women and that did not involve councilling. Moreover he was pressed by his own women to avoid encountering such an exotic creature. She did, however, sleep with the King for the first time, and that was – and was probably intended to be – a way of forcing the issue.

It was the discovery of her pregnancy in January 1533 that necessitated rapid action. The amenable Archdeacon of Taunton, Thomas Cranmer, had already been summoned back from a diplomatic mission in Germany to the see of Canterbury. Cranmer was not the most obvious man for such a promotion but he had already declared himself to be the King's man over his annulment issue with a respectable show of theological conviction, and that was what mattered. He had also spent some time in the Earl of Wiltshire's household and was well known to Anne, although not her servant. The fact that he had secretly married in Germany was at this time known to no one but himself and his wife's family. Although he knew something of Cranmer's antecedents, Clement VII made no difficulty about confirming his appointment – perhaps he was anxious to oblige the English king over some matter that was within his power. Cranmer received his temporalities on 19 April and was duly enthroned. By that time Henry and Anne were already married in a private ceremony, probably about 25 January, although we do not know where, by whom the ceremony was conducted, or who the witnesses were.[14] Henry may have been confident, both in his new Archbishop and also in the understanding that he had reached with Francis at Calais but he was not prepared to come into the open. Even the sharp-nosed ambassadors in London did not find out what had happened until 12 April. As we have seen, convocation dutifully declared the King's first marriage null and void, and Cranmer, acting in defiance of the papal ban on any further action in the matter, used his consistory court to pronounce a formal verdict. All this Catherine, Chapuys, and many Englishmen of all degrees rejected with varying degrees of contempt.[15] However, the King's conscience was now satisfied, and on Thursday, 29 May a visibly pregnant Anne was paraded from Greenwich to London by barge in preparation for her coronation.

Everything possible was done to make the occasion seem joyful and spontaneous. She was escorted along the river by 'all the worshipful Crafts and Occupations in their best array, goodly beseen'. The King received her at the Tower, and graciously thanked the citizens for their welcome. Over the next couple of days he made 65 new knights, and on the Saturday she processed through London from the Tower to Westminster, escorted by bishops, noblemen and 'ladies of honour'. The following day, Whitsunday, 1 June, she was solemnly crowned, and at the banquet that followed, her 'service' was led by Henry Bourgchier, Earl of Essex, as Carver. 'These noblemen' declared the official observer, 'did their service in such humble sort and fashion as it was a wonder to see the pain and diligence of them, being such noble personages'.[16] Within a few days, Wynkyn de Worde had published an authorized account for the benefit of any loyal (or not so loyal) subject who might have missed the show. The whole display was splendidly choreographed and a masterpiece of political showmanship, but it could not entirely disguise the unease and even downright hostility that many people felt. The King's own sister, the Duchess of Suffolk, boycotted the celebrations, as did his daughter Mary and the Imperial ambassador. Sir Thomas More, who had resigned the Chancellorship when the clergy had capitulated to royal pressure in the previous summer, was also conspicuous by his absence.[17] Catherine had already refused to hand over her jewels to 'the scandal of Christendom' but her complaints to her nephew were becoming shrill and his own council advised him that his aunt's troubles were a private matter, and that Henry's stance towards himself gave no pretext for action – an opinion that he no doubt received with relief:

> ... although the king has married the said Anna Bulans he has not proceeded against the Queen by force or violence, and has committed no act against the Emperor which [he] could allege to be an infraction of the treaty of Cambrai ...[18]

Catherine had now become a cause but she was not a leader and her supporters were at a loss. They could not complain of evil counsel because the policy was obviously the King's and they had no desire to depose Henry because there was no plausible alternative. They could (and did) endlessly remonstrate with him and urge him to change his mind, but he could afford to ignore such representations. In July, Catherine was formally deprived of her title and told the delegation of peers that was sent to urge her to submit that she would do no such thing because her conscience took priority over all earthly considerations.[19] That position she was not to change but she had effectively been shunted into a siding. Anne (and her family) had won, but it remained to be seen what use they could make of their victory. On 7 September she was delivered of a daughter and although this was in a sense a disappointment, the omens were good. She had conceived promptly, had an easy labour and the child was healthy and perfectly formed. The Christening, which took place in the Church of the Observant Friars at Greenwich on 10 September was another political demonstration. Many of Catherine's friends were pressed into services that they would no doubt have preferred to avoid. The Marchioness of Exeter stood Godmother, whereas the Marquis bore the taper; and Lord Hussey helped to carry the canopy. Cranmer was the Godfather and the ceremony was dominated by the Boleyns and the Howards, but no one was allowed to stand apart from this celebration of the King's new heir. The Parliament, which met early in 1534, duly placed its seal of approval on these proceedings. The submission of the clergy to the royal supremacy was confirmed; annates and applications for dispensations were no longer to go to Rome and it became high treason to deny the validity of the King's second marriage. A second session, later in the year, finally abrogated all papal claims in England.[20]

It could be argued that it was Thomas Cromwell rather than Anne who emerged as the victor from these political battles and that the Queen was a mere pretext or catalyst. However, that would be to underestimate her power. Of course her whole position depended upon the establishment of the royal supremacy but it was the King's will that counted in these matters, not Cromwell's, and her opportunities for access were absolutely unique. Anne later acquired the reputation of being an early Protestant, and a patron of reformers such as John Frith and Robert Barnes. John Foxe saw her in that light and so did George Wyatt (Sir Thomas's grandson) who, writing in the 1590s, spoke of the 'thrice excellent Queen Anne Boleyn', whom he saw as a key promoter of the 'blessed splendour of the gospel beginning then to shew her golden lustre upon our world'.[21] She is supposed to have shown Henry a copy of Tyndale's *Obedience of a Christian Man*, which elicited the response that this was a book for all king's to read, and Mathew Parker was one of her chaplains. The 'evangelicals' as they were called, were Henry's natural allies against the Pope, and that was probably the main reason why Anne patronized them. Her position might have been one of conviction but it might equally have been calculated. The fact that she was clearly not a Lutheran suggests that she was matching her religious position carefully to the King's and there is no indication that she was ever reluctant to attend mass or any of the other religious ceremonies in which Henry took part. It must be remembered in this context that despite his break with Rome, the King continued to see himself as an orthodox Catholic prince, so his wife could not have afforded to disturb that conviction. There is no doubt that evangelical preachers and writers looked to her for promotion and support, or that her influence in that direction was effective, but she never stepped outside the parameters that Henry laid down. It was her enemies who tried to claim that she was a heretic.

Chapuys, who never ceased to describe her as 'the concubine', also blamed her for the sufferings of the Lady Mary but in that respect, too, he may have exaggerated. Henry had at first been inclined to be indulgent towards his daughter and when Catherine was provided with a diminished but still honourable household as Princess Dowager, he prepared to do the same for Mary. On 1 October 1533 a generous establishment of 162 persons was decreed, headed by her old governess, the Countess of Salisbury. However, when the royal commissioners visited her to receive her formal submission, they were treated to a tirade of dissent, and on 2 October Mary wrote to her father, lecturing him on the error of his ways. Even Chapuys was apprehensive at such an act of defiance. Yet when Mary's whole establishment was dissolved and she was consigned to a supporting role in the household of the infant Princess Elizabeth, the ambassador was quick to blame 'the concubine'. No doubt Anne was hostile to Mary and may well have urged severity but no such influence is required to explain the King's decision. He was very angry – as well he might be. Whenever she got the opportunity, which was usually when Anne was visiting her daughter, Mary went out of her way to be as offensive as possible. The Queen seems to have made several attempts at conciliation but was consistently rebuffed and eventually became angry in her turn. Whether she ever urged Henry to execute her, as Chapuys believed, we do not know. If so, her advice was ignored, because despite her outrageous behaviour, the King continued to be fond of his daughter and in the event she survived to (metaphorically) dance on the Queen's grave.

Anne was by this time about 33 but, unlike Catherine at the same age, had kept both her figure and her physical attractiveness. Whereas four or five pregnancies had exhausted the latter's fertility, Anne conceived again within about three or four months of Elizabeth's birth. By February 1534 this was generally known and in April Henry ordered his goldsmith to make an especially elaborate silver cradle for the anticipated prince. Then, during the July progress, and perhaps assisted by the strains of travelling, the Queen miscarried. We know very little about the circumstances, which were deliberately concealed, but she never got as far as a lying in (which would have necessitated withdrawal from the progress) and we do not even know whether the foetus was male or female.[22] What we do know is that Henry was bitterly disappointed, and began to entertain doubts about his second marriage. Could his critics have been right all along? Was God now punishing him again for a similar offence? Anne was put on her mettle because her relationship with her husband was in danger. Chapuys was highly gratified and immediately began spreading rumours that Henry was having an affair with 'another very beautiful maid of honour'. The ambassador was probably exaggerating a very superficial attraction – or perhaps not, the evidence is not clear. What is clear is that Anne reacted badly. Catherine had put up with numerous such flirtations but Anne's position was different. She had relied for seven years on her feisty sexuality to keep the King in line and up until now she had succeeded. So instead of shrugging off such an affair as an adolescent prank she became shrewish and threw tantrums. On this occasion her reaction seems to have worked because a marriage that was as purely emotional as hers was bound to be afflicted by such spats, and Henry knew that perfectly well.[23] Child or no child, he still loved her and did not want to upset her.

Nevertheless, this incident was a sign of a deeper malaise. Despite her intelligence, political shrewdness and considerable intellectual powers – or perhaps because of them – Anne had never learned to be a conventional wife. She did not know how to be meek, submissive or long-suffering. So she continued to hold on to her husband in the same way that she had done during their prolonged courtship – with emotional outbursts and passionate reconciliations. Henry, who was extremely conventional in this respect, was first puzzled and then irritated by this behaviour. Did she not realize that a wife and a mistress were different things and their behaviour was governed by different rules? The fact seems to have been that as long as Catherine was alive and Mary still allowed to bait her, Anne was never able to relax into her role and her lack of a son made the situation worse. It would be an exaggeration to say that their marriage began to deteriorate after the summer of 1534 but it did become more erratic and Henry's sexual performance, which had always been inclined that way, became even more so. It was the summer of 1535 before Anne conceived again.[24]

This situation, and her own peace of mind, was not helped by the fact that she continued to be very unpopular. With the promotion of Catherine's cause now prohibited by law, her friends and supporters built up their whispering campaign against the Queen. Every indignity, real and imagined, which was suffered by the ex-Queen and her daughter, was blamed upon the malice of 'that whore Nan Bullen'.[25] She became the equivalent of the medieval 'evil councillor', the scapegoat for all the King's unpopular actions. When the London Carthusians, John Fisher and Thomas More, were executed in the summer of 1535: 'The people, horrified to see such unprecedented and brutal atrocities, muttered in whispers about these events, and often blamed Queen Anne …'[26]

These were insinuations that Eustace Chapuys was only too keen to encourage. Chapuys was also alert to the popular implications of Anne's Francophilia. Given her background, and the nature of her position, she was bound to favour a French alliance but anti-French sentiment in England ran deep and particularly in the City of London, which depended for so much of its prosperity on trade with the Low Countries. Unfortunately the Anglo-French friendship was based on nothing stronger than a mutual antipathy to the Emperor, and the only way to strengthen it was by resurrecting the old proposal for a marriage between Mary and the Dauphin. This must have been Henry's own idea, because Anne was mortally offended, and the King's rather clumsy attempt to redeem the situation by offering instead a marriage between Elizabeth and Francis's second son, Henri, was poorly received. It seems that despite all professions of friendship, the French were still reluctant to accept the Princess's legitimacy. The offended Queen contributed notably to a chill, which began to afflict Anglo-French relations in the summer of 1535, but diplomatically she had nowhere else to go, because any understanding between Henry and the Emperor would have been even worse news from her point of view. Whatever the realities of the situation, the Council continued to regard her as a pro-French adviser with access to the King's ear. And not only to his ear; by November 1535 the Queen was pregnant again and if her relations with Henry were 'on/off', they had certainly been 'on' during the late summer. It was far too soon to regard Anne as a spent force.

At the beginning of 1536, her position again appeared to be strong. Her father was Lord Privy Seal, her brother a nobleman of the Privy Chamber and the Archbishop of Canterbury was her staunch friend. At the same time her enemies had disappeared or had been weakened. The Duchess of Suffolk, one of her most implacable critics, had died in 1533, leaving her husband encumbered with debt, and on 7 January, Catherine died at Kimbolton. If the child that she was carrying should be a son, then her position would be assured for the foreseeable future. However, with hindsight we can see that all was not entirely well. Catherine's death cut both ways. Although it removed any possibility of pressure on the King to take her back, for that very reason it made her successor more vulnerable. If Henry should tire of Anne, he could now start again with a clean sheet. At the same time Thomas Cromwell, the King's powerful secretary and her erstwhile ally, was becoming ambivalent. Catherine's death opened the possibility of a rapprochement with the Emperor, to which Anne was an inconvenient obstacle. As the year advanced, Cromwell became increasingly keen on building bridges to Brussels. Finally the Duke of Norfolk, another erstwhile ally, had drawn back and was keeping a low profile. Probably he was offended with her patronage of evangelical clergy and scholars. He himself favoured the most conservative interpretation of the royal supremacy, and had no time for Cranmer, Cromwell or Anne, who all seemed to be tarred with the reformist brush. There is no reason at all to suppose that Henry and Anne were on bad terms at the time of Catherine's death. In October 1535 there had been the usual rumours that when pregnancy made his wife unavailable, Henry started turning to other women. There was probably no substance in them, and by the end of the month the royal couple were apparently 'merry' together. In November the Queen was described by one well placed observer as having more influence with the King than Thomas Cromwell, which was praise indeed.

Nevertheless, it seems that Anne's reaction to Catherine's death was a good deal more complex than the King's. He was just relieved, and declared that there was now no more risk of war with the Emperor. She was having a difficult pregnancy, and had become depressed and fretful. It is very unlikely that, as Edward Hall declared, she 'wore yellow for mourning'. It was also reported later that she was distressed by her husband's relationship with Jane Seymour, and had bitterly reproached him for it, which is plausible because Jane represented just the kind of threat that she had now most to fear, but it cannot be substantiated.[27] What did happen was that Henry had a heavy fall in the hunting field on 24 January, and was left unconscious for two hours. He recovered quickly but was badly shaken. Five days later Anne miscarried of a son. The king, still not fully recovered, was distraught, and is alleged to have given vent to his anguish by abusing his wife. He had been seduced into this marriage; it was null and void and he would take another wife. He had clearly offended God again – was his punishment to have no end? The trouble with this graphic account is that it comes from a suspect source – it is what the Marquis of Exeter told Chapuys. Exeter was a warm supporter of Mary, and no friend to Anne.[28] It is also unlikely that he would have been close enough to the King to have heard this outburst for himself, so that he was relying on hearsay. Altogether the story is unreliable, and the idea that the King determined at that point to get rid of Anne is not consistent with other evidence. What probably did happen is that there was a quarrel between the King and Queen and that is supported by a story that, many years later, George Wyatt heard from one of Anne's ladies: 'Being thus a woman full of sorrows, it was reported that the King came to her, and bewailing and complaining unto her the loss of his boy, some words were heard to break out of the inward feeling of her heart's dolours, laying the fault upon unkindness …'[29] This is equally uncorroborated, but much more plausible. Two thoroughly miserable people having a go at each other because they did not know what else to do.

Whether there was any link between these events at the end of January and Anne's sudden fall at the end of April is problematic. Many years later Nicholas Saunders repeated a story to the effect that the foetus that Anne miscarried had been deformed in some way and that the King had leapt to the conclusion that he could not have begotten it. As it was commonly believed at the time that a deformed birth was the result of the sexual misconduct of one or both parties such a story is plausible. On the other hand, there is not a scrap of contemporary evidence that there was anything wrong with the foetus, which died only because it was premature. It was apparently inspected and declared to be male, but nothing else was said at the time. Nevertheless it is reasonable to suppose that such a miscarriage, followed by misery, quarrels and recriminations, would have destabilized a relationship that had had its rocky moments before. What seems to have happened is that these events impinged upon two longer term situations to create a crisis of confidence upon the King's part. In the first place, Anne seems to have been quite unable to control her flirtatious instincts or her sharp tongue and, in the second place, Thomas Cromwell decided that she was a serious obstacle in the way of his chosen foreign policy. It was the latter development that was the more important, because complex negotiations were in train at the time to persuade Charles to endorse Henry's repudiation of the papacy in return for a recognition of Mary's legitimacy using the argument of *bona fide parentum* – in other words that Mary was legitimate because at the time of her birth both her parents believed that they were legitimately married. To this Anne was vehemently opposed and, although Chapuys was prepared to change his tactics far enough to be polite to her, he did not succeed in moving her position. In taking this line she was not defending herself, but her daughter Elizabeth, who would automatically lose her right to the succession if Mary should be so recognized. The story is far more complex than this simple outline would suggest but as April advanced Cromwell became increasingly convinced that Anne was standing in his way. Negotiations with the Emperor would be so much easier if this woman, who had been the cause of the Anglo-Imperial breakdown in the first place, could be removed and replaced with a new wife – perhaps Jane Seymour. About 20 April Cromwell changed sides and began to seek for ways to destroy Anne's relationship with the King – and this would not mean divorce, but death.

Within a few days he was consulting with his erstwhile enemies, Mary's supporters, and putting together a sort of dossier consisting of unsubstantiated gossip about Anne's behaviour, and midwives' evidence about the aborted foetus. All this was intended to arouse the King's suspicions, not to be the kind of evidence that could be produced in court. The device seems to have worked. Henry must already have been in a volatile state of mind, but it must also be remembered that he trusted Cromwell to a degree that he would not have trusted anyone else, with the exception of Archbishop Cranmer – who was not a party to any of these intrigues. By the end of April Henry was half convinced that his wife was a scheming whore and then she presented him with what appeared to be tangible evidence. On 30 April she had a furious quarrel with Sir Henry Norris of the Privy Chamber, during which she accused him of seeking her hand in marriage 'if aught came to the King but good'. Norris was horrified, as well he might be, by such an irresponsible charge, which he was quite unable to refute except by denial.[30] The Secretary's intelligence was good, because the same day his agents picked up one Mark Smeaton, a Privy Chamber musician who seems to have been mooning after the Queen for some time. With the aid of a little privately administered torture, Smeaton was persuaded to admit to an adulterous affair with Anne, which almost certainly existed only in his own imagination. Emboldened by this success, on 2 May, Cromwell ordered the arrest of Norris, and for good measure, Anne's brother George. George had naturally been on intimate terms with his sister, and there were many occasions that could be misrepresented by a sufficiently perverted mind. Incest, moreover, was particularly calculated to horrify a king whose sexual morality was nothing if not conventional. On the same day Anne was also arrested and taken to the Tower.

So far, so good but, as one of Cromwell's agents put it 'no man will confess anything against her, but all-only Mark of any actual thing'.[31] This, he judged 'should much touch the king's honour if it should no further appear'. In other words, it would do Henry's reputation no good at all to charge his wife upon such flimsy grounds.[32] Ironically, it was Anne herself who partly solved this dilemma. The shock of imprisonment seems to have unhinged her, and she began to chatter. She did not confess to any actual misdeeds because there were (almost certainly) none to confess, but she did recount a whole string of indiscreet conversations, going back some time, and admitted that she had mocked Henry's occasional fits of impotence. All this was promptly relayed to Cromwell, with the result that Sir Francis Weston, Sir Thomas Wyatt and William Brereton, a Groom of the Privy Chamber, were also arrested. With the aid of some forensic imagination and a few perjured witnesses, a detailed and circumstantial list of the Queen's alleged adulteries was built up over the next few days, and on 10 May Weston, Norris, Brereton and Smeaton were all tried at Westminster and convicted by a hand-picked jury of Boleyn enemies. The Queen and her brother were tried by their peers two days later but the conviction of their 'accomplices' made the verdict a foregone conclusion. Anne was charged not merely with adultery and incest but with poisoning Catherine, attempting to poison Mary and conspiring to bring about the death of the King. Completely amazed by this catalogue of iniquities, she could only respond, 'If any man accuse me, I can but say "nay" and they can bring no witnesses', which was true but quite unavailing.[33] With the King's eye upon them, the peers knew their duty and found both the defendants guilty. Six days later, on 18 May, they both went to the block on Tower Hill.

The exact chronology and circumstances of Anne's fall have been much debated. Was she secretly opposing Cromwell's plan for the dissolution of the monasteries? That might have given him an additional reason for wanting to get rid of her. When did he turn against her? His own claim that he only abandoned the Queen when he saw that the King had decided against her was disingenuous. He was moving against her at least by 24 April.[34] The King's critical role is even more mysterious. He was apparently fully supportive as late as Easter, which was on 16 April, yet by 2 May he had completely changed his mind. The conclusion that he was 'bounced' into a fundamentally irrational decision seems unavoidable. The agent must have been Cromwell, who seems to have seized upon the opportunity created by Henry's genuine perplexity. Anne was awkward, independent and sometimes abrasive; he admired her, loved her and sometimes feared her. Yet she had now miscarried twice and he still had no legitimate son. Was there something sinister in the fascination that had held him in thrall for nearly ten years? Then the magic word, 'witchcraft', was mentioned. Henry had a strong superstitious streak in his make up, mixed up with his rather eclectic intellectualism and erratic emotions. If Anne was a witch, suddenly everything fell into place; her obvious sexuality, her power over him, her failure to bear a son. It was all part of a diabolical conspiracy! Cromwell had no desire to see witchcraft feature among the legal charges. It was too subjective and emotive, and besides it was not within the jurisdiction of the Lord Steward. Fortunately for him, he did not need it. Once the King's mind was made up, there was no shortage of more orthodox charges, no matter how implausible. Both the London commission and the Lord Steward's Court could be persuaded to do the King's bidding – provided it was clearly known. For whatever reason – and there must remain some doubt about that – in the space of about a week between 24 April and 1 May 1536, Henry became convinced that his bedfellow was a whore and a witch. Of course that meant that she had never been properly his wife. Attainder had already stripped her of her title of Pembroke and on 17 May Cranmer was forced to preside over a special session of his consistory which dissolved her marriage on the grounds of consanguinity – an impediment that had been perfectly well known three years earlier when he had pronounced the marriage valid. Only the King's manic insistence can account for such an unworthy *volte face* on the part of a man otherwise known for his integrity.

So Anne went to her execution, abandoned and despised, for no good reason other than that the King would have it so. Her family-based political faction was destroyed overnight and her young daughter left in a limbo of bastardy. As a result of his own quixotic actions, Henry now had three illegitimate children but no heir, either male or female. However, on 19 May, the day after Anne suffered, he was betrothed to Jane Seymour. There was at the time, and has been since, a school of thought that attributes Henry's vindictive determination to erase Anne to an intense infatuation with this new love. However, that would seem to be an exaggeration. Anne had to die because she was too dangerous to leave alive and that was Cromwell's judgement rather than Henry's. The secretary seized the opportunity created by the King's suggestibility to pile Pelion on Ossa, because he feared her revenge if she were left alive. In a way her death was a tribute to her power. By the beginning of May, Jane was clearly at the top of Henry's agenda, but how long she had been there is another matter. She had been a member of the Queen's privy chamber for some time, and Henry must have known her well by sight. However in September 1535, when the royal couple visited Wulf Hall, the Seymour residence in Wiltshire, during their summer progress, Jane was probably not even there. The reason for a visit to Sir John Seymour had more to do with the rising career of his elder son, Sir Edward, than with any charms of Jane. Moreover only hindsight links her with Anne's tantrums in January 1536. It may be that the King was becoming seriously interested by then but it cannot be proved. In fact the chronology of their relationship is hazy. At some point, probably in March or early April, the King seems to have propositioned her, to be told firmly that 'she had no greater treasure in all the world than her honour, which she would rather die a thousand times than tarnish'. He is also alleged to have sent her a letter and a generous present, both of which were returned with dutiful humility. All this sounds a bit like hindsight and a family plot intended to unseat Queen Anne, but the source of most of it is Chapuys, who was a keen meteorologist when it came to storm signals. It is quite probable that Henry's decision to marry her was as sudden as his decision to abandon Anne, and was conditioned more by her immediate availability and by her father's proven breeding record than by any deeper or longer term considerations.

In moving as he did on 19 May, Henry outpaced all the observers. As soon as Anne's fall was known, Pope Paul III, convinced that she had been the sole cause of the King's straying, began to anticipate negotiations to end the schism. The Emperor was similarly speculating about the possibility of a Habsburg marriage to bring Henry back into the mainstream of European diplomacy. Both knew about Jane, but both chose to regard her as a casual 'amour' rather than an intended bride. They were wrong because Henry's needs, both sexual and dynastic, were now urgent and he had no intention of plodding through the endless rounds of negotiation necessary to secure a European bride. Nor had he any intention of re-negotiating his ecclesiastical policy. In that respect the Seymours were neutral, perhaps more conservative than otherwise. Cromwell seems to have favoured Jane as a means of healing the deep divisions in the court that had characterised the Boleyn ascendancy – but he had no hand in prompting his master's decision, and seems to have adopted this attitude only after the *fait accompli*. Henry and Jane were married with what can only be described as indecent haste at Whitehall on 30 May. Jane was 27: a somewhat plain and dumpy virgin if her portraits are anything to go by, although her unmarried status probably had more to do with her hard-up father's inability to provide a suitable dowry than with any lack of attractiveness. Of course, with this dramatic turn in her fortunes no dowry was required.

She was not at all the kind of girl who would have appealed to the young Henry, but he was now 44 and his priorities had changed. What he needed now, apart from a son, was a spot of peace and quiet. Anne had been a challenge in every sense of the word. She had been sexy, edgy and opinionated; a stormy and emotional companion but a shrewd and well-informed adviser. She had had her own supporters, her own networks, even her own policies. Jane was none of these things. What she did have was a good natured and imperturbable common sense. As Henry told Chapuys soon after his marriage, 'her nature was gentle and inclined to peace' – in short, Jane was everything that Anne had not been.[35] When she urged Henry to take his elder daughter into his grace – which must have been within a few weeks of their wedding and before Mary's surrender – the King told her effectively to mind her own business. Anne would have sulked furiously at such a rebuff but Jane took it all in her stride. She probably did not have any share in Mary's submission, which came towards the end of July, but was on hand to make sure that Henry took it in good part and that the younger woman's household was fully and sensitively restored. She was more like an elder sister than a stepmother to Henry's daughter, who was now 21 and the two became firm friends. Jane clearly did not have any religious opinions, which grated on Mary's sensitive conscience. Conservatives like the Marquis of Exeter regarded her as a friend but it is an open question whether she had any opinions of her own at all.

In the latter part of 1536, Henry had need of as much domestic peace as he could get. On 18 July his son Henry had died at the age of about 18. He may, or may not, have ever entertained ideas of legitimating him, but he was fond of the boy and felt his loss keenly. Fitzroy's widow, Mary Howard, we are told 'handled herself very discreetly' but she was only 17 and they had never lived together. The young Duke's main legacy, apart from his father's grief, was a large tidying-up operation of people, lands and jobs because he had no direct successor in any of his functions. More importantly, the north of England was swept by rebellion. This had a number of specific causes, which have been exhaustively discussed, but the timing seems to have been mainly occasioned by the discovery that Anne's death had made not the slightest difference to the main thrust of the King's policies. She had been cast as the evil influence from which all his errors and abuses had stemmed and when she fell her enemies waited expectantly for everything to change. Mary had been the first to be disillusioned in this respect and she had submitted and come to terms with Thomas Cromwell. The conservative leaders (or some of them), however, now felt that Cromwell had betrayed them and he became the arch-enemy whom the King must be pressed to repudiate. The rebellions, known collectively as the Pilgrimage of Grace, were powerful, but messy and ill directed. Above all the great conservative magnates, the earls of Derby, Shrewsbury and Northumberland, who had been expected to back the movement, held aloof. The Emperor, who might have felt compelled to support them a year earlier, was now not interested at all. The Pilgrimage collapsed under its own weight with only a few discreet pushes from the King and the Duke of Norfolk. Mary, who might have been its figurehead, instead confirmed her newly established favour by repudiating it absolutely and making it clear to Charles that she was no longer prepared to be used against her father.[36] Jane, whose peacemaking role had certainly played a part in keeping Mary 'on side', had by Christmas become a symbol of the new stability. Henry spoke of her as his first 'true wife', which was legally the case since Parliament had confirmed Anne's displacement back in July.

The new queen had the immense advantage of carrying almost no political baggage. Unlike Catherine, or even Anne, she had no pretensions to noble birth and no established political persona. The King had made her to suit himself. She even dressed to please him and he made her magnificent. She was given the usual consort's jointure and her attendants were chosen with great care. Jane was not flirtatious but in the light of the recent past it was essential that no breath of scandal should touch her entourage. Jousts and entertainments were provided in her honour and several royal palaces were lavishly refurbished. Altogether there was a sense of new beginnings and Christmas was kept at Greenwich with exceptional splendour in the midst of ferociously cold weather that prevented any movement upon the river. Jane, however, was not crowned. A great ceremony was being discussed, but just before Christmas the Queen's father, Sir John Seymour, died, and that required a fixed period of mourning. Then in February she was found to be pregnant. That had not inhibited Anne's coronation four years earlier, but there was no comparable point to be made this time and talk of a coronation was quietly dropped. The Queen's health appeared to be good, but nothing must threaten her at this most delicate time. By June, all seemed still to be well but Henry was taking no risks and cancelled his summer progress in order to remain within reach. Quite apart from the fact of conception, the King seems to have been exceptionally solicitous of Jane's welfare and it may be that he was genuinely more fond of her than of either of her predecessors. Perhaps her straightforward dependence touched him. Here was a woman with no independent resources. He was even concerned to reassure anyone who would listen that it was not she who had asked him to cancel the progress, because 'she can in all things well content, satisfy and quiet herself with that thing which we shall think expedient.'[37]

Throughout the summer the astrologers were predicting the birth of a prince. They knew that that was what the King wanted to hear, and they had a 50 per cent chance of being right – perhaps rather higher, given the number of times they had been wrong in the past. Henry was sufficiently convinced to have a stall prepared in the Garter Chapel at Windsor for the new Prince of Wales, but again perhaps he was whistling in the dark. Like many women at the time, Jane seems to have been quite uncertain when her time was due. She withdrew into the customary seclusion at Hampton Court in late September, which suggests that she expected to give birth in late October. In fact she went into labour within a fortnight, on 9 October. After an easy pregnancy the birth was bitter and protracted, lasting two days and three nights and leaving Jane exhausted. However, the agony appeared to be worthwhile for the child was a boy, alive and perfect. Henry is said to have wept with emotion, as well he might considering what suffering he had created in the quest for this child. Rejoicings thundered round the country in a way that had not been heard since the ill-omened birth of Prince Henry 27 years before. The new Prince was named Edward, and on 15 October was christened with great splendour in the chapel of the palace where he had been born. The godfathers were the Archbishop of Canterbury and the Duke of Norfolk; the godmother the Lady Mary. No more complete a symbol of reconciliation could be wished for. On 18 October the infant was created Duke of Cornwall and Earl of Chester and on the same day his maternal uncle, Edward Seymour, Viscount Beauchamp, was promoted to the Earldom of Hertford.

Unfortunately, the Queen did not make a good recovery. On the day of the christening she had been well enough to sit in the ante-chapel and receive the congratulations of the guests, but three days later puerperal fever developed; by 23 October she had become delirious and late on the night of the 24 October she died. Henry's dynastic ambitions had claimed one more life, although it would be hard to blame him in this case. Jane had been such a gentle soul, and her passing was bitterly mourned: '... and of none in the Realm was it more heavelier taken than of the King's Majesty himself, whose death caused the king immediately to remove into Westminster, where he mourned and kept himself close and secret a great while ...'

His father had mourned likewise in similar circumstances 34 years before. Henry, who had been relieved by the death of his first wife, and gratified by that of the second, was genuinely and deeply distressed by that of the third. She was, he declared, the dearest of them all and when his own time came he chose to be buried beside her. However, for the time being life went on and he had the son for whom he had longed.

Henry had had little experience as a widower. In fact he had lacked a wife for barely a month out of the previous 28 years. This time, however, he was to remain unwed for over two years, and when he was tempted back into matrimony it was into the disastrous alliance that we have already noticed, with Anne of Cleves.

Physically, Henry was almost spent. Almost, but not quite, and on the rebound from Anne he married Catherine Howard, who was so unusual that she merits a whole chapter to herself. The King emerged from that experience chastened, humiliated, and feeling his age. He was not, however, prepared to admit defeat and as his councillors continually pointed out, one son was not enough to secure the dynasty. Whether he was still capable of begetting a child remains an open question, but in 1543, at the age of 51, he married for the sixth and last time. The statute which had condemned Catherine Howard had made elaborate provisions against any such event being repeated. It was now high treason for anyone to conceal the prenuptial infidelities of any future Queen. Moreover two of Henry's wives had now ended on the block for adultery. There was consequently no rush of candidates. Nor did any courtly family wish to embrace the fate of the Boleyns or the Howards. For about a year after Catherine's fall, the King occupied himself in renewing his alliance with the Emperor, and in provoking the Scots into the invasion that ended so disastrously for them at Solway Moss in November 1542. Henry now had no Thomas Wolsey or Thomas Cromwell to lay potential policies before him, but his experience was vast and he was able to manage quite satisfactorily on his own. He did not, however, like living on his own and although no one was now prepared to take the risk of introducing nubile damsels into his presence, he nevertheless kept an eye open for himself and, early in 1543, he became friendly with another Catherine, the 31-year-old Lady Latimer.

Catherine came, like Anne Boleyn and Jane Seymour before her, from a major gentry family with marginal links to the peerage. She was the oldest child of Sir Thomas Parr of Kendal in Westmorland, who had made his mark in the early days of Henry's reign as a companion in arms but who had died young in 1517. His widow did not remarry and the details of Catherine's upbringing are obscure. She was highly intelligent, but not notably well educated and it is probable that she stayed in her mother's modest establishment until she married in 1529 at the age of about 17. Her mother, Maude, had retained links with the court and managed to secure for her a match with Edward Borough, the son and heir of Thomas, Lord Borough. This was a good match in every respect save one: Edward's health was poor, and he died in 1532 leaving his widow childless and probably still a virgin. By that time Maude had also died but the family rallied round and in 1533 she had been married for a second time, to Lord Latimer of Snape in Yorkshire. John Neville was a man of about 40, with two grown children by his previous (two) marriages. Catherine was passably good looking and sexually frustrated but she made a good job of being Lady Latimer and ran her husband's great Yorkshire household with firmness and competence. The Latimers survived the Pilgrimage of Grace with difficulty and the experience seems to have ruined

John Neville's health. They moved to London in 1537 and Catherine was able to establish (or re-establish) a network of friendships at Court. This seems to have happened through the Seymours, who were riding high at that point. Through Jane she met the Lady Mary, about four years her junior. The Seymour position was not affected by the death of the Queen, and Catherine, whose husband was by this time an invalid, became emotionally involved with Thomas Seymour, Jane's dashing and unscrupulous younger brother. Catherine was wise and discreet and no scandal attached to their friendship, but he was clearly on the look out for a rich widow, which he hoped she would shortly become. By January 1543 Lord Latimer was in a bad way, and it looked as though the couple's wishes were about to be fulfilled. And then Henry became interested.

Henry was no longer looking for excitement, sexual or otherwise. What he wanted was a calm and sensible companion – someone who could soothe his increasingly violent fits of bad temper, ease the pain of his various ailments and quietly do as she was bidden. About 16 February he sent her his first recorded gift and message. On 2 March, Lord Latimer died. Left to her own devices, she would almost certainly have married Thomas Seymour. Several years later she wrote to him, '… as truly as God is God, my mind was fully bent, the other time I was at liberty, to marry you before any man I know …'[38] However, the King took precedence, and daunting though it must have been, the prospect of becoming Queen was also attractive. By June 1543 Catherine's presence in the Privy Chamber was sufficiently conspicuous to attract comment, and on 12 July Henry married her in the Queen's closet at Hampton Court and another gentry family had made it to the top.

Catherine was not a political animal except in one very important sense – she was an evangelical. Quite how this had come about is not clear, but Lady Latimer appears to have become interested in things intellectual after her return to London in 1537. Within two years the court was dividing along religious lines, into evangelicals and conservatives. At first the latter appeared to be carrying all before them. Firstly the Act of Six Articles, then the fall of Thomas Cromwell and finally the King's marriage to Catherine Howard appeared to give them an unassailable advantage. The latter, however, turned out to be a liability and the Howard ascendancy that she brought with her alienated many – including the Seymours. By 1543 the Earl of Hertford and his brother were firmly in Archbishop Cranmer's camp and Catherine went with them. The evangelicals, however, were not Protestants and her friendship with Mary was not impeded; in fact it seems very likely that Mary coached her in her belated struggles with Latin and encouraged her to read the Bible. The Queen enjoyed having theological discussions with her much more learned husband, and was not short of opinions, although always (as she thought) strictly deferential. She wrote and published a book of *Prayers and Meditations* in 1545, which was a unique achievement for any of Henry's queens, and in consequence attracted rather more praise and attention from humanist scholars and ecclesiastics than she strictly deserved. Whether she had any hand in selecting the evangelical tutors whom the King appointed for his son Edward is more problematical but those who saw her as gently steering her erratic husband in that direction in the last years of his life were probably not wrong.

Too much should not be made of this. John Foxe later told a long and circumstantial story about how the conservative faction at court, led by Stephen Gardiner the Bishop of Winchester, sought to bring about her downfall by incriminating her in the heresy of Anne Askew. Anne was certainly a heretic (as even Cranmer admitted) and she seems to have had supporters within the Queen's Privy Chamber, but the Queen herself was not touched. The story as told is that Henry had become irritated with his wife for 'lecturing' him on theology and that Gardiner seized the opportunity to persuade the King to draw up articles of accusation against her. A copy of these articles then came 'by chance' into the Queen's possession. In spite of her agitation, she hastened to abase herself before her Lord and Master assuring him that her only desire was to learn from his wisdom. Perfect reconciliation and collapse of hostile party![39] Whether these events actually occurred or not there is a kind of symbolic truth about the story because the Queen and her allies (notably Sir Anthony Denny, the Groom of the Stool) were clearly in the ascendant at Court in the last months of Henry's life and that accounts for the shape of Edward's regency Council. When the King went to war in France for the last time in 1544, he left Catherine as governor in his absence and although this was little more than a formality, it was also a studied gesture of confidence as it had been with her predecessor in 1513 – only this time there was no Scottish invasion and the Queen did not have to go to war.[40] There are some indications that she expected to be named as Regent in the King's will but in the event she was completely ignored. When it came to the real work of government, Henry was not prepared to entrust it to a woman – why else had he moved heaven and earth to beget a male heir?

Despite her reputation among the evangelicals, there was nothing oppressive about Catherine's piety. Although she was a keen reader of improving books, her chief delights were in clothes, music and dancing. She loved animals and flowers, kept jesters both male and female and generally gave the impression of enjoying the good things of life. Mirth and modesty are the two words most commonly used by contemporaries to describe her and she was a conspicuously successful stepmother to two broods of children, first the Nevilles and then the Tudors.

Her friendship with Mary survived the increasing divergence of their religious views and although she saw less of Elizabeth (who was 12 in 1545) and Edward (who was 8), relations appear to have been relaxed and amicable. In the case of the younger children there was no religious tension and Catherine may well have had a hand in appointing their tutors. She was spared the agonizing trauma that afflicted most of Henry's other queens. Although the succession act of 1544 spoke dutifully of any children to be begotten between the King and his present wife, everyone knew that it was not going to happen.[41] The unfortunate woman was into her third virtually sexless marriage and although nobody was going to tell Henry that, he must have known it perfectly well. The statute confirmed what everyone knew – that Edward was his heir – but what followed thereafter must have come as a surprise, because if Edward were to die without 'heirs of his body lawfully begotten' the Crown was to pass to Mary and after her on the same terms to Elizabeth, neither of whom was legitimated. This was altogether unprecedented, and an expression of how far the power of statute had advanced, even since the last succession Act.

Catherine was not with Henry when he died. Whether this was by custom, inadvertence or someone's decision is not clear because the King's demise took no one by surprise. She attended his funeral but only as a spectator. As Queen Dowager she was left at the age of 35 with no political role but a substantial jointure and an unassuaged sexual appetite. For the time being the latter dictated events and within weeks she was secretly married to Lord Thomas Seymour, now the brother of the Duke of Somerset, the Lord Protector. Somerset disapproved of their union for a variety of reasons, not least its haste and a furious quarrel developed between the brothers over the jewels that Catherine claimed had been given to her personally by the late king and which the Protector claimed were Crown property. For about 18 months she was Lady Seymour of Sudeley, presiding over a large household, which also included for a while the King's sister Elizabeth. She was soon to discover that there were risks attached to having a real man at last and while she was pregnant in the summer of 1548 she found her husband making passes at Elizabeth, now a precocious 14-year-old. The girl was sent away in disgrace but Seymour himself was above reproach. Having at long last conceived a child, Catherine was brought to bed at Sudeley Castle and, on 30 August 1548, gave birth to a healthy daughter. Six days later she contracted puerperal fever as Jane Seymour had done and died with her erring husband beside her. After Henry's death she had published a second religious work, the *Lamentation of a Sinner*, which was unequivocally Protestant. When she was buried in September 1548 it was with the Protestant rite, which would not become legal until the following year. The ceremony was performed by her almoner, the Protestant scholar and future bishop, Miles Coverdale. Catherine had not enjoyed her hard-earned status as Queen Dowager very long. Indeed, apart from her pregnancy it is likely that she did not enjoy it much at all because every time she appeared at court she had to fight a petticoat war with the Duchess of Somerset, as each claimed precedence; and as we have seen, her husband had a roving eye which in due course was to contribute to his downfall. That, however, is not part of Catherine's story; her legacy is to be found in the reign of Elizabeth and the Protestant ascendancy.

7

The Queen as Whore: Catherine Howard

Anne Boleyn had been condemned for political reasons on the pretext of adultery because that was what had been necessary to touch a raw nerve in the King's psychology. No such shadow had ever hung over Catherine of Aragon – indeed if it had done it would have been much easier to get rid of her – or Jane Seymour, or Anne of Cleves, although Henry found her displeasing for several reasons. Catherine Howard was an altogether different proposition. According to the author of the only full study of Catherine:

> The Queen was accused of having been a woman of 'abominable carnal desires' who had craftily and traitorously misled her royal spouse into believing that she was 'chaste and of pure, clean and honest living'. Worse still, she had followed 'daily her frail and carnal lust' …[1]

Very similar language had been used of Anne, but this was different because the charges against Catherine were true – or substantially so. The traitorous intent may be questioned, because Catherine had no political agenda and doing away with her husband never crossed her mind, but she certainly behaved like a whore both before and after her marriage. Although she was sufficiently streetwise to declare at one point that 'a woman might lie with a man, and yet have no child by him unless she would', errant sexual behaviour posed an obvious threat to the succession.[2] If a woman was sleeping around, how did anyone know whether a child she might bear had been begotten by the King or not? There were no DNA tests in the sixteenth century. So even the most serious charge of treason was justifiable in contemporary terms and it was also treason for the Queen to will the actual bodily harm that her lovers were inflicting upon her. Although to modern eyes Catherine Howard was a stupid and oversexed adolescent who did not remotely deserve to die for her sins, at the time she was a moral outrage. No one ever successfully cheated on Henry VIII, but Catherine tried, uniquely among his consorts, and paid the ultimate price.

She was a younger daughter of Lord Edmund Howard, who was himself a younger brother of the Duke of Norfolk, and his wife, Joyce Culpepper. The couple had ten children altogether and it is not clear where in this

brood Catherine belonged. She had been born in about 1521, and had been
offloaded at the customary age of seven or eight into the grand household kept
by her step-grandmother, the dowager Duchess.[3] This was no doubt thought
to be an advantageous placement, but it turned out to be a disastrous mistake.
The Duchess's young ladies, of whom there were several, were not adequately
chaperoned and in a sense were left to bring themselves up. It is difficult to be
certain how much formal education they received. Catherine was later to be
literate in English but not in Latin as far as anyone can tell; she could dance,
play the lute and knew how to present herself in a courtly setting. She could also
probably sustain a conversation in French but she had little or no book learning.
In other words, her training was that of an aristocratic damsel destined for the
court and a husband among the minor peerage or upper gentry. It was on the
disciplinary side that the Dowager Duchess's regime was particularly deficient. The
'maids quarters' in the great rambling Howard mansion at Horsham resembled
nothing so much as a modern student dormitory, and the girls entertained their
admirers more or less at will. Catherine's first affair came at the age of 14, when
she 'had to do' with a young music teacher named Henry Mannox.[4] This lasted
for about a year, and then Mannox was replaced by a lover of more wealth and
status, Francis Dereham. Dereham could have been a serious candidate for her
hand in marriage and that may have been why the Duchess, who knew perfectly
well what was going on, did not put a stop to it. Agnes Howard may have had her
own somewhat eccentric notions of teaching girls how to look after themselves.
Because Catherine and Dereham were lovers in the full sense of that word, the
latter must have possessed more contraceptive knowledge than a young lady was
supposed to have. As we have seen, she admitted as much, and such expertise
must have come from somewhere.

In 1539, when she was about 18, Catherine moved out of this somewhat
overheated environment into a place in the Chamber establishment of Queen
Anne of Cleves. She was described as being very small and of 'mediocre beauty'.
She had none of the courtly accomplishments of Anne Boleyn but was sufficiently
presentable and her kinship with the powerful Duke of Norfolk would have
done the rest. There was probably nothing particularly calculated about this
appointment. When it was made, no one knew that Anne would turn out to be
a pudding or that Henry would react so adversely to her. The requirement was
for young ladies with good aristocratic credentials, not for great beauties, nor
for sexual educators, although as we have seen the latter were certainly needed.
So Catherine came within the King's field of vision, rather as Anne had done
though the household of Catherine, or Jane through that of Anne. There was,
however, one big difference. Where Anne had been a flirt, and Jane had offered

calm, Catherine was a skilled seductress. It is reasonable to suppose that with her peculiar background she had more sexual experience than any of her colleagues – even the married ones – and it was this quality that caught the King's attention. He had failed to consummate his union with Anne, and was full of self-doubt, looking for reassurance, and this adolescent sex-pot was just what he was hoping for.[5] By about March or April of 1540, Henry was beginning to show a serious interest in her, and the Duke and the Dowager Duchess were quick to perceive a political opportunity.

It was not known at that point that the King had decided to end his failed marriage but it would not have required much skill to realize that Catherine's best initial response should be coy. It worked, and Henry quickly became infatuated. Gossip had already identified her as the King's latest 'amour', long before Anne had any inkling that anything was wrong. Lavish presents began to be sent as early as April, and unlike Jane in similar circumstances, Catherine did not refuse them, so that when convocation dutifully declared the King's marriage null and void on 9 July, expectations were already formed. The ground was carefully prepared in spite of the shortness of the time. The king's non-consummation of his existing marriage was ascribed to his having acted under compulsion, a transparent fiction that was aimed against his fallen minister, Thomas Cromwell, then in the Tower awaiting the attentions of the executioner. Moreover Parliament, which now had jurisdiction in such matters, helpfully abolished the impediment of consanguinity insofar as it applied to first cousins – which was the relationship between Catherine and Anne Boleyn. Henry's marriage to Anne might have been declared null but he had no desire to deny that he had slept with her. Both the French and Imperial courts greeted the repudiation of Anne of Cleves with theatrical displays of incredulity and disgust, which made the English ambassadors' lives difficult for a few weeks, but neither had the slightest intention of taking any action. If even the Duke of Cleves was not prepared to break off diplomatic relations, why should anyone else? Henry and Catherine were married at Oatlands on 28 July and it was observed that he was so uxorious that he could not keep his hands off her, even in public. 'The king's affection was so marvellously set upon that gentlewoman, as it was never known that he had the like to any woman', wrote Cranmer's secretary Ralph Morice, and most of the comment was similarly indulgent.[6] There were great hopes that the succession would now be put beyond all reasonable doubt.

Unfortunately it was not to be. Henry's health and spirits noticeably improved. He took to rising early, and hunted with renewed enthusiasm, but Catherine did not conceive. It is possible that the Queen herself was infertile and it was that rather than any precautions that had protected her during her earlier affairs, but it is unlikely in view of her knowing comments. It seems more likely that Henry's grasp exceeded his reach and in spite of his evident desire, his performance fell far short. It is hard to imagine even so sexually active a girl as Catherine acting in the way that she subsequently did if her relationship with her husband had been entirely satisfactory. Henry was at best erratic and this drove his young bride wild with frustration. Somehow or other he managed not to notice that her maidenhead had already been taken but this was probably due to his absolute (and quite irrational) conviction that she was young and pure rather than to any lack of experience on his part. After all, he had suffered from the opposite delusion about Anne. Although Catherine did not conceive, for the time being she concealed any disappointment that she may have felt and all appeared to be well. Although her education seems to have been neglected and she had no intellectual pastimes, in some respects she was an ideal consort. She was, or appeared to be, totally submissive and chose (or had chosen for her) the appropriate motto 'Non autre volonte que la sienne' – 'no other will but his'. She was a courtier and a member of a courtly family, so it was not difficult for the King to become the centre of her world. However, her attitude was paradoxical. On the one hand she seems to have thought that her husband was omniscient, and on the other hand set out to deceive him with quite inadequate precautions. She knew how to make all the correct physical responses to his passionate advances but emotional commitment seems to have been lacking from the start. She needed a young and athletic lover, not this elderly and overweight fumbler. Moreover it soon transpired that his own ardent spirit was outrunning his flagging body. He could no longer dance all night and hunt all day and an awareness of his own declining powers made him irritable and fretful. Nor was there any genuine companionship in his marriage to fall back on when the physical flames burned low; in other words it was a one-dimensional union. Then in March 1541 the King fell ill. He suffered from a chronic ulcer on his leg, the result of numerous falls in the tilt yard and the hunting field as a young man, which suddenly closed up. He was in excruciating pain and it was feared for some time that he would die. The condition eased, but the optimism and apparent vitality of the previous autumn were now only memories. He became savage and morose and if he had been an unreliable lover in the past, he was now virtually *hors de combat*.

There was also a political context to the King's fifth marriage, because, as we have seen, Catherine was a Howard, and a niece of the Duke of Norfolk. Norfolk was the arch-enemy of Thomas Cromwell, and the opportunity to use Catherine against him was too good to be missed. Although the politics of the court could be Machiavellian, it would be an exaggeration to say that the Duke 'dangled' his niece under the King's nose with the intention of ruining the marriage that Cromwell had brought about. Henry had already decided that he wanted rid of Anne before Catherine came on the scene. Nevertheless his infatuation did ensure that there was no going back on that decision. At the same time the Cleves marriage was not the only, nor even the principal, cause of Cromwell's fall; but it created a dissatisfaction in the King's mind that could be worked on to the minister's disadvantage, and that certainly happened.[7] How much the Duke actually knew about his niece before he encouraged the King to marry her, we do not know. Perhaps, in the light of the outcome, not very much. However, for the time being she symbolized a Howard ascendancy at court which brought many political advantages. It also created a time bomb, because the Howards were greedy and the way in which the Queen filled her household with her kindred and their hangers on created great resentment. It was expected that the consort would do her best for her relations, and both Anne Boleyn and Jane Seymour had done the same, but Catherine went a step too far. She was given a lavish jointure, to the tune of £4,600 a year, which was more than any of her predecessors, and a good deal of freedom as to how she used it. It included a substantial part of the estates of the late Earl of Essex (Thomas Cromwell) and of the newly dissolved abbeys of Reading and Glastonbury, which was ironic in view of the fact that the Howards were notorious religious conservatives. Catherine was genuinely grateful for Henry's generosity, but had no idea how to use such largesse wisely. Within a few months the memory of Thomas Cromwell began to appear much less obnoxious. When the King was low, in the spring of 1541, he began to look back on his great minister with regret, and (more ominously) 'to have a sinister opinion of some of his chief men ...'; in other words to blame his present councillors for having destroyed 'the best servant he ever had'.[8] This was not entirely fair, because the responsibility for Cromwell's fall lay with the King himself but he was not likely to acknowledge that and the blame game had sinister implications.

Catherine simply lacked the resources to cope with the black royal moods that now became increasingly frequent. A suitable toy or pet when his fits of youthful exuberance were on him, she was incapable of being pleasing or supportive when he most needed her. For about a fortnight while he was ill in March, he declined to see her at all. This was not because she had displeased him, but because he was aware how unattractive an object he had become and although that self-awareness does him credit it was not a hopeful sign for their future together. The Queen simply could not cope, and perhaps to escape from an intolerable situation, or perhaps out of irresponsible habit, in the spring of 1541, Catherine renewed a relationship with one of her former lovers, a young gentleman named Thomas Culpepper. At the time, Culpepper was a junior member of the King's Privy Chamber, so the opportunities for encounter would have been numerous.

Culpepper was an unscrupulous womanizer, and his intention seems to have been to establish a claim to Catherine if (or when) the King's deteriorating health carried him off.[9] The Queen may have encouraged him more out of ingrained habit than with any deliberate intent, but if so, her indulgence soon backfired, because what may have started as a mild flirtation soon became emotionally serious – at least on her part. She started writing passionate love letters to her paramour – an extremely dangerous course in a world where privacy was virtually unknown and anything committed to paper gave a hostage to fortune.[10] Although Culpepper's visits were no doubt as surreptitious as they could be, it was not long before the principal lady of her Privy Chamber found out what was going on. Jane Rochford should have gone immediately to the King and declared what she knew – but she did no such thing. Perhaps out of loyalty to her mistress, or perhaps heavily bribed, she kept quiet and became in effect an accomplice. Throughout the royal progress to the north in the summer of 1541, Culpepper kept up his secret assignations with Jane Rochford's connivance. Every time that the court stopped overnight (on its progress), there were backstairs adventures. It is hard to believe that others of the Queen's entourage did not also know what was going on, but no one said anything, and it may be that Jane had her own methods for maintaining discipline.

At the same time, Francis Dereham also reappeared. He may have threatened to disclose their previous relationship but for whatever reason, Catherine appointed him her private secretary. No one was surprised that she should have promoted an old friend but then nobody knew what the nature of that friendship had been. Throughout the progress, it seems that Culpepper and Dereham were in and out of the Queen's bedroom like characters in a modern farce, but nobody dared to say anything to the King. All this activity exposed Catherine to blackmail and so did her earlier liaisons, given the misconception which her husband had of her. On 12 July Joan Bulmer, who had been one of Catherine's 'bedfellows' at Horsham, wrote to the Queen demanding a place at court as the price of her silence. It was duly provided, and it is possible that several other places in the Queen's service were similarly filled.[11] That might explain the silence which enveloped her later misdemeanours. That may have been part of the bargain. Unfortunately for Catherine, there were others who were interested in her behaviour who were less easy to silence. Gossip began to circulate and Henry must have been the only person at Court who did not harbour some suspicion of the Queen's activities. At the same time, as we have seen, her kindred was not popular, because the Howards did not bear their good fortune lightly. Cromwell had had few committed friends at court, but there were many who owed obligations to him, and mostly the evangelical writers and preachers whom he had patronized. John Foxe was later to lament the passing of his Godly influence, and that may well have been an exaggeration, but there were certainly some evangelicals on the look out for a chance to avenge him.[12]

One of these was a man called John Lascelles. Lascelles was a Protestant whose life was to end at the stake five years later, but at this time he was a key witness for the prosecution. His sister, Mary Hall, had been in the service of the Dowager Duchess at the time of Catherine's upbringing at Horsham and knew a great deal about what that young lady had been up to. Whether Mary herself was a Protestant is not clear, but at some time in the summer of 1541 she told her brother all that she knew. She may have been motivated by sheer malice because she is alleged to have said of the Queen at the time, 'Let her alone, for if she holds on as she begins, she will be nought within a while.'[13] Lascelles, however, had no intention of leaving her alone and on 1 November he sought out the Archbishop of Canterbury and unburdened himself. The King had by this time returned to Hampton Court, and by a supreme irony had ordered that very day a special mass of thanksgiving for the happiness that his Queen had brought him. He was living in a fool's paradise, because Cranmer realized at once that so convincing and circumstantial a story must have substance to it. He was also, although discreetly, an enemy of the Howards and the opportunity was too good to miss. What Mary Hall knew, of course, related to the days before Catherine's marriage to the King, so it did not constitute evidence of adultery. What it did do was to demonstrate that the Queen had not been the innocent bride that Henry had taken her for. It also provided some evidence for a pre-contract with Dereham, which, if established, would have nullified the royal marriage altogether. On 2 November Cranmer passed the King a discreet note while he was at mass, with the request that he read it privately.[14] By this time the Archbishop had also communicated his knowledge to the Lord Chancellor, Sir Thomas Audley, and to the Earl of Hertford, both also enemies of the Howards.

Henry's reaction was surprisingly low key. He was inclined to dismiss the story as a slanderous forgery, cooked up by a jealous woman. Nevertheless he instituted an inquiry in order, as he put it, to clear his wife's name, and entrusted it to William Fitzwilliam, the Earl of Southampton, one of his most senior and trusted advisers. Southampton examined Lascelles, who repeated his story, and then went down to Sussex to interview Mary Hall, who also told the same tale. Meanwhile, almost certainly without the King's knowledge, Dereham and Mannox had been detained by Sir Thomas Wrothesley, the former on a rather far-fetched charge of piracy. Henry was not yet convinced, but Catherine was ordered to keep her chamber and await his pleasure. By this time the Howards' numerous enemies had sensed their opportunity. On 6 November the King returned to London without seeing his wife, which was an ominous sign. By this time several of Catherine's ladies had also been arrested but, most seriously, Dereham had broken down under interrogation. Not only did he confess his earlier intimacy but also his more recent access and in the process implicated Culpepper. By the time the King met his Privy Council in emergency session after his return to London, the whole issue had escalated alarmingly. Henry had proved credulous when confronted with the evidence against Anne Boleyn but this time credulity was not in question. Not only had he misjudged his young bride, but she had made him a cuckold into the bargain. When confronted by the full evidence that had now been painstakingly assembled, the King exploded with fury and threatened to torture the ungrateful girl to death.

As had happened with Henry before, the measure of his infatuation was now the measure of his disillusionment. When his rage subsided, he collapsed into an embarrassing orgy of weeping and self-pity. The realization that he had not only been unable to satisfy his young wife but had also been unable to prevent her from finding her satisfaction elsewhere was the ultimate humiliation. For the time being nobody ventured to mention either courtly 'amours' or the prospect of a Duke of York. Of course, none of this was his fault. The responsibility lay partly with Catherine herself, and partly with those who had persuaded him to take such a wanton slut into his bed. The fact that the choice had been entirely his conveniently escaped his memory and just as Anne's fall had brought down the whole Boleyn party in ruin, now the Howard ascendancy was destroyed at a stroke. Servants and minor members of the family began to be rounded up. On 10 December the Dowager Duchess of Norfolk was arrested, and on 13 December Catherine's aunt, Lady Bridgewater, Catherine Daubeney. The Duke himself was neither arrested nor charged but was forced to abase himself and then retreated tactfully to his estates. On 22 December the entire family, except for the Duke, was found guilty of misprision of treason for concealing the Queen's offences. This could have resulted in perpetual imprisonment and the loss of all property, and was indeed premature because Catherine had not yet come to trial and the fact of her treason was not yet established. Most of them were entirely innocent of any intention to deceive and were pardoned and released over the next few months. Agnes was in a rather different position, because not only had she known perfectly well what was going on under her roof, but she was also found to have destroyed some of Dereham's papers. However in this case the King did not prove to be vindictive and she too was released in May 1542. No doubt she had learned a salutary lesson, but the shock of this experience had a paralysing effect upon the whole clan. The Duke did not forfeit his office of Lord Treasurer, and soon recovered a measure of favour, so that he was leading the King's forces into Scotland by the autumn. He was brought down finally by the indiscretions of his son the Earl of Surrey in 1546, and was in the Tower awaiting execution on the night in January 1547 when King Henry died. He lived to be restored under Mary and to die in his bed in August 1554.

Catherine was less fortunate. The day after the Council meeting, on 7 November, Cranmer went to Hampton Court to interrogate her and to make sure that she remained under restraint. At first she wept copiously and denied that she had been guilty of any offence but the following day either broke down or decided that confession was the best way to turn aside wrath. The whole story came out, interspersed with fits of hysterics.[15] Meanwhile, Francis Dereham had confessed to intercourse with her at Horsham but claimed that there had been a contract of marriage between them. If that had been the case, it would of course have meant that her marriage to Henry had been null from the start and, since she could not cuckold a man to whom she had never been married, the whole charge of treason would have fallen to the ground. She would have been guilty of deception, and possibly of bigamy, but not of adultery. It was, perhaps, a measure of Catherine's stupidity that she would not entertain this line of defence. Either she was unable to understand its implications, or she was too proud to consider that a Howard could ever have married a Dereham. For whatever reason, she denied that any such pre-contract had ever existed, and thus effectively laid her head on the block. A few days later she wrote out a full and abject confession and threw herself on the King's mercy.

In this confession, which still survives, she described her relations with both Mannox and Dereham in graphic detail, but claimed that her affair with the latter had ended '... almost a year before your majesty was married to my lady Anne of Cleves' – that is in January 1539. 'I was so desirous', she went on, 'to be taken into your grace's favour and so blinded with the desire of worldly glory that I could not, nor had grace, to consider how great a fault it was to conceal my former faults from your majesty, considering that I intended ever during my life to be faithful and true unto your majesty after ...'[16]

The line of defence is clear. Yes, she had been guilty of deception and had not come to Henry as a virgin bride but that was all. All charges of adultery since her marriage, she continued to deny vehemently. The council did not immediately respond, being concerned at that point mainly with the issue of pre-contract, which was not even mentioned. However, shortly after they were confronted with Dereham's confession, and as a result Thomas Culpepper was arrested. He in his turn confessed to a sexual relationship with Catherine since her marriage – during that problematic summer progress. This was confirmed in a sense by Jane Rochford, who was now struggling painfully in the toils that she had created for herself. She declared that to the best of her knowledge, Culpepper was right, and that intercourse had taken place.[17] Catherine continued her denials, but her attempts to draw a line under her earlier indiscretions were now fatally compromised. If she had behaved in such an irresponsible fashion before her marriage, what was to prevent her from carrying on in the same manner? She was removed from Hampton Court to the former monastery of Syon, with four ladies and a dozen servants. On 13 November her household was closed down and her jewels were inventoried. All the accused were now in desperate straits and Cranmer and Wriothesley made another attempt to persuade the Queen to confess. As a result the story became more circumstantial – and more tangled. Catherine admitted indiscreet nocturnal meetings but continued to deny that they went further than dalliance and talk. Culpepper also changed his story. While admitting that he had intended sexual intercourse, a desire which he claimed was mutual, he now denied that it had taken place and that the sexual relationship which had admitted to earlier had amounted to no more than that. At the same time he claimed that these encounters had been arranged by Jane Rochford, who was thus made to appear as Catherine's pander.[18] Although it would have been convenient if the Queen had admitted her guilt, it was not really necessary. The statute of 1534 had laid down that if any person should '… by craft imagine, invent, practice or attempt any bodily harm to be done or committed to the king's most royal person, or the Queen's, or the heir apparent's …'[19] then that person was guilty of treason. Culpepper had certainly 'by craft imagined' bodily harm to Catherine, so that the fact that he had not actually succeeded in violating the Queen did not matter in terms of defining the crime. The fact that the Queen had condoned and even encouraged his action was neither here nor there. By not denouncing his actions at the time, she was guilty of conspiring her own bodily harm. Had she fallen pregnant, it would automatically have been assumed that the child was the King's and a gross deception would have been practised on the realm.

Throughout the third week of November the interrogations continued intensively, and it is likely that both Culpepper and Dereham were racked. Despite the King's threats, Catherine was not subjected to any such ordeal – indeed the only woman known to have been tortured throughout this period was the heretic Anne Askew, who added defiance to her demerits.[20] Nevertheless, the case against Catherine built up damningly and by 22 November the Council was convinced of the guilt of all three. On that day it was decreed that Catherine was no longer to be styled Queen but only the Lady Catherine Howard. This had no judicial significance, but was perhaps a pointer to the way in which it had been decided to proceed against her. On 1 December the two men were arraigned and both pleaded guilty. In fact Dereham's guilt was by no means established because, despite the opportunities that his position in the household had created, there is no proof that he had either resumed or attempted to resume, an intimate relationship. He seems to have been mainly the victim of the King's malice for having 'spoiled' his innocent bride. However, his plea of guilty resolved the matter so far as the court was concerned and both men were taken to Tyburn on 10 December. Because he was a member of the Privy Chamber, Culpepper was beheaded 'by the king's mercy' but Dereham suffered the full penalty of hanging, drawing and quartering. Both men allegedly 'made a good end', confessing their faults and asking the assembled people to pray for them. What the crowd's reaction may have been is not recorded. It was not every day that gentlemen were despatched in such a fashion and curiosity probably assembled a good number. As was customary, their heads were displayed on London Bridge, and Catherine's fate was sealed.[21]

As the French ambassador commented, Dereham had been executed because '... his coming to the queen was to an ill intent', and by the same criterion, the Queen had 'traiterously imagined and procured' that he should be so positioned 'that they might resume their wicked courses'. In other words, Catherine was as guilty as her lovers.[22] The appointment of another of her former associates, Katherine Tylney as a chamberer (like Joan Bulmer who was not named), was also construed as 'proof of her will to return to her abominable life ...' The same observer also remarked that Culpepper had been sufficiently intimate with the King as to 'share his couch' – by which he meant that he had been trusted with guard duty in the royal bedchamber, which involved sleeping on a pallet bed at the King's feet – and 'apparently wished to share the Queen's too'. For whatever reason, Catherine was never brought to trial. Anne Boleyn had been tried by her peers, but this time an Act of Attainder was used. It may have been felt that the public trial of a second Queen for adultery within the space of six years would have brought the King to ridicule, but it is more likely that the usefulness of such a procedure had been demonstrated in the meanwhile by the case of Thomas Cromwell, and it was simply selected as a convenient way of sparing Henry's feelings, which were still pretty raw at the end of December 1541. Lord Chancellor Audley apparently had some qualms about proceeding in this fashion, fearing that justice would not be seen to be done, but the King's wishes prevailed.[23] After a singularly cheerless Christmas, Parliament reconvened on 16 January and the Bill of Attainder was introduced in the House of Lords on 21 January. This confirmed the attainders of those who had already been executed, which was a standard procedure, and declared Catherine to have been guilty of treason. Rather surprisingly, the other person who was similarly condemned was Jane Rochford. Jane had (by modern standards) not been guilty of anything except crass stupidity, but her own confession told against her. If, as she claimed, Culpepper had been guilty of intercourse with the Queen, then she was guilty by association. However, as we have seen, there is every reason to doubt whether that had actually happened and while the wish might have been sufficient to condemn the principals, such an outcome should have exonerated Jane. On the other hand it could well have been argued that if she was an unsuccessful pander, it was not for want of trying. The Bill passed its final reading in the Commons on 8 February, and would normally have had to await the royal assent at the end of the session, on 1 April. However, Henry did not want to prolong the business any further, and a special assent was delivered by Letters Patent on 11 February. The two women were warned for death.

Catherine's mood over the previous two months or so is hard to assess. Under interrogation she had been by turns tearful and hysterical and that phase seems to have been succeeded by violent fluctuations. Sometimes she would collapse in weeping and lamentation but sometimes she appeared more preoccupied with her clothes than with the fate that hung over her. As late as Christmas she seems to have been unable to grasp the seriousness of her situation. On 10 February, the decision having been made, she was moved by river from Syon to the Tower, not to the royal apartments but to an appropriate dungeon, and two days later her fate was communicated to her. At this point she seems to have collapsed into a sort of numb acquiescence. As far as we know, she did not even appeal to her erstwhile husband for mercy – perhaps she realized that it would be pointless. All she did was to request a swift and secret death. The former was granted, and the latter refused, because it was necessary to have witnesses to so important a sacrifice. So it came about that a large crowd was gathered on Tower green in the bleak dawn of Monday, 13 February. An eyewitness account of the event survives in the reports of Charles de Marillac, the French ambassador, who was present.[24] The hapless Catherine was almost too distraught to know what was happening, and almost too weak to ascend the scaffold. She was able to utter just a few words, confessing her faults and 'desiring all Christian people to take regard to her worthy and just punishment'. It was generally agreed that she made a Godly and Christian end, more becoming of respect than anything that she had done in her life. She was just 20 years old, a mere child, broken on the wheel of her own desires. Jane Rochford reacted very differently. She had far more cause to feel that she had been unjustly used, but no such sentiment was aired. It would have been almost unthinkable for anyone condemned for treason to protest their innocence, or rail upon their judges. Under the stress of the occasion, however, Jane became voluble to the point of incoherence. Her confession and pious exhortation rambled on until the patience of the officials and of some of the crowd was exhausted. Both women died cleanly under the axe and both were interred in the nearby chapel of St Peter ad Vincula.

Jane was expendable, and in the circumstances a fitting object of the royal wrath, but whether Catherine would have suffered the ultimate penalty if she had not been the tool of a powerful aristocratic faction is another matter. If she had not been the Queen, the confessional and a suitable penance would have awaited her rather than the headsman's axe. The fate of a disgraced and repudiated woman in the sixteenth century was not enviable, but many ordinary girls endured it and lived to tell the tale. It was typical of the period that a woman guilty of such offences should be ostracized and condemned, whereas her male partner would escape unscathed unless he was identified as the father of a bastard child. Fornication was not an offence in the common law but was reserved to the Church Courts, and the judgement of society. However, none of this applied at the highest level and the Queen as whore was an almost unthinkable insult to the royal honour. Catherine, moreover, carried a heavy load of political baggage, just as Anne Boleyn had done. Anne had had to die because she was personally dangerous, Catherine had to die because her kindred were. There can be little doubt that Catherine's disgrace was more than personal; it carried an indictment of the whole Howard family. There would have been little point in arresting the Dowager Duchess of Norfolk if her offence had been merely bad household management. The charge of misprision of treason was based upon the thesis that she had been party to a conspiracy to foist a wanton girl on the King – not as a mistress (which might have been acceptable) but as a wife. Such charges were sufficient to destroy the family as a political force and for that same reason Catherine's status as a whore had to be substantiated and the full penalty of treason exacted. It was probably a guilty awareness on Henry's part that he had contributed to his own humiliation, which prevented the charges against Agnes from being pursued. By the time that she was pardoned they had had their political effect – and Catherine was dead.

The infliction of capital punishment upon women was comparatively rare in the early sixteenth century. Females were executed for murder and robbery but on nothing like the scale of their male contemporaries and Anne Boleyn was the first gentlewoman to suffer on the block in living memory. Witchcraft, while claiming many women's lives in the early seventeenth century, was hardly an issue in the reign of Henry VIII. A few female Lollards had been burned, but the execution of Anne Askew in 1546 was notorious partly because it was so rare. Margaret Pole had been despatched for high treason in the summer of 1541, but adultery was the treason of Queens and the simultaneous despatch of two women for that offence in February 1542 was a very notable event. Nobody has ever had much good to tell of Catherine. She was an instrument of her family, who was broken in the effort largely because of the defects in her own personality. She was obviously very attractive to men and may well have had others, in addition to Henry Mannox, of whom we know nothing because it was in no one's interest to disclose them. Having discovered this fact at an early age, she was quite unable to discipline herself and became, in effect, a 'girl who couldn't say no'. In her original confession, she claimed to have put her wanton past behind her and after her marriage to have kept herself for the King. What she did not, of course, say was that Henry was a very unsatisfactory lover and that, even by her own admission, she had sought solace in flirtations which were second nature to her. Her confession was not accepted as satisfactory at the time, and has become no more convincing today. She was in effect just a silly girl in the wrong place at the wrong time – and for that her family can be largely blamed.

As we have seen, Henry took her behaviour very hard. She had inflicted more psychological damage upon him in a few short months than several successive Popes, or Francis of France over many years. By the summer of 1540 his abortive encounter with Anne of Cleves had warned him that all was not well but Catherine had appeared to offer rejuvenation. The lustful, potent Henry who had wrought havoc with the damsels of the court was back! Then he was forced to confront the truth. He was old, tired and periodically sick. His once magnificent frame was now grossly overweight and regularly overtaxed. The sexual potency that had once kept Catherine of Aragon in a state of regular pregnancy was now unable to satisfy a young girl who had fewer years than his own daughter. A consort was supposed to maintain a King's honour, but this ignorant child had humiliated him in the most intimate possible way. Fortunately, international affairs did not await the King's mood or convenience. During the ill-fated summer progress of 1541 Henry thought that he had persuaded James V of Scotland to meet him at York. James's council persuaded him otherwise, and the English king took his non-appearance as an insult. Then at about the same time, on 10 July, Charles and Francis resumed their interminable conflict, and these two events shook the diplomatic kaleidoscope. Negotiations had been going on for a marriage between Mary and the duc d'Orleans, but these had foundered on the reef of Mary's illegitimacy. Early in 1542, at the same time that Catherine was awaiting the attentions of the executioner, Henry began secret negotiations for a renewal of his old Imperial alliance. In June plans were settled for a joint invasion of France in 1543, and through the autumn ships and guns were gathered for the impending action.[25] No doubt these bellicose preparations restored a measure of vitality and confidence to the King, and perhaps they were intended to do just that. However, the first action came against Scotland. Remembering what had happened a generation earlier, Henry was minded to exclude the Scots from the forthcoming action, by a treaty preferably, but if not by intimidation. The treaty option did not work, and in October 1542 the Duke of Norfolk launched a brief but savage raid into the lowlands. It was by doing his master's bidding in such ways that the Duke crept back into favour after his niece's disgrace. James could not fail to respond to such provocation and early in November he launched 20,000 men into the debateable ground north of Carlisle. His army walked into a well-laid trap and was routed at the battle of Solway Moss on 23 October. It was not a bloody defeat like Flodden but it left a lot of Scottish nobles as prisoners in English hands. It also took Scotland out of the forthcoming continental war because not only had its main field army been destroyed but James V himself died about a week later of unrelated causes, leaving his infant daughter Mary as his heir. These events, and the prospect of action in France, restored some youthful bounce to the decrepit Henry, and as his black moods retreated he began to contemplate marriage again. As we have seen, by March 1543 he was showing a serious interest in Lady Latimer.

The damage that Catherine had done to Henry was severe, but not irreparable. In a sense she had done him a favour, because she had proved conclusively that he was not the man he had been, and that sort of realism was necessary. He lowered his sights, and did not make the same demands upon his sixth wife that he had attempted to make on all the others. Of the six, Catherine stands out because she was the only one to be actually guilty of serious misconduct. Unlike Catherine of Aragon or Anne Boleyn, she had no political presence of her own. In that respect she resembled Jane Seymour but there the similarity began and ended. Jane's sexuality had been gentle and passive, Catherine's was devious and manipulative. Unlike any of Henry's other wives, she was the creation of a family faction, rather than the founder of one. The Boleyns and the Seymours would have had a presence at Court, even if their leading women had not shared the royal bed – the Parrs probably not. But neither the Boleyns nor the Seymours were powerful in the same sense as the Howards. Anne Boleyn had been more a councillor than a consort, but she had always been meticulous in her preservation of the King's honour and even her alleged misdemeanours had produced anger rather than humiliation or depression. Like Anne, but in a completely different way, Catherine did not know how to be a consort. She accepted all the privileges and wealth of her position but gave nothing in return except a sexual complaisance, which turned out to be fraudulent. She is not known to have been the patron of any group, or of any particular style of piety, nor did she receive petitions soliciting her arbitration. Her time, admittedly was short, but then so was that of Jane, who was a conspicuous peacemaker in the royal family. Catherine was at daggers drawn with Mary, who seems to have suspected her motives from the start, and who was a dedicated spinster five years her senior. Paradoxically the only member of the royal family with whom she seems to have been on good terms was her immediate predecessor, Anne of Cleves. It must have been an attraction of opposites because no two women could have been more different, except in one important respect – both were relatively uneducated, and when Anne was at court the Queen may have sought her company as a relief from the demands of her more learned compatriots. Judged by the standards normally applied to a consort, Catherine had almost no redeeming feature, and the fact that it took a major crisis to convince Henry of that fact is probably a better indication of his declining judgement than either the Boulogne campaign or the rough wooing, which as we shall see, was a seriously counterproductive policy.

8

The Queens who Never Were: Jane Grey and Mary Stuart

These women were both claimants or pretenders not to the role of consort but to the Crown in their own right. They therefore belong in a different league from the ladies we have so far considered. Mary was Queen of Scotland in her own right almost from birth, and for about 18 months was also Queen Consort of France. Her claim to the throne of England was by what was called 'indefeasible hereditary succession', a custom or rule recognized in both England and Scotland (but not in France) whereby the oldest legitimate descendant of the last monarch to produce offspring was recognized as heir. By this custom males took precedence over females, irrespective of seniority, but in the absence of men, the right of women to succeed was recognized. Mary was the daughter and only surviving child of James V of Scotland, born just a week before his death, and thus the granddaughter of Margaret Tudor, Henry VIII's elder sister, who had married King James IV. If it was claimed – as it was in Catholic Europe – that both Henry VIII's younger children were illegitimate, then the lawful Tudor line was represented on his death by his elder daughter, Mary, and after her by Mary of Scotland. The English, however, did not see it that way. As far as English law was concerned, Edward, Henry's son was legitimate because Papal sanctions were not recognized, and he was the heir in 1547.[1] Mary also recognized his right, and did not put forward a claim. Although unchallenged, Edward's position was nevertheless ambiguous, because he had also been declared the heir by his father's last succession Act in 1544, and by the will which that Act had authorized. In other words an Englishman could choose whether he recognized Edward by hereditary right, or by statutory authorization. When Edward died childless, the issue returned, but was resolved, as we shall see, in favour of the statute. In neither of these situations was any claim by Mary of Scotland considered, but when Mary Tudor also died childless, the issue returned.

In 1558 there were two possible claimants representing different principles of succession. Elizabeth represented the statutory policy laid down in 1544, whereas Mary of Scotland, whose claim had been ignored in the Succession Act, represented indefeasible hereditary right. At the time it was no contest, because Mary was betrothed to the Dauphin, and England was at war with France. Moreover the Succession Act was universally respected. The issue arose over who should be recognized as Elizabeth's heir should she, like her siblings, die childless. As we shall see, that problem was to afflict English politics for over twenty years.[2] By comparison, Jane Grey was a very short-term problem. She was not the direct heir by anyone's standards, except those of Edward VI. Edward issued (or tried to issue) Letters Patent recognizing Jane as his successor when it became clear that he was mortally ill in the summer of 1553.[3] It looked at first as though his wishes would be obeyed, but the superiority of Mary's claim, both by hereditary right and by the Succession Act, was soon apparent. Jane was consigned to the Tower, and eventually to the block. She became a footnote to history. However, because her pretension came first chronologically, and it was she rather than either of the Marys who can claim in a sense to have been England's first ruling Queen, Jane takes priority for consideration.

Jane was the eldest of three daughters of Henry Grey, Marquis of Dorset, and his wife Frances Brandon. She was born at Bradgate Hall in Leicestershire in October 1537. Frances was the elder daughter of Mary, Henry VIII's younger sister by her second marriage to Charles Brandon, Duke of Suffolk, and by the Succession Act of 1544 was next in line to the throne should all Henry's own offspring die childless. That was not the case in the summer of 1553, when both Mary and Elizabeth were very much alive. Frances was also alive, and indeed Edward's 'device for the succession' had started by naming any son who might be born to her. Only when it was apparent that his time was very short did the young King switch his option to Jane, who should have had no claim by anyone's standards. The reason for this implausible change was that Edward knew Jane and liked her. Her education and theological tastes matched his own and she was almost exactly his age. For several years there had been talk of a marriage between them and Jane seems to have been brought up with that in mind. Her early education at Bradgate was ordinary enough, except that she seems to have been taught Latin from the beginning, which was not normal for a girl. At the age of about 9 she went to live in the household of the Dowager Queen Catherine and for a year or so appears to have shared the education of the precocious Edward there, which elevated her onto an altogether new plane of learning.[4] For two or three months Mary, Elizabeth and Jane all continued in Catherine's establishment. The latter's controversial and somewhat hasty marriage to Lord Thomas Seymour prompted Mary to move out. She could afford to do so, since she was of age and the estates conferred upon her by the terms of Henry's will were promptly assigned. Elizabeth and Jane stayed put. Elizabeth was 13 and her estates had not yet been assigned. Jane stayed by a special arrangement between the Marquis of Dorset and Lord Thomas Seymour, in the course of which Lord Thomas hinted broadly that he was in a position to arrange her marriage to the young king. 'You will see', one contemporary observed, 'he will marry her to the king.'[5] Why he should have thought that – and still more why the Marquis should have believed him, remain something of a mystery. Grey paid Seymour something like £2,000 for the privilege.

In the summer of 1548, while Catherine was pregnant, she discovered the indiscreet Lord Thomas with his arms around Elizabeth. The girl was sent away in disgrace and, having nowhere obvious to go, retreated to the home of Sir Anthony and Lady Denny at Cheshunt. Then, early in September, Catherine died in childbirth, leaving Jane apparently unprotected in the household of a notorious womanizer. Lord Thomas, however, was not a child abuser and the Marquis appears to have continued to trust him. His first thought was to break up the overlarge household that he had kept up while married to the Queen Dowager, and after a friendly exchange of correspondence, Dorset took his daughter back to Bradgate, where she arrived on about 20 September. Seymour, meanwhile had changed his mind, and decided for political reasons to retain a much larger establishment than he could really afford. Jane's role in all this was obvious, so he opened negotiations with Dorset to get her back. The latter, meanwhile, may have grown sceptical of these ambitions because he had also opened a correspondence with the Lord Protector for a marriage between Jane and the Earl of Hertford, his eldest son. It is probable that Dorset was simply keeping his options open because, within a couple of weeks Lord Thomas had persuaded him to allow his daughter to return to Hanworth. On 1 October the girl herself wrote to Thomas, expressing her gratitude for his kindness and describing him as her 'loving and kind father'. His charm seems to have been working overtime because at the same time her mother, Frances, also wrote to him as her 'very good lord and brother'. It may have been Lord Seymour's friend and associate Sir William Sharrington who got on so well with the Marchioness but relations between the two establishments could hardly have been more cosy.

Within weeks, Thomas was in trouble up to his neck, for reasons that had nothing directly to do with Jane and the Greys were, understandably, very worried. The Lord Admiral had been plotting a coup against his brother, whom he detested by this time, and boasting about how many armed men he could raise. At the same time, Sharrington had been filtering off money from the Bristol Mint, for which he had responsibility. The intention seems to have been to get the Lord Protector's patent overturned by statute, but other, more direct action was also suspected. In January 1549, Lord Thomas Seymour was arrested, interrogated, and charged with treason. This charge was not derived from the plot against his brother, which would not have been treason because the latter was not the King, but from an alleged intention to marry the Princess Elizabeth. The Princess was also interrogated, and although she behaved with admirable self possession, the charge was deemed to be proved. Lord Thomas was condemned by Act of Attainder and executed on 20 March 1549.[6] The Protector seems to have been genuinely perplexed as to what to do but his temper was not sweetened when he discovered that his brother had been endeavouring to sabotage his marriage plans for his son by continuing to dangle Jane before the King – a circumstance of which the Marquis of Dorset had not informed him. Jane's reaction to the loss of her 'kind father' in such dramatic circumstances is not known but all Seymour's property was forfeit by his attainder, so the ground was literally swept from under her. By the end of March, and still short of her twelfth birthday, she was back at Bradgate.

At such a distance from the Court there was no longer any question of her sharing the King's lessons (if that is what had been happening), but the Greys decided to persevere with the quality of education that she had been receiving and engaged John Aylmer, the future bishop of London, as her tutor. Aylmer was a learned man, and strong Protestant, and in friendly correspondence with such leading continental reformers as Heinrich Bullinger and John ab Ulmis. Aylmer was hugely impressed with his charge and was soon encouraging her to correspond directly with his friends, who were equally impressed with her piety and her Latin.[7] It seems clear that at this point, in the summer of 1549, Dorset still had more than an eye on Jane marrying Edward, and wanted to make sure that she would be a fit companion for him. Like over-anxious parents in any period, the Marquis and his lady fretted over their eldest child, and according to her own account were 'sharp and severe' with her. Roger Ascham, who visited Bradgate that summer, declared that it was her parents' 'taunts, pinches, nips and bobs' that caused her to seek solace in the company of Plato, and 'gentle master' Aylmer. Perhaps, but Ascham's work was more than a little hagiographic and it may well be that Jane was not quite the humble and polite bookworm whom he portrayed. As one recent biographer has observed, she was probably 'a priggish, opinionated teenager, contemptuous of her parents'. She knew what was expected of her but a taste for 'playing, dancing and being merry' can also be glimpsed through his record. The one thing that is quite clear is that she was formidably intelligent, a quality that she does not seem to have inherited directly from either of her parents. Her younger sisters, Catherine and Mary were much more truly their parents' children in that respect.

Jane stayed at Bradgate, or other Grey residences as appropriate, for the next four years. Her prospects changed as the political events of the reign unfolded but neither she nor indeed her father had much control over those events. The disturbances of July and August 1549 did not touch Bradgate, and the Marquis played no leading role in their suppression. Nor was he active in the coup that overthrew the Protector in October. What he did succeed in doing was to ingratiate himself with the man who effectively took over the Protestor's position – John Dudley, Earl of Warwick. After the coup, Warwick was locked in a three-month battle with the religious conservatives on the Council, whose main motivation in getting rid of Somerset had been to check England's progress towards Protestantism. Warwick's own incentives had been quite different and he was happy to see the Reformation continue, but in order to secure control he needed allies in the Council, and that meant Protestants. That was where the Marquis came in. He may not have been a very shrewd politician, or even a good administrator, but he was a Protestant and he was sworn of the Council on 28 November 1549.[8] This raised his political profile substantially and he came to be regarded as one of Warwick's closest and most reliable allies.

Meanwhile, Jane's matrimonial prospects were ebbing away. One of the obstacles in the way of her union with the King had always been the fact that he was supposed to be committed to Mary of Scotland by the treaty of Greenwich of 1543. However the Scots had repudiated that treaty and numerous English attempts to resurrect it had finally ended in failure in 1548 when Mary was betrothed to the Dauphin, Francis. War with France had followed, from August 1549 to March 1550, and with the peace that ended that war came talk of a matrimonial alliance. Negotiations proceeded for over a year and were finally concluded in June 1551, whereby a marriage was agreed but was not to take place until Elizabeth, Henry II's eldest daughter, had passed the age of 12 (she was, at that point, 6) which was the minimum canonical age for co-habitation.[9] The marriage never took place because Edward died when Elizabeth was 8, but he was considered to be committed, and that shut off Jane's chances – if they had ever existed. Similarly, relations with Edward Seymour chilled noticeably after Dorset's choice in October 1549. He became so close to the Earl of Warwick that when the latter had himself raised to the Dukedom of Northumberland on 11 October 1551, he caused the Marquis to be created Duke of Suffolk at the same time. Shortly after the Duke of Somerset was arrested, and with his execution for felony in February 1552, his title was extinguished and his property forfeit. The Earl of Hertford disappeared into limbo and another matrimonial option was closed.

The dukedom of Suffolk brought further wealth to the Greys and by the summer of 1552 they had moved their main centre of operations from Bradgate to the former Carthusian monastery of Sheen, in Surrey. There Jane seems to have lived until her ill-fated marriage to Lord Guildford Dudley in June 1553. Guildford was the Duke of Northumberland's last unmarried son, and his father's intentions had not originally focused on Jane at all. He had been negotiating for some time for the hand of her cousin, Margaret Clifford, the daughter of her Aunt Eleanor, Frances's sister, and Henry Clifford, Earl of Cumberland. His purpose seems to have been to establish a firm link with one of the northern peerage families, but Clifford was having none of it.[10] As early as July 1552 the Privy Council had written to both peers to 'grow to some good end', concerning the marriage, which was probably Northumberland's way of putting pressure on his colleague – but to no avail. Frustrated in his quest, Northumberland turned to his complaisant ally, the Duke of Suffolk, and on 21 May 1553 effected a series of prestigious marriages. His daughter Catherine was married to Henry Hastings, heir to the Earl of Huntingdon, Jane's sister, also Catherine, to Henry Herbert, son of the Earl of Pembroke, and Jane herself to Guildford Dudley. This appears to have been an act of parental oppression on the Greys' part, because all the indications are that Jane loathed her spouse and was only compelled to sleep with him by 'the urging of her mother and the violence of her father, who compelled her to accede to his commands with blows'. Jane had become a bluestocking, perhaps as much by force of circumstances as by taste, and some of her stilted, elaborate letters to Heinrich Bullinger testify both to her accomplishments and her ambition. At the age of 16 she was fluent in Latin, proficient in Greek and anxious to learn Hebrew. In an earlier generation she would have been a natural candidate for the cloister, an abbess in the making. As it was, she was forced into bed with Guildford Dudley.

It has been argued that this marriage was part of a deep-laid plot by the Duke of Northumberland to divert the Crown into the Dudley family, but at the time even the suspicious Jehan Scheyfre, the Imperial ambassador, merely noted that Jane was a cousin of the King's. It is likely that, in late May, Northumberland did not even know of that schoolboy exercise on the succession, known as the 'King's Device'. Edward had been ill since February, but the nature of his ailment was not understood, and in late May he was in remission. It was only about a week into June that his condition deteriorated alarmingly, and the physicians who had been glibly talking of a complete recovery, suddenly decided that his death was not only certain but imminent.[11] This desperate news concentrated minds, not only Northumberland's but also the King's, and caused the school exercise to be brought out. When he had written it, Edward had been obsessed with the male succession and his order started with any son who might be born of the Lady Frances (the Duchess of Suffolk), followed by any son who might be born to Jane. There was much more in the same vein but the important thing was that it ignored the Succession Act of 1544 and excluded both Mary and Elizabeth as being not only female but also illegitimate. After that, its provisions followed the Act in excluding the Scots, and including the 'Suffolk line'. However, in the emergency that had now arisen, it was not much use. Frances had not conceived for years, and was probably passed what was known at the time as her 'climacteric'. Jane was newly married but had scarcely had time to get pregnant, even if the will had been there. Reluctantly, therefore, the King altered his 'Device', settling the Crown upon 'the Lady Jane and her heirs male', by a simple insertion in the text.[12]

It was clearly Northumberland's intention to get this 'Device', which had no legal status, confirmed by Parliament, which in so doing would have repealed the Succession Act – but there was no time. As June advanced the terminal nature of the King's illness became more apparent and he ordered that his 'Device' be embodied in Letters Patent. There was much resistance to this, the lawyers pointing out that an Act of Parliament could not be overruled by Letters Patent and that, in any case, the King was a minor who could not even make a valid will. Edward, however, insisted and, put upon their allegiance, his council all swore to uphold his wishes.[13] On 6 July the King died and Jane's eccentric claim was put to the test. Bearing in mind that it could not be treason to obey the personal commands of a king, they could have felt uncommitted and free to obey the law as it then stood. Northumberland, however, thought differently. Whether out of loyalty to his late master, or out of family interest, he persuaded (or forced) the Council to follow its oath, and Jane was duly proclaimed. The King's death was kept secret for two days (a standard precaution), and on 8 July revealed to the Mayor and Aldermen of London, who were sworn to Queen Jane. A contemporary observer wrote: 'The 10 of July, in the afternoon about 3 of the clocke, lady Jane was conveyed by water to the Tower of London, and there received as Queene ...'[14]

A couple of hours later the King's death was publicly announced, and 'how he had ordained by his letters patent ... that the lady Jane should be heire to the Crowne of England.' The news was received in ominous silence and there were protests. It was pointed out that the King had been solely motivated by his desire to preserve his 'godly reformation' against the threat of Mary's known conservatism but even that (which was true up to a point) could not move the citizens. If the largely Protestant city of London could not be persuaded to support so Godly a claimant, what chance was there in the rest of the country?

Jane's 'rule' lasted just nine days. She had no time to appoint officers of State, and the Council of Edward VI simply carried on.[15] By 12 July it was clear that Mary was 'making a power' in East Anglia and that military action against her would be necessary. Letters were sent out in Jane's name to the Commissions of the Peace, urging loyalty to the Queen, and the suppression of Mary's pretensions. In some places these letters were taken seriously but events were moving too fast. The Council's first thought was to send the Duke of Suffolk against Mary, but the Queen 'with many tears' asked that he be allowed to remain with her, so Northumberland went instead. This turned out to be a fatal mistake. Northumberland was a better soldier than Suffolk but as soon as his dominating presence was removed from London, the Council began to split. By 16 July the split had become open and Mary's adherents were in the majority. On 19 July Mary was proclaimed in London with general rejoicing and Northumberland, stuck at Cambridge with a dwindling force, was left out on a limb. The Duke of Suffolk himself took down the canopy of state under which Jane had sat, and informed her that she was no longer Queen.[16] Instead, she and her father and all their adherents were prisoners. She was removed from the royal apartments to the Keeper's lodgings. The hapless girl had had no time to rule and we have no idea what sort of a job she would have made of it. She did, apparently, indicate very firmly that she had no intention of conferring the Crown Matrimonial upon her husband and if that had ever come to an issue it would have been a revolutionary move. She appears to have been a mere pawn in a power game that the Duke of Northumberland played, and lost, with Mary. What might have happened if she had been a boy is a fascinating but pointless speculation. Whichever way the issue had gone in July 1553, England would have had its first ruling Queen.

As soon as Mary reached London on 3 August, the wheels of political justice began to turn. Stephen Gardiner, the Bishop of Winchester, the Duke of Norfolk and Edward Courtenay were released from the Tower. The Duke of Northumberland and his sons replaced them. In due course all were arraigned and condemned to death, although in the event only the Duke suffered.[17] Two of his followers suffered with him, but the delicacy of the political balance that had brought Mary to the throne was reflected in the outcome. Jane, it is clear, was not rigorously confined. She had her servants and was allowed to move around within the Tower. An anonymous chronicler recorded how on 29 August:

> I dined at Partrige's (the Keeper) house with my lady Jane ... she sitting at the bordes end ... emongst our communication at dyner; this was to be noted ... saythe she "The queens majesty is a mercyfull princes; I beseche God she may long continue, and sende his bountefull grace upon hir ...[18]

They spoke of religion and Jane asked if the mass was set up again in London. Being told that it was so, she proceeded to comment on the recent conversion of the Duke of Northumberland, 'who woulde have thought', saide she, 'that he would have done so'. She clearly had no sympathy with his predicament and proceeded to blame him bitterly for bringing 'me and our stocke in most miserable callamytye'. As she wrote to the Queen in a letter not now surviving '... in truth I was deceived by the Duke and council, and ill-treated by my husband and his mother ...' She would, she declared, in spite of her youth, never seek to save her life by any such apostasy as Northumberland had been guilty of. She was yesterday's woman but as such presented something of a problem to Mary, who was inclined to pardon her, as she confided to Simon Renard, the Imperial ambassador. Her father was indeed pardoned during November in a somewhat inexplicable act of clemency, considering the extent of his involvement. However, she had pretended to the throne, and the proprieties had to be observed. Consequently on 13 November she was tried at the Guildhall, along with her husband and the Archbishop of Canterbury, 'The lady Jane was in a blacke gowne of cloth, tourned down, the cappe lined with fese velvet ... a blacke velvet booke hanging before hir ...'[19]

They were all, of course, condemned to die. Nevertheless, it is likely that she would have been pardoned eventually if it had not been for her father's reckless involvement in the Wyatt rebellion in January 1554. This was a dangerous protest against the Queen's plan to marry Philip of Spain, but once it had collapsed the government chose to represent it as an attempt to rescue and restore Jane to the throne. There was no desire to admit that Philip would be so unpopular, and Jane was expendable. Consequently, on 12 February she and her wretched young husband were executed as a sacrifice to expediency. The Queen sent the persuasive John Feckenham, the Dean of St Paul's, in an attempt to convert her to the old faith. They parted with mutual respect but without agreement. It was her powerful religious faith that enabled her to die with assurance:

> 'Good people' she said, 'I am come hether to die, and by a lawe I am condemned to the same. The facte, in dede, against the queens highnesse was unlawfull, and the consenting thereto by me, but touching the procurement and desire thereof ... I doo wash my handes in innocencie ...

She then repeated the Misere, 'and so ended'.[20]

Because of her place in Protestant hagiography this scene has been often described and was a favourite with the kitsch Victorian painters of historical scenes but it was an unnecessary tragedy, which brought Queen Mary no ultimate advantage. She would probably have done better to release Jane into the obscurity of a failed aristocratic marriage.

Mary of Scotland was a completely different kind of animal. None of the problematic and arbitrary thinking that had been required to create Jane's claim was necessary in her case. She represented the clear principle of undisputed legitimacy. Very little is known about her early years when her realm was in the hands of Regents and her person in the care of her mother, Mary of Guise, except that she was crowned as an infant on 9 September 1543. One thing, however, is very clear: Henry VIII wanted her as a wife for his own son, Prince Edward. There were several reasons for this but the most important was an imperial ambition to gain control over the neighbouring kingdom. Had this marriage taken effect, Mary would have been Queen Consort in England, and would have been expected to live there, while Edward would have held the Crown Matrimonial of Scotland, and would have governed the kingdom (with his wife's consent, of course) through his own appointed agents. Any child of the marriage would have had an equal claim to both countries and when the Crowns were so unified the greater political and financial weight of England would have guaranteed it the role of senior partner. It was this medium- and long-term threat to their independence which turned the Scots against the marriage and although they were in no position to resist after the defeat at Solway Moss, the parliament nevertheless repudiated the subsequent Treaty of Greenwich and never recognized the betrothal of the children. Henry was very angry at what he saw as a betrayal and, despite his primary concern over war with France, kept up an erratic and totally ineffective military pressure upon Scotland. These campaigns, known collectively as 'the rough wooing', served to alienate those in Scotland who had at first been in favour of the union and led to a marked increase in French, and Catholic influence north of the border.

This orientation was confirmed when Edward's Lord Protector, the Duke of Somerset, launched a new campaign, in accordance, he claimed, with his late master's wishes, in September 1547. The French were apparently taken by surprise, and the Scots suffered another heavy defeat at Pinkie Cleugh near Musselborough. Realizing that he lacked the resources for a systematic conquest and unable to force the regency government to the negotiating table, Somerset dispersed his victorious army into some two dozen garrisons, from Dundee in the north-east to Dumfries in the south-west. This turned out to be useless. The garrisons could not be supplied or reinforced and were under constant guerrilla pressure, being abandoned or falling into enemy hands steadily over the following year. Scotland's plight also belatedly stirred Henry II into action, and on 19 June 1548 a force of 10,000 French troops landed in the Firth of Forth. In August the Franco-Scottish treaty of Haddington not only tilted the military balance decisively in Scotland's favour but also killed off the treaty of Greenwich by betrothing the 5-year old Mary to the Dauphin, Francis. The same month she was smuggled out of Ayr, landing at Roscoff on 13 June and was received with open arms at the French Court. For the next ten years she was to be cosseted, educated and trained to be a French princess and sometime Queen Consort. She was not, apparently, even taught to write in English (or Scots), and certainly felt closer to her Guise kindred than to anyone in Scotland. Meanwhile her northern realm continued to be run by regents, culminating in the Queen Mother in 1554, and became increasingly disrupted by aristocratic and religious feuds. Although much influenced by events in England, Scotland had its own band of indigenous reformers who, in 1547 and 1548, had learned to their bitter cost the folly of looking south of the border for support. From their point of view, however, the total failure of English policy in Scotland and its virtual withdrawal by the autumn of 1549, had its own advantages. No longer thought of as being English agents, and seeking their inspiration instead directly from Geneva and Zurich, between 1550 and 1558, the Scottish Protestants made huge strides. On a level playing field, the French were no more popular in Scotland than were the English, and after 1548 they were there, while the English were not. By 1558 the Protestant Lords of the Congregation of Jesus Christ were in full rebellion against the Regent and her French backers.

Meanwhile Mary had grown up tall and beautiful. An accomplished linguist, dancer, needlewoman and horsewoman, she had been given only the most perfunctory instruction as to how to run her problematic northern kingdom.[21] It seems to have been assumed that she would remain in France, and govern Scotland through agents. On 24 April 1558, Francis and Mary were married and both Mary as Queen and Francis as King Consort swore to uphold the laws and liberties of Scotland. At the same time Francis guaranteed that, in the event of Mary dying childless, he would not press any claim to the Scottish throne but would let it come to the next inheritors by Scots law. This was disingenuous, not to say dishonest, because three weeks before her wedding Mary had signed another instrument whereby, in the event of her dying without issue, she assigned the Crown of Scotland – and any claim which she had to the Crown of England – to the King of France. In the event, both instruments were dead letters because Francis died first, but their existence amply justifies the suspicion with which Mary was always regarded in official circles in England. When Queen Mary Tudor died on 17 November, Francis and his consort promptly added the arms and title of England to their achievement. The claim was explicit, but low key and

Henry II was not anxious to exploit it. When the Franco-Spanish-English war was brought to an end at Cateau Cambrecis in April 1559 he made no difficulty about negotiating with Elizabeth as Queen of England. When Henry died, however, in a tournament accident following the signing of the treaty, his son, now Francis II, did not scruple to use the titles of all three kingdoms, irrespective of the fact that so far nobody in England had canvassed his wife's claim at all.

Meanwhile the political situation in Scotland was deadlocked. Mary of Guise, with only minimal French support, was not strong enough to suppress the rebels, while they, plagued with internal quarrels, lacked the muscle or support for a complete victory. The English, having now committed themselves to the Protestant side in any future European conflict, regarded this situation with anxiety. When one of the rebel groups approached the English council for support, the response, although cautious, was positive. William Cecil persuaded Elizabeth to intervene and the Queen in turn was at great pains to distance herself from the father's imperialist claims.[22] The intelligence of this approach was quickly demonstrated and despite a spectacular military failure at the siege of Leith in 1560, by the summer the issue had been forced to a treaty. The French position had been fatally weakened by the fact that internal dissentions in France made it virtually impossible for Francis to send reinforcements and then, in June 1560, Mary of Guise had died. By the Treaty of Edinburgh, both English and French forces were withdrawn, and Scotland was left in the hands of the Protestant Lords, who wasted no time in establishing a reformed Kirk and a council of regency. The French troops duly went home but neither Francis nor Mary ever ratified the treaty, despite the fact that it remained the *de facto* basis of Anglo-Scottish relations for the next 40 years. This non-ratification continued to be a bone of contention between Mary and Elizabeth, at least until Mary was detained in England. In spite of the fact that the English were ignoring her, and she them, Mary's fortunes were at their zenith in 1559–60, when she was 18. Thereafter it was downhill all the way.

The first blow was the death of Francis II in December 1560. He had never been anything but a sickly youth and it is unlikely that his marriage with Mary was ever consummated. This not only left her childless, but deeply frustrated – a frustration that was to be reflected in some highly irresponsible behaviour within a few years. It also left her without a role in France because the powerful Queen Mother, Catherine de Medici, was bitterly opposed to the Guises. The second blow was consequently that her uncles, the Duke and Cardinal of Guise, became so preoccupied with the internal troubles of that kingdom that they had scant time or attention for their niece and began to press her to return to Scotland. They pointed out, rightly enough from their point of view, that that kingdom had much need of its Catholic ruler. Once the 40 days of her official mourning were over, there was much talk of her remarriage, both Don Carlos, Philip II's son and the Earl of Arran being mentioned, but Mary's own thoughts were turning consistently to her northern kingdom, which had been without any sort of royal government since the death of her mother. She appeared to the English ambassador in Paris, Sir Nicholas Throgmorton, to be a very competent and self-possessed young woman:

> Since her husband's death the Scottish Queen has showed ... that she is both of great wisdom for her years, modesty, and also of great judgement ... which increasing with her years, cannot but turn greatly to her commendation ...[23]

Meanwhile, the Scots themselves were warming to the thought of her return, especially as she was beginning to acquire a reputation for flexibility in matters of religion. It was Maitland of Lethington, who was keenly aware of the international dimension, and of Mary's English claim, who urged that she be invited to return, so that that claim might benefit Scotland rather than France.

As early as January 1561 she had notified an intention to return. The emissaries passed to and fro and by the beginning of August a deal had been struck. On 19 August her French galleys reached the port of Leith. And Mary, at the age of 19, returned to the country of her birth, which she had not seen for 13 years. Her deal had been with Lord James Stuart, her half brother, and had included an undertaking to 'work along' with the Protestant ascendancy. Within days she had issued a proclamation protecting that ascendancy, and established a council the leading members of which were Lord James and Maitland of Lethington.[24] It was expected at first that the Queen would be little more than a figurehead, but she soon began to demonstrate an unexpected intelligence and grasp of politics. Her willingness to work with a Protestant council had largely marginalized the fiery John Knox and when she confronted him in a number of disputations, although his intransigence reduced her to tears, he gained no political advantage thereby. At first, as Mary quickly realized, the Anglo-Scottish amity of 1560 was fundamental and she was happy to retain that for reasons of her own. Her eyes were fixed on the English succession. This was not an immediate issue, because although she never withdrew her alternative claim, Elizabeth was a young woman not much older than herself. Mary's intention was not to replace Elizabeth (least of all as a Catholic claimant), but to obtain an official recognition of her position as heir should the Queen die childless. In this she made no progress at all. Elizabeth refused even to discuss the issue of the succession, and when she was seriously ill in 1562 it quickly transpired that Mary had no backing in the English Council.

Meanwhile, the Scottish Queen was proving as energetic as she was sensible. Between 1562 and 1564 she undertook numerous progresses, going to the Catholic stronghold of the north east in 1562 and getting as far as Inverness in 1564, where the court donned highland dress in honour of the place! The Gordons were so alienated by her pro-Protestant policies that the Earl of Huntly staged a small-scale rebellion during the 1562 progress, which only served to demonstrate the weakness of his following. He died (apparently of apoplexy) on the field of battle.[25] Lord James Stuart became Earl of Moray and the Huntly title was temporarily extinguished. The Anglo-Scottish amity was put under some strain, not only by Mary's persistence over the succession issue but also by the failure of a planned joint initiative in Ulster involving the Earl of Argyll. However, that failure was largely William Cecil's fault and the amity still held into 1565.[26] At that point it was seriously disrupted by Mary's need for a man. A widowed Queen, young and beautiful, was an inevitable subject for matrimonial speculation and all sorts of suitors were canvassed, including Eric of Sweden, who had failed with Elizabeth and had no desire to try again. Much more serious, particularly in its political implications, was the proposal of Don Carlos, Philip's somewhat unpromising son. By 1563 Anglo-Spanish relations were coming under strain and the prospect was regarded in England with undisguised alarm. So exercised was she that Elizabeth decided to take an initiative with the 'good sister' and offered her the hand of Lord Robert Dudley. By the time that this happened the English Queen had abandoned any intention of marrying Lord Robert herself, but he was still unquestionably her favourite and the question of her sincerity in making this offer has often been discussed.[27] Was she trying to do the best that she could for a man that she loved, but would never have? Or was she trying to establish a vicarious control over the Queen of Scots? Perhaps it was a bit of both. In any case Mary was not amused at being offered Elizabeth's 'cast off lover', even when he was created Earl of Leicester in 1564.

At this point, however, Mary's shrewdness and political judgement, both of which had been much in evidence since her return to the north, appear to have deserted her completely. As a result of the manoeuvrings of Scottish aristocratic politics, and a dash of English intercession, the exiled Earl of Lennox returned to Scotland in September 1564 and was restored to the title that he had forfeited in 1545, on 4 October. Lennox's countess was Margaret, the daughter of Eleanor, the younger sister of Frances Brandon, Duchess of Suffolk, and thus had a remote claim to the English throne. Both Eleanor and Frances were dead by 1564, and although Mary Tudor had taken Margaret's claim seriously, Elizabeth and her council had never done so. However, the Lennoxes had a son, the 18-year-old Henry, Lord Darnley, and he was the only male with even a remote claim by that time. Darnley joined his father in Scotland in January 1565 and shortly after met the Queen. He was, apparently, a 'long lad', boyish but tall and handsome.[28] Mary fell head-over-heels in love with him, and all her hard-earned common sense went out of the window. There was soon talk of marriage and the alarm bells began to ring in England. Darnley professed to be a Protestant, but his mother was a notorious Catholic (which was why Mary had approved of her) and his claim to the throne made him dangerous. If they should wed, two quite different claims would be united. It has been argued that, having rejected Dudley, there was no realistic alternative if Mary was determined on marriage but in fact she could have had her pick of the princely houses of Europe – even those currently pursuing Elizabeth. The fact is that she wanted him. Darnley was created Earl of Ross on 15 May 1565 and on 29 July Mary married him. He was proclaimed King the same day.

The dispensation that the rules of the Catholic Church demanded did not arrive until September and Elizabeth was completely alienated: 'All their sisterly familiarity was ceased…' as one contemporary put it.[29] There were even rumours of war.

Even at this early stage, Darnley was not a popular choice in Scotland but the prevailing attitude was 'wait and see'. The minor rebellion known as the Chaseabout Raid in September was premature and resulted only in the flight to England of the earls of Arran and Moray on 6 October. Meanwhile, Mary's primary need had been satisfied because within a couple of months or so of her wedding she was pregnant. The Queen's little weakness had been spotted, or presumed, as early as 1562, when in the course of her progress, she had been handed a 'lewd bill', which left nothing to the imagination. Elizabeth's reaction to such presumption can only be imagined! The price that Mary paid for that gratification, however, was high. The rupture with England remained at the diplomatic level but the Chaseabout raid left her with the need for a new Council and that saw the rise of David Rizzio. Rizzio was never a member of the council, but his appointment as French secretary gave him influence – and access. By October the Queen's brief honeymoon with Darnley was over – a sure sign of its unstable foundation. He swiftly confirmed what many had realized before: that he was both vain and stupid and had a unique talent for upsetting everyone. That included the Queen, who by the end of October had refused him the Crown Matrimonial, which left him with only the empty title of King and a monumental grudge.[30] Whether it was Darnley's behaviour or some other factor, Mary seems to have been thrown completely off balance by these events. By January 1566 she had abandoned plans to conciliate the exiles in England and bring them home. Instead she called a parliament for the express purpose of forfeiting them and at the same time turned against the Protestant establishment with a plan to legalize the mass. The alarm that these moves created led to a plot against her, to which Darnley was recruited by a promise of the Crown Matrimonial. The plotters clearly intended to seize power but whether they aimed to replace Mary with Darnley seems much more problematical. On Saturday 9 March 1566 they invaded the royal apartments, seized the unsuspecting (and ill-protected) Queen, and they murdered David Rizzio. Rizzio was not the main target, but he was in the wrong place at the wrong time. Mary was imprisoned and the parliament dismissed without having pronounced either on the forfeitures or the mass. The Queen was accused of listening to evil council, but whatever the plotters aim may have been it was quickly frustrated by her escape. With the aid of the Earl of Bothwell, she got away to Dunbar and swiftly raised an army, which swept her back to power. The plot had been only skin deep in terms of support, and the plotters (except Darnley) now fled in their turn. Their action, however, had not been entirely in vain, because the Queen did, in fact, pardon and recall the earlier exiles and no further attempt was made to legalize the mass. It was in the interval of calm following these events that Prince James was born on 19 June.

The labour was difficult. Mary only recovered slowly, and was then ill again in October. It was November before she was fully operational again, and in a position to tackle the thorniest problem of all – what to do about Darnley? Despite Rizzio's murder and her own rough handling, she seems to have decided to write off the events of the spring, perhaps as the only way of resolving the issue of her husband. Divorce was out of the question, and annulment would have jeopardized their child, so conciliation was in the air. Joseph Rizzio was appointed to his brother's former position, and on 24 December the March plotters were pardoned.[31] Religion seems not to have been an issue, although James was baptized on 17 December with full Catholic rites, a ceremony from which Darnley, most of the Scots Lords and the English ambassador conspicuously absented themselves. There was, however, another possible way to deal with Darnley. A conspiracy of some kind existed by the end of November, and then on 10 February 1567 he was spectacularly blown up at Kirk o' Fields. James Hepburn, Earl of Bothwell, the same man who had supported Mary the previous year, is generally held to have been responsible. Mary's complicity is reasonably certain, although she may not have known that the plot extended to murder. There was an immediate and vociferous outcry, which owed nothing to Darnley's popularity, and he suddenly became a cause. In this crisis, Mary's wit and good sense seem to have deserted her again, leaving her a political and emotional wreck. Bothwell was duly tried on 12 April and acquitted by a rigged court, an event that did nothing to placate the furore. The Earl's intention seems to have been clear. He wanted to marry the Queen, and had hastily divorced his existing wife for the purpose. He tried to raise some support for such a project but made little progress and the Queen, with a last flicker of good sense, rejected him. So fragile was Mary's security, however, that he was able to kidnap her as she returned from Stirling to Edinburgh on 24 April, and he then proceeded to rape her. There is, it has been asserted, no evidence of love on her part, nor of any kind of collusion, but if collusion did not precede the fact, it certainly followed it. On 6 May she returned with Bothwell to Edinburgh, on 15 May proceeded to marry him with Protestant rites. One contemporary observed that 'the Queen could not but marry him, seeing he had ravished her and lain with her against her will …'[32] but it is hard to imagine Elizabeth being so supine if such an unthinkable event had occurred in England. Mary was ill, and understandably deeply distressed but she had now dug herself into a political hole from which there could be no escape.

A powerful confederacy of outraged lords now combined against her and Bothwell. Even her loyal Catholic familiars were alienated by the circumstances of her marriage. Their pretext was to avenge Darnley, but their real purpose was to get rid of the Queen. She was defeated at Carberry Hill early in June, and Bothwell was allowed to withdraw into exile, making nonsense of the original reason given for their action. Mary, in a state of virtual collapse, was captured and taken to Edinburgh. The confederates then declared that their main purpose was to uphold Protestantism, and on 16 June they removed the Queen to Lochleven castle, where on 24 June she was forced to abdicate in favour of her year-old son.[33] Soon after she miscarried of twins, clearly the result of her enforced intercourse with Bothwell, and was for several weeks extremely ill. She would probably have been executed out of hand if it had not been for the fact that the English Council, with whom the confederates were clearly in close touch, had not interceded on her behalf. Emotions were running high in Scotland at that point and there was precious little sympathy for Mary – now an ex-Queen and seen by most as a fallen woman. However, although her judgement appears to have deserted her completely by this time, her courage and resilience remained unimpaired. Despite all that she had been through, she was still only 25, and remarkably tough. Through the winter of 1567–8 she gradually recovered, physically if not emotionally, and with the aid of a few loyal followers escaped from Lochleven Castle on 2 May 1568, and headed for Dumbarton, a stronghold of the sympathetic Earl of Argyll. Now that Bothwell was out of reach, it appears to have been the confederates intention to justify her continued imprisonment by charging her, belatedly, with the murder of Lord Darnley.

However, her escape brought a temporary end to any such intention. Mary was not without supporters, from the Earl of Argyll to the countrymen who cheered her as she made her way to the south-west, but it soon transpired that they were not enough. When they were worsted in a brief and almost bloodless encounter at Langside on 13 May, Mary (rather uncharacteristically) panicked and fled due south – over the Solway and into England. At first Elizabeth appeared to be supportive. She had a very low opinion of Mary's behaviour since the early part of 1565 – behaviour that she attributed (probably correctly) to a female weakness that the English Queen was only too familiar with, but always contrived to conquer. However, Mary was an anointed Queen and her abdication had clearly been enforced. Elizabeth therefore set out initially to negotiate her restoration in Scotland, on suitable terms and conditions.[34] Whether the Scots Queen herself would have found those conditions acceptable is highly problematic but, in any case, the Earl of Moray, now regent for the young James VI, would have none of them. Instead he caused the Casket letters to be concocted and sent into England as evidence of the Queen's complicity in her husband's death. The English Council was not convinced, and in any case its competence to judge in such a case was questionable. Mary's fate was a political matter, which could not be decided judicially. Elizabeth had three options. Either she could use her political and military weight to enforce Mary's restoration, which would have meant an end to the Anglo-Scottish amity; or she could let her withdraw to France, where she would have been welcome personally, but not politically; or she could keep her in England on one pretext or another. After a good deal of dithering, she decided on the last option, and laid up a store of trouble for herself in the process.

It has been rightly pointed out that for several years Mary's situation was that of house arrest rather than imprisonment. She had substantial revenues from her jointure as Queen Dowager of France and a household of about 40 persons for which she paid, including a confessor and a secretary. She also had a Council, which operated in France under the leadership of James Betoun, the exiled Archbishop of Glasgow. The Queen herself, however, saw her position as one of durance. She was moved from Bolton castle to Tutbury in Staffordshire late in 1569, to avoid any possible intention by the northern rebels to free her, and from Tutbury to Sheffield in 1570, where she was to spend the next 14 years under the watchful eye of the Earl of Shrewsbury. When the move from Bolton to Tutbury was proposed, she declared that she would have to be 'bound hand and foot' to make such a frightful journey in the middle of winter. Nevertheless – she went. In view of her later reputation as a Catholic martyr it is interesting to notice that her religious practice during her captivity was nothing if not ambiguous. Mass was said privately for her by her confessor, but she regularly attended Protestant services, and for several years after her Protestant wedding in 1567 was *persona non grata* in Rome. Most, but by no means all of her servants were Catholics and it seemed for some time that her conversion was a distinct possibility. Mary's own policy for coping with her situation was by no means consistent. On the one hand she professed friendship with Elizabeth and denied any intention of harming her but on the other hand she looked increasingly for Spanish support, and became involved in plots that were aimed at her 'good sister's' life. In 1570 and 1571 she inclined with some enthusiasm to the plan to marry her to the Duke of Norfolk. Norfolk, although confused, was not a Catholic and such a marriage would probably have involved her conversion, but as the Protestant Duchess of Norfolk her position in respect of the English succession would (she believed) have been greatly strengthened. In fact Elizabeth was vehemently opposed to the whole idea, and the Ridolfi Plot muddied the waters irredeemably.[35] Norfolk was executed for treason and Mary's status as a security risk was greatly enhanced.

At the same time, Mary's prospects of an eventual return to Scotland were withering away. There had from the time of her flight been a residual party in her homeland committed to her restoration. When the Regent, the Earl of Moray, died in 1570, the Earl of Argyll and the Hamiltons briefly made common cause for that purpose, but their alliance lasted less than a year before Argyll pulled out. The casualty rate among regents was high. The Earl of Lennox was killed in a skirmish in 1571 and his successor, the Earl of Mar, died in 1572. This left James Douglas, Earl of Morton in control, and Morton was strongly pro-English. The unsettled conditions produced by the rapid turn over of governors between 1570 and 1572 brought some of Mary's supporters out into the open in what was a *de facto* rebellion. They seized Edinburgh Castle but that was the limit of their success and when the regent was able to call upon English artillery to bombard the castle in 1573, they were forced to surrender. In 1579 there was a brief flutter of returning hope. James was now 13 and his personal preferences were beginning to matter. At that point his preference was for his French kinsman, Esme Stuart, who became Earl of Lennox in 1580 and Duke in 1581. Esme's rise signalled the downfall of Regent Morton, who was overthrown in 1580 and executed in 1581. The English Council was briefly exercised about the possibility of a revival of French influence in Scotland, and Mary became optimistic. However Henry III had no desire to destabilize his delicate relations with Elizabeth. The Guises began a new round of intrigues with Mary's agents in France but before they could come to anything a group of Protestant lords seized control of the young King of Scots and arrested a number of Lennox supporters. The Duke himself fled to France and the last chance of there being a role for Mary in Scotland disappeared.

The Earl of Shrewsbury was vigilant to prevent unauthorized access to Mary but he made no attempt to prevent her from communication with the outside

world and she conducted a series of restless and futile intrigues with her supporters, mainly in France but also to some extent in England. The Earl moved
her around his residences for reasons of convenience and hygiene but she never
went far from Sheffield, except for periodic visits to Buxton to take the waters.
This was fashionable as well as therapeutic and she may well have conducted
unauthorized discussions there. The Council feared that, but took no effective
attempts to stop it. Meanwhile her constant attempts to earn by good conduct
the ultimate prize of recognition as Elizabeth's heir made no progress at all.
Since the Ridolfi plot William Cecil (now Lord Burghley), the Queen's senior
adviser, was particularly strong in his opposition. The Anglo-French treaty of
Blois (1572) held firm through the 1570s, and Mary at last realized that this
cut off any chance of substantial aid from France – as distinct from a little surreptitious encouragement – so in 1580 she set out in a radically new direction.
Through her agent in Paris, she offered to place herself, her realm and her son,
under the protection of the King of Spain.[36] At the same time she reaffirmed
her Catholicism and repaired her damaged fences in Rome. The cause of the
catholic Church, both in England and in Scotland, was the cause of Spain. Philip
himself was cautious and non-committal but his agent in England, Bernardino
de Mendoza, was enthusiastic and a new round of intrigues began, not this time
involving the succession but rather Elizabeth's removal by a combination of a
large-scale Catholic rising and substantial Spanish military support. As neither of
these conditions was likely to be satisfied, all these plots have an air of unreality
about them and how much Mary herself knew of them is uncertain. Whatever she
knew, she was playing a double game because on the one hand she was writing to
Elizabeth about the possibility of a condominium in Scotland, which, she argued,
would secure French and Spanish recognition for James and, on the other hand,
she had written to Philip in October 1581 proposing that James be sent to Spain
while she returned to Scotland on the back of a Spanish army. By this time, it
seems clear that her professions of friendship for Elizabeth were worthless and
that her own grasp of political reality was wearing distinctly thin.

At about the same time that Mary was writing to the King of Spain, the Duke
of Guise was spinning another web of intrigue with the assistance of Mendoza.
This time the foreign invasion was to be mounted by the Guise party with Spanish
financial backing and was heavily dependent upon the Catholic network in
England, which a young man by the name of Francis Throgmorton claimed to be
able to mobilize. The object was ostensibly to be Catholic toleration but in reality
it was regime change. Mary knew of these intrigues and their real purpose but was
not deeply involved. Philip appears to have known nothing about it. The threat
was not serious. As Holinshed pointed out, 'there wanted two things, money and

the assistance of a convenient party in England to join with the foreign forces.'[37] Throgmorton's network was real enough but quite inadequate for his purpose. The main consequences of the plot, apart from the execution of Throgmorton, were the expulsion of Mendoza in 1584 and the convincing demonstration that had been given of the effectiveness of Walsingham's 'anti-terrorist' system. There was insufficient evidence to proceed against Mary but suspicion of her intentions had been jacked up another notch. A less direct consequence was something of a panic about the succession, because the more of these plots there were, the more likely it was that one of them would eventually succeed. A Bond of Association was drawn up in 1584 and signed by over a thousand gentlemen, committing themselves never to accept anyone on the throne in whose name the present queen had been made away. Mary was not named but the target was obvious. Then in 1585 Parliament passed an Act 'for ... the surety of the Queen most Royal Person', which not only gave legal status to the Bond of Association but laid down detailed procedures as to how the guilty parties were to be dealt with. It was under the terms of that statute that Mary was shortly to be tried.[38]

The Queen of Scots seemed to be quite incapable of learning from her own mistakes. She had got away with a marginal involvement in the Throgmorton plot, partly for lack of firm evidence but rather more because there was no obvious law under which she might be tried and no certainty that any court in England had jurisdiction over her. The statute of 1585 supplied both those defects but in spite of knowing that perfectly well and professing a desire to retire altogether from the political arena it was not long before she was up to her eyes in another plot. In January 1585 the Earl of Shrewsbury was relieved of his charge, and Mary was moved from Sheffield back to Tutbury, this time in the custody of Sir Amyas Paulet. Paulet was a puritan, and soon proved to be an exceptionally zealous guardian. In December of the same year he moved his charge to the nearby manor of Chartley and deliberately deceived her into believing that she had discovered a way to correspond that evaded his vigilance.[39] Nothing could have been further from the truth, and the next time a plot was being hatched, Paulet and Walsingham made certain that she walked right into the trap. The scenario was familiar. Mendoza, the Guises and Mary's French agents were plotting in Paris what was virtually a re-run of the Throgmorton conspiracy, only this time the English agent was a young man named Anthony Babington. Babington was a former servant of Mary's, and appears to have been quite bowled over by her charms. He was also far more zealous than discreet and on 6 July 1586 wrote her a highly explicit letter, seeking her approval for another assassination attempt against Elizabeth. This letter fell into Walsingham's hands and he read it before she did. Altogether this was a very leaky conspiracy because another of the plotters, a priest named Ballard, was already in custody and had made damaging allegations, so Babington was a marked man. Then on 17 July the unsuspecting Mary replied to Babington, explicitly approving his scheme and giving him various advice as to how to set about the task. Walsingham, of course, read the letter. He now had the evidence which he needed, but still faced the daunting task of persuading the Queen to act. However, circumstances had changed since 1584. England was now at war and Mary had exposed herself to the charge of being a Spanish agent; even Elizabeth could not ignore so blatant a threat. Had not William of Orange fallen to just such an assassin's bullet two years earlier?

This combination of pressures forced the Queen to act. In October 1586 she set up a commission to try her cousin and notified her of the intention:

> Whereas we are given to understand that you, to our great and inestimable grief, as one void of all remorse of conscience, pretend with great protestations not to be in any sort privy or assenting to any attempt either against our state or person, forasmuch as we find by most clear and evident proof that the contrary will be verified and maintained against you ...[40]

She had authorized the commissioners to proceed to trial. Mary did not attempt to challenge the jurisdiction of the court but instead adopted the futile expedient of protesting her innocence. However, even her own secretaries testified against her. Elizabeth knew perfectly well that compassing the death of a heretic would incur no censure from the Catholic Church, but she still insisted on conferring with the commissioners before they delivered their verdict. On 4 December her guilt was proclaimed in accordance with the terms of the 1585 Act, and James was reassured that his mother's exclusion from the English throne did not affect his own claim.[41] As a result very largely of her own folly, all Mary's schemes for the English Crown or succession, which had occupied her for quarter of a century, had now come to nothing and her life was on the line. Elizabeth, for reasons that are entirely creditable in humane terms, was most reluctant to see the woman who had professed to be her 'most dear sister' suffer on the scaffold. On the other hand, she was now convinced of Mary's treachery and her councillors, aware of her reluctance, stirred rumours of new plots. At length she was convinced. 'Aut fer, aut feri; ne feriare feri' (suffer or strike; strike in order not to be stricken), she is alleged to have said, and signed the death warrant on 1 February 1587. Mary was executed on the morning of 8 February, making her exit with far more theatrical flair and dignity than she had lived. Despite her dubious relations with the Church, she presented herself as a Catholic martyr and as such was accepted by subsequent Catholic historiography. She died at Fotheringhay, where she had been tried, and was buried in nearby Peterborough Cathedral. James professed great sorrow and indignation but he did not allow either to disrupt his developing relationship with Elizabeth. After all, he had not seen his mother since he was a baby. What he did do years later in 1612, was to have her remains moved from Peterborough to Westminster Abbey – as though she had been Queen indeed.

Mary was unique. She was Queen of Scotland effectively only from 1561 to 1567 and, after a good start, made a catastrophic mess of her responsibilities. Before 1561, although she bore the title, she was little more than a figurehead and after 1568 she was an exile and a prisoner. For the six years of her reign when she was in Scotland she was a serious political rival to Elizabeth but, after her marriage to Darnley, her position disintegrated. In fact she fell into the trap that Elizabeth narrowly avoided, of allowing her physical and emotional needs to take precedence over the political demands of her position. This worked both positively, in her marriage to Darnley, and negatively in her involvement in his murder. Despite her intelligence and shrewdness she behaved as a woman rather than as a queen. After 1568, if she had converted to Protestantism and had come to terms with the English Council, she might have been recognized as heir. On the other hand if she had been a different kind of woman she might have ended her days as Queen of Scotland and England would not have been troubled with her. Eventually she drifted into the position of being the Catholic pretender and – given the way in which English opinion was moving – particularly after 1570 – that was a formula for failure. In the context of this study, she is an admirable foil for Elizabeth. Scotland's misfortune was England's gain.

7. Anne Boleyn by Unknown artist (National Portrait Gallery, London)

8. Jane Seymour by Hans Holbein the Younger

KATHARINE PARRE

9. Catherine Parr by Unknown artist (National Portrait Gallery, London)

ETATIS   SVÆ ·21·

10. Unknown woman, formerly known as Catherine Howard after Hans Holbein the Younger (National Portrait Gallery, London)

11. Lady Jane Dudley (née Grey) by Unknown artist (National Portrait Gallery, London)

STVART

12. Mary Queen of Scots by Unknown artist

13. Queen Mary I by Hans Eworth (National Portrait Gallery, London)

14. Queen Elizabeth I attributed to George Gower (National Portrait Gallery, London)

9

The Married Sovereign: Queen Mary I

In July 1553 Henry VIII's earth-moving efforts to prevent a female succession were finally brought to nothing. When his only surviving son died without achieving his majority there was no man with a respectable claim in sight.[1] Henry had provided against such an eventuality both in his last succession Act and in his will, decreeing that in the event of both himself and his son dying without further heirs the Crown was to pass to his elder daughter, Mary. It was, of course, hoped that this would not arise. As we have seen, Edward tried to divert the succession away from Mary but since his chosen candidate was also female and with an inferior claim the attempt made on his behalf after his death was unsuccessful. On 19 July Mary was proclaimed and, as her reign was officially dated from the time of Edward's death, Jane was erased from the record. Mary, although passionately convinced of her right to succeed, was only too aware of the problems that she faced. As the Church taught, custom decreed, and everyone believed, women were naturally inferior to men and it was their destiny to be ruled and not to rule. In her youth, a girl was controlled by her father, or by some male surrogate; when she married, she passed under the authority of her husband and as a widow she was 'protected' by her sons. Of course many women did not fit into these tidy categories. There were unmarried heiresses whose fathers had died; spinsters who were not heiresses; and widows without offspring. It was among such unattached women, as well as among those families where the number of daughters outran the parental capacity to provide dowries, that the religious houses had carried out their main recruitment. Mary, however, even at the time of her deepest affliction, had been no more inclined than her mother to take the veil. Both were far too keenly aware of their royal credentials to wish to exchange them, even for the kingdom of heaven.

Mary had enjoyed a happy childhood and had seen a great deal more of both her parents than was normal with royal offspring of the period. Her education was carefully planned in the Renaissance mode, with much emphasis upon biblical and classical reading but it had been a girl's education, designed to make her a fit companion for a great king and a mother to his children. It was not designed to make her a ruler of men. For Henry to have brought up his daughter for that purpose would have been an admission of defeat that he was not prepared to countenance. Catherine needed to look no further for a model than her own upbringing, which had likewise been learned, and feminine. Juan Vives, to whom her mother had turned for advice, and who was an advocate of women's education, designed his scheme for a girl's supposedly inferior capacity and conscientiously steered clear of both lechery and politics.[2] How much Mary knew of her parents' marital problems while she was in Wales we do not know but it is reasonable to suppose that the Countess of Salisbury protected her against the salacious gossip that focused on Anne Boleyn before 1529. When she came back from the Marches in the latter year and walked into the storm she was already 13 and no longer a child by the standards of the time. She had been twice betrothed and twice abandoned but it is unlikely that these essentially political games had had much impact on her personally. The independent household that she had enjoyed in Wales continued and, although she spent quite a lot of time with her mother, the Countess of Salisbury continued in post, and Mary was, in theory at least, very much her own mistress. However, during the sensitive adolescent years between 13 and 16, she became a very partisan spectator of the 'sex war' going on between her father and her mother and when the whole situation exploded in 1533 she was very much in the firing line. When she furiously declined to be termed 'The Lady Mary' her whole establishment was closed down and she found herself under virtual arrest in the household set up for her supplanter, Elizabeth. Her formal education had in any case ceased by that time and she was left to draw what consolation she could from the piety and classical learning that she had absorbed

Her mother's death in January 1536 dealt her a severe blow and worse was to follow in May, when she discovered that the shameful ways in which she had been treated sprang not from the influence of Anne Boleyn but from her father's own political and ecclesiastical convictions. Undermined by this discovery, she surrendered to his will in July 1536, and was immediately restored to favour becoming 'the second lady of the court' after Queen Jane Seymour.[3] Over the next 11 years, as queens came and went, she ran her own household, living partly at court and partly in one or other of the royal residences in the Home Counties. Marriage proposals were mooted from time to time and she even met one of her suitors but despite her diminished official status, her marriage was primarily a political issue over which she had (and could expect to have) very little control. She is said to have lamented at one point that as long as her father was alive she would never be wed, but would remain 'only the Lady Mary, and the most unhappy lady in Christendom'.[4] What Mary really thought, either about this or about anything else, during these years is extremely hard to reconstruct. Her subsequent conduct suggests that she was dissembling and remained secretly a committed papist – but no contemporary evidence shows this. It would, of course, have been a very dangerous line to have taken, but even her warmest admirer, Eustace Chapuys, does not give any hint that that was what was happening. Indeed he seems to have been totally puzzled by her attitude. She quarrelled with Catherine Howard – a girls' spat over jewels and precedence – but was warm friends with both Jane Seymour and Catherine Parr. She remained devoted to the liturgies and practices of the old faith – but then so did her father so there was no basis for disagreement there.

She must have realized that her views were seriously at odds with those of Henry's last queen and her circle but that does not seem to have impaired their friendship and indeed there is at this stage no sign of her later reputation for intolerance and bigotry. She was living in Catherine's household with every sign of contentment when Henry died.

As we have seen, she made no bid for the succession at that point, being apparently quite satisfied with her lawful position of 'second person'. However, in other ways the King's death transformed her circumstances. Henry was hardly buried before Lord Thomas Seymour resumed his attentions to Catherine, who obviously found them welcome. Feeling ill at ease in this love nest, Mary moved out. Her father had bequeathed her lands to the value of some £4,000 a year and several houses including two of her favourites, Hunsdon and Beaulieu or New Hall. This made her for the first time, not only fully independent, but a magnate in her own right, and the Council made haste to confirm the arrangements and formalize the grants.[5] Mary now needed not only household officers but Stewards and Receivers for her manors and a council of lawyers and advisors. She was 31 years old and her unmarried state was an anomaly but at least it gave her invaluable experience in management. For about four years, until her half sister Elizabeth was similarly endowed in 1551, she was the only woman who could be classed as a major peer in her own right. She held no title or public office and did not sit in the House of Lords, but in other respects she was a Prince of the Blood. She denied any intention of meddling in the politics of her brother's reign and declined any role in the conspiracy that overthrew Protector Somerset in October 1549 but in one critical respect she made a highly political statement. On the ground that it offended her conscience she absolutely refused to use or countenance the use of the Book of Common Prayer.[6] Furious quarrels and ruthless pressure from the Council, both under Somerset and under his successor, John Dudley, Earl of Warwick, could not budge her. Her father's settlement, she declared, was absolute and final, and could not be touched – least of all while the King was a minor.

Not only was this defiance highly embarrassing to the Council – it also put relations with the Emperor into the freezer. Charles had been mystified by Mary's apparent quiescence in the latter years of her father's reign but this stand he understood, and supported to the hilt, threatening war if the law was enforced upon his cousin.[7] Whether he would (or could) have gone so far is uncertain, but the minority Council could not afford to take the risk. Stalemate ensued. By 1553 Mary was thus not only an experienced manager in terms of her estates, and the patronage which went with wealth and status, but she was also in this particular respect a political leader. All those (and they were very numerous) who found Edward's religious settlement unappealing, and who hankered after 'religion as king Henry left it', looked to her as their standard bearer and leader. In spite of her almost hysterical exchanges with the council, she had proved extraordinarily tough and shrewd in her campaign against the Prayer Book, and had used her status quite ruthlessly to expose the weaknesses and limitations of Edward's government. In the light of this, and of her quarrel with the King that had resulted, it is not surprising, that as his death approached in the summer of 1553, the young Edward should have become fully convinced that her succession to the Crown would be a disaster.

As we have seen, he tried to will the throne to his young cousin, Jane Dudley, and for a few days everyone thought that the 'King's party' would prevail. However, within about a fortnight it had turned out to be no contest. In the first place, Mary was ready for a fight because she knew about the conspiracy against her, and believed passionately in the rightness of her cause. Her servants had written out numerous copies of her proclamation of accession and the gentlemen of her retinue had mobilized their friends and put their own retainers on standby. When the moment came and she was fully convinced that her brother was dead, the machinery immediately went into action. Within days her proclamations were being read all over the country, and a sizeable military force began to assemble at Kenninghall in Norfolk, in the heart of her own estates.[8] By contrast, the Duke of Northumberland was not prepared. His theoretical command of resources depended upon men whose primary allegiance was elsewhere. Some were the King's men, and their loyalty in such a crisis was uncertain. Some were dependent upon his fellow councillors, and would remain loyal only as long as their masters did. His own *manred*, when it came to the point, was pitifully small. He was a great man, with commensurate wealth, but his estates were in constant flux, producing no large body of committed tenants and followers. Consequently, he could not count on nearly as many loyal supporters as Mary could. Added to which, his action was of dubious legality, whereas Mary was supported both by statute and the old King's will. Even the Protestants, who with the benefit of hindsight can be seen to have had the most to lose, on the whole declared for her. When the majority of the Council deserted him, between 16 and 19 July 1553, taking their men with them, Northumberland was left with a rump retinue, which was no match for Mary's large and increasing forces, and he gave up. Robert Wingfield recorded the whole of Mary's triumph and although his account is replete with hagiography and special pleading, the outline of the story that he tells is accurate enough.[9] Mary moved her base from Kenninghall to Framlingham on 12 July, was proclaimed in London on 19 July and then advanced steadily on the capital, sweeping up further peers and former councillors as she advanced. She entered London in triumph, to universal acclamation, on 3 August.

Five years later she died, if not quite unlamented, certainly much less popular than at the time of her triumph. So what went wrong and to what extent can her failure be blamed on the fact that she was England's first ruling Queen? Neither Mary nor her subjects had any doubt of her right to the throne. To some she was the old King's only legitimate child but to most she was his heir by law established and her known commitment to the old faith was no handicap at all. Edward's Protestant government had been remarkably effective but it had never been popular except in parts of London and the Home Counties. What most expected their new Queen to do was to restore her father's settlement. That, after all, had been the slogan under which she had campaigned against the Prayer Book. However, Mary's particular brand of piety led her to ascribe her success against the Duke of Northumberland to direct Divine intervention. Those Englishmen, nobles, gentlemen and others, who had been the effective cause of that success, had been merely acting as the agents of the Will of God. This meant that she believed herself to have a Divine mandate to right all the wrongs of the previous 20 years and that she had been deliberately preserved by God in all her troubles for precisely that purpose.[10] So God had intended her to succeed to the Crown, but God had also created her as a woman with all that it implied in contemporary perceptions. On the one hand, executive responsibility was now hers – given directly by God – but on the other hand she was naturally created to be ruled by men. There is no evidence that Mary pondered these matters deeply but her instincts did sometimes lead her in contradictory directions. On the one hand she told her council and the Imperial ambassadors that she intended to restore the Pope's authority; on the other hand she issued a conciliatory proclamation, indicating her intention to make a religious settlement in Parliament, as both her father and her brother had done.[11] When her much admired kinsman, Reginald, Cardinal Pole, wrote to warn her against repealing statutes that had been *ultra vires* in their creation, she paid no attention. At first, this worked well enough, and corresponded with the general expectation. Her first parliament repealed

Edward's ecclesiastical statutes, and returned the Church to the situation that King Henry had left, with the mass and all the traditional ceremonies back in place but still subject to the Royal Supremacy. 'The Queen's Godly proceedings', as they were known in conservative circles, were widely popular.[12] Leading Protestants were either arrested or fled into exile and the Queen clearly won this round by a large points margin.

With her council she was less successful, largely because her experience of affairs was confined to running a private estate. Despite having been close to the politics of her brother's reign, she had no executive training whatsoever, both because of her gender and because of her religious stand. Her first and most natural instinct was to cling to those whom she knew and trusted – men like her controller, Robert Rochester, or Sir Francis Englefield, and they formed her initial Privy Council, which met for the first time on 8 July. Unfortunately, although the loyalty and Catholicism of these men was exemplary, they had no more experience of high politics than their mistress. In short, they were quite unsuited to be a monarch's council. To her credit, Mary realized this quite well and knew that she would have to recruit from among the experienced councillors who had only recently signed a letter urging obedience to Queen Jane. She did this pragmatically, and roughly in accordance with the speed with which they had abandoned Northumberland when the tide turned against him. By the time that she reached London, therefore, she already had a large and heterogeneous council, to which she then added three victims of the previous regime, Stephen Gardiner, the Duke of Norfolk and Cuthbert Tunstall. Gardiner was a valuable acquisition, who rapidly became Lord Chancellor, but the other two were very elderly, and were recruited largely for nostalgic reasons. By the end of August, her Council numbered nearly 50 and she had in effect gone back to the older, more amorphous type of council that had preceded the reforms of 1540. This was a retrograde step in every sense of that word. What she should have done at this stage was to drop most (if not all) of the 'Framlingham' council – and never appoint Tunstall and Norfolk. However her affection for councillors such as Rochester and Englefield was out of proportion to their usefulness and what happened was that the council broke up into 'factions', with the old councillors accusing the new of disloyalty, and the new accusing the old of being out of touch.

Added to this problem was the fact that the Queen never really trusted her new councillors, who were without exception compromised by their support for the regimes of either Edward or the later Henry. Even Stephen Gardiner, despite his exalted position and his opposition to Edward, was contaminated by his earlier support for the royal supremacy. Whether this lack of trust was in any way connected with her gender is uncertain – a man might have behaved similarly – but it was seen at the time as female indecision and emotionalism.

This lack of confidence was immediately accentuated by the debate over the Queen's marriage. Had Mary been a king this would have been an important but essentially secondary issue, mainly inspired by considerations of the foreign policy implications of any such match. However, because she was a woman, it became an intense debate over who was fit to wear the Crown Matrimonial and share the government with her. The Queen was 37 and if there was to be a child of the marriage it would have to happen very soon. That was the purpose that was in the front of everyone's mind (including Mary's) but it was not the only concern. England had never had a King Consort before, and there was great uncertainly over what the role would entail. The Queen was not only concerned to find an agreeable companion (and one who would get her pregnant) but also to have 'a man about the realm'. So much of the traditional imagery of monarchy was male and military, she felt that she needed someone to discharge that function. There was also the question of protection, not just of her person but also of her kingdom. She needed a prince with power and connections of his own. Unfortunately that ran directly counter to her very keen sense that God had entrusted the realm of England to her – and to her alone. All these problems were to become apparent in due course. First it was necessary to look at the possibilities, and it was in this connection that Mary made her first serious mistake. Many years before, when she had been under severe pressure from her father, the Emperor Charles V (who was also her cousin) had been her champion. At that time she had declared that he was her true father and that she would never marry without his advice. This insult to Henry VIII had been overtaken by events and in any case he was no longer around to dictate. So she remembered her promise and consulted Charles through his ambassador, Simon Renard. Charles in turn remembered that they had once been betrothed but he was now, he declared, too old for such an adventure. His son Philip, on the other hand, was by happy chance a widower.[13] By comparison, the other candidates were non-starters. There was Dom Luis, the brother of the King of Portugal (who had been considered before) but the Emperor successfully blocked his candidature. There was Edward Courtenay, now Earl of Devon. Courtenay was the domestic candidate, and attracted much influential backing, but he was a foolish and irresponsible young man who had spent most of his youth in the Tower. That was no fault of his, but it had left him seriously inexperienced in life and there is no evidence that Mary ever seriously considered marrying him. That left Philip and, of course, Simon Renard. Renard was an ingratiating fellow with an agenda of his own, and because of the sensitive nature of the issue that he was discussing, soon won an exclusive place in Mary's confidence. He dominated the negotiations, to the virtual exclusion of the Council, and that caused considerable resentment. His confidential relationship with the Queen was unprecedented and should never have been allowed to arise. Mary should never have committed her choice of husband to the arbitrament of any outside party and should never have admitted Renard to the confidences that he enjoyed.

When the matter came into the open there were protests. Parliament petitioned her in November to marry within the realm and was brusquely told to mind its own business. In January 1554 there was a briefly dangerous rebellion in Kent, led by Sir Thomas Wyatt, which demanded that she change her mind. It was suppressed but the sentiment lingered on. In the event, the Emperor's keenness on the match worked very much in England's favour. Charles was not much interested in England but marrying its Queen would give Philip an ideal power base from which to fight off rival claims to the Low Countries when Charles himself either retired or died. He was planning retirement and was mindful of the fact that he had gerrymandered the Imperial constitution in order to settle the succession of the Netherlands on Philip, who would in addition receive Spain – but not the Holy Roman Empire.[14] In other words there were issues about the Low Countries that the English marriage would resolve. He was therefore inclined to be generous with concessions when it came to defining the role of the King Consort. The draft articles, drawn up on 7 December, ran:

> Prince Philip shall so long as the matrimony endures, enjoy jointly with the Queen her style and kingly name, and shall aid her in her administration. The prince shall leave to the Queen the disposition of all offices, lands and revenues of their dominions; they shall be disposed to those born there. All matters shall be treated in English ... There may be made another contract, wherein the prince shall swear he will not promote to any office in England any foreigner ... If no children are left, and the Queen dies before him, he shall not challenge any right in the kingdom, but permit the succession to come to them to whom it shall belong by right and law ... England shall not be entangled in the war between the Emperor and the French King ...[15]

There was a lot more in the same vein, making provision for dower and for any children of the marriage but these are the essential limitations that Charles was willing to accept on his son's behalf in order to secure the title of King. When he found out about them, Philip was not amused. This was not at all the kind of kingship that he had envisaged – in fact it was downright dishonourable. He considered abandoning the whole project, but then reflected that once he was established in England there might be ways around the various obstacles in his path – a suspicion that had also occurred to some of the English – so he accepted the treaty with an apparently good grace. At the same time he entered a secret reservation, declaring that he had only signed the terms to enable his marriage to take place – and that he had no intention of observing them! Fortunately the English did not find out about that.[16]

The treaty was duly concluded in January 1554, proclaimed, and in due course ratified by Parliament. This last step was unprecedented in respect of a royal marriage but then the circumstances were also unprecedented. Meanwhile, treaty or no treaty, there was a legal ambiguity to be resolved. By English law a married woman (or *femme couvert*) surrendered her property on marriage to her husband, in whom it remained vested for the duration of his life. Did the same apply to the Crown, and if so, where did that leave the marriage treaty? It was generally assumed that the law did not apply to the Crown but the issue was open to dispute. Again, resort was had to statute, and when Parliament reconvened on 2 April an Act was passed declaring that the Imperial powers of the Crown of England were the same, whether vested in male of female. In other words the Queen was also King and no legal or other gender limitations applied.[17] Meanwhile, Philip appeared to be sulking. His formal betrothal to Mary took place in March but he was represented by his father's servant the Count of Egmont and he sent neither message nor token. Nor did he communicate the reason for his delays to Simon Renard, who was left jumping up and down with frustration and rapidly running out of excuses. In fact he seems to have had genuine difficulties, both in settling the government of Spain (where he was regent) and in raising the money that Charles insisted that he bring with him to pay the northern armies, but none of this was explained. Eventually, in early June, he set off from Valladolid on his leisurely way towards La Coruna, and as soon as word of this reached England, a group of English nobles set off to meet him – arriving in Galicia before he did. Philip's English household was assembled at Southampton to meet him and the Queen travelled to Bishop's Waltham in Hampshire, where Philip's harbinger, the Marquis de las Navas, found her early in July. He bore the long-expected token from her betrothed, a magnificent table diamond[18] and, although the household at Southampton was getting restive, the long period of waiting was almost over.

On 20 July he landed at Southampton, was honourably received and girded with the Order of the Garter. He then made his way to Winchester where the Dean's lodging had been prepared to receive him. The Queen meanwhile had moved into the Bishop's palace, a distinction of status that was not lost upon the Prince's vigilant entourage. The couple met for the first time the same evening, and Mary's feelings can only be imagined. She was on the brink of a political and sexual encounter that should, by the normal rules of royal marriage, have occurred at least 20 years earlier. We are told that both were magnificently attired and honourably accompanied and that they greeted each other affectionately and 'chatted pleasantly'.[19] The whole thing was carefully staged for what would now be called 'the world's press', and their real feelings are unknown. It is not even known what language they used for their pleasant chat. Mary understood Spanish but spoke it very hesitantly while Philip's French was in the same state. He (of course) spoke no English so perhaps they used Latin, in which both were fluent. The marriage duly took place on St James's day, 25 July, in Winchester cathedral. The day was chosen as a careful compliment to the bridegroom, whose nose was otherwise put comprehensively out of joint. During the ceremony his seat was placed lower than hers and he stood on her left, which would normally have been the bride's position. The royal sword was only borne before him after the wedding and his jealous servants claimed that even at the wedding banquet he was served from silver while the Queen was served from gold.[20] Nevertheless he was duly recognized as King of England when their elaborate titles were proclaimed and the crowd outside the cathedral gave him an unexpectedly warm reception, noting particularly how affectionate his demeanour towards his new wife appeared to be. The whole symbolism of the occasion had been designed to emphasize that Philip's status in England depended upon his wife, but that was virtually ignored in the spate of Habsburg propaganda that celebrated his triumph in England.[21] Simon Renard may have known differently but continental observers were clearly expecting the new King to dominate his wife and to use his position in England for his own (largely international) purposes.

It might be expected that Mary would have been traumatized by having sex for the first time at the age of 38. Following custom, she remained secluded for a few days after the wedding but by all accounts was blissfully happy. Philip was less enchanted. From hints that were soon being dropped by his Spanish servants, he found her disappointing 'para la sensualidad de la carne', which may well have been the case as she was 11 years his senior and totally inexperienced.[22] Nevertheless he had done his duty and when, three months later, there was talk of her being pregnant, he retained a discreet silence. As a sexual encounter, their relationship seems to have worked reasonably well and it may be significant that, despite the fact that he had many enemies, no scandal attached to him while he was in England. The 'bakers' daughters and other poor whores' whom he was accused of using after his departure do not feature, so presumably he found his wife satisfactory. However, there were other problems. Philip must have been aware that a full English household had been appointed for him. After all, he had signed a treaty that bound him to the use of English servants. Nevertheless, he brought a full Spanish establishment with him, which included not only a

Chapel Royal (which had been expected), but also a Majordomo and a complete set of Chamber servants (which had not). It can only be supposed that Philip had yielded to pressure from his Spanish officers, who had declared that their beloved lord could not be expected to entrust himself to a bunch of barbarians whose language he did not even understand. Of course, there was immediately trouble, which the King must have anticipated. He immediately decreed that he would be served in public by his English officers, in accordance with the treaty, but in private he would retain his Spanish servants. Both sides immediately and loudly complained – the Spanish that they were dishonoured and the English that they had no access to the privy apartments. The issue was never really resolved but both sides had to live with the compromise. More seriously, the lower servants on both sides were full of hatred and contempt towards each other and there was violence ('knife work' as one contemporary put it) even within the precincts of the court. There was also murder and robbery on the streets and the English were not always to blame. Both the King and the Queen were distressed by this blatant racism but neither could do much to halt it. Philip made the largest contribution by sending the majority of his noble followers and their retinues to join the army in the Low Countries, but the problem was never completely solved as long as Philip was in England.

The King was in a very difficult situation. Despite his harmonious relations with his wife she had given him no English patrimony. This was unprecedented because consorts had always hitherto been endowed with lands of their own and expected to dispense their own patronage as well as paying some of their own expenses. Such lands had varied somewhat in value but had usually produced an income of between £3,000 and £4,500 a year. Philip might reasonably have expected to have received the Duchy of Cornwall or Lancaster, which would have given him an English clientage and English resources. Instead of which he received nothing and had to pay all his English bills out of his Spanish revenues. These were large, but already over committed and when we remember that he also felt obliged to pay substantial pensions to the members of the English Council and to other selected courtiers, it becomes apparent that the Crown of England was an expensive honour.[23] Nor did he have much of a role in the government of England. All state documents were dutifully issued in both their names and he regularly accompanied the Queen on ceremonial occasions but most of his working life was spent with his own Council, dealing with the affairs of the Empire and of Spain. The proceedings of the English council were translated into Latin for his benefit and he consulted regularly with those councillors (notably Gardiner) who were fluent in that language but his fingerprints appear very little on the routine processes of English government. What he did do was rather more subtle. Throughout the winter of 1554–5, and into the New Year, he encouraged courtly entertainments, and staged 'war games' – mostly tournaments. Mary had virtually neglected the Revels before her marriage. Her coronation in October 1553 had been the only one that century not marked by jousts and similar celebrations and Christmas 1553 had been exceptionally quiet. Philip had two motives for wishing to change this. In the first place he wanted to make an impact on the Court, both to encourage loyalty and to cheer everyone up; in the second place he wanted some popular approval and some recruits for his armies. Both these aims were served by tournaments and if the King took part in person (as he sometimes did) so much the better. After all, as a knight of the Garter, he was supposed to be a showpiece of English chivalry – and that meant more than being affectionate to his wife.

The other thing that the King did during his first few months in England was to end the 20-year-old ecclesiastical schism. This was the outcome of a long-maturing scheme by the Emperor and was mainly in the interest of securing Habsburg influence in Rome. As we have seen, one of Mary's earliest expressed wishes was to return to the papal obedience and in that she was fully supported by Cardinal Pole, who had been appointed Legate to England as soon as news of her accession had reached Rome. However, as soon as the possibility of a marriage between the Queen and his son was raised and the extent of his influence over Mary became clear, Charles began to urge caution.[24] The English were deeply sunk in heresy, the French might try to intervene – and so on. His real motive, however, was to ensure that the credit for such a reconciliation should go to Philip rather than to Mary and her English advisers. Through his agents in England, he managed to sabotage a unilateral declaration of allegiance proposed by the Lord Chancellor in the second parliament of the reign but as soon as the marriage was completed, his opposition evaporated and he began to encourage Philip to seize his opportunity. This was realistic enough, because opposition to the reconciliation in England (apart from the Protestant minority) came largely from those who had purchased former ecclesiastical property and who saw their investment disappearing. Philip understood this and quickly determined that the easiest route to success would be by persuading Pope Julius III to write off the English monasteries, relying on the piety of future generations to re-establish them. After some negotiation, he succeeded in doing that, and the way to reconciliation was thus opened.[25] Mary simply did not have the influence in the Curia to have accomplished that – nor was she convinced of its necessity. In this respect the Queen showed markedly less political judgement than her husband, whose Catholicism was fortunately above suspicion. Consequently, having secured his main objective in Rome, Philip then had to persuade both

Cardinal Pole and his wife to accept the deal. Pole was reluctantly convinced by early November and the formalities of reconciliation were then completed but it was Christmas before the King talked Mary round, and what method he used we do not know.[26] There was then a question over the legal title to the secularized lands and this was resolved (with Philip's support) by incorporating the terms of the papal dispensation into the statute that repealed the Royal Supremacy. Altogether, the reconciliation was very much Philip's doing and was celebrated as such with thunderous applause all over Catholic Europe.[27] Mary was barely mentioned, except by Julius in his official correspondence and decrees.

Just why the Queen allowed herself to be so comprehensively sidelined is not known. The idea of bargaining with heretics (or 'possessioners') was repugnant to her but her duty required no less. Perhaps she was compensating for her failure to give Philip a more active role in regular government by delegating this extremely important task to him; perhaps she was becoming increasingly preoccupied with her supposed pregnancy, or perhaps she was just ducking the issue. No sooner had the reconciliation been completed than the imprisoned Protestant leaders began to be put on trial. Philip had nothing whatsoever to do with this. He had no objection to persecuting heretics but judged that such an initiative in England was inexpedient. He also knew his own lack of rapport with the English people and realized that if the policy of burning the recalcitrant turned out to be unpopular (as it showed every sign of being) then he would be blamed. He made cautious dissenting noises but did nothing to check the persecution.[28] This was fronted by Reginald Pole as Cardinal Legate but the real driving forces were Lord Chancellor Gardiner, and the Queen. Mary was quite convinced that so-called Protestants were merely avaricious opportunists, seeking to ruin the Church both morally and financially and their pretended constancy under affliction was just a trick to win sympathy. The mere threat of burning would have them recanting in droves! Up to a point she was right; many did recant. However, when some of the leaders proved willing to suffer the ultimate penalty, Gardiner soon realized that, as a policy, this was not going to work. Unfortunately, the Queen showed no such sensitivity. As far as she was concerned, burning heretics was not a policy that could be picked up or laid down but a solemn religious duty. Insults to the Holy Mass seared her conscience to the bone and no punishment could be too severe for such blasphemy. She had defended the rite when it was under attack and would do so now from a position of much greater strength.

As 1555 advanced, Mary's condition became more pronounced and Philip, with his eye on his father's affairs, became restless. It required firm guidance from the latter to persuade him to remain in England until his wife should be safely delivered. Once he was the father of an heir to the throne, his position would be infinitely stronger. Simon Renard dutifully conveyed the message but one of the benefits of Philip's arrival had been the ending of his confidential relationship with the Queen. The King neither liked nor trusted him, and although he remained at his post until the autumn of 1555 he had no real influence.[29] In that respect at least, Mary observed her husband's wishes. No one seems to have known when the Queen's 'hour' was due, which was perhaps a sign of the impending disaster. About 20 April she retired into the customary female seclusion, and the government of the country simply carried on without her. No doubt some matters were referred to Philip but his role did not noticeably increase. Fortunately no major issues pressed upon the Council. Meanwhile the court waited ... and waited. Nothing happened. Observers declared that birth was imminent and then withdrew their predictions. Scandalous tales began to circulate: the Queen was ill or bewitched; there was an elaborate substitution plot masterminded from Spain;[30] the Queen was not really pregnant at all – and so on. Still nothing happened and the upbeat predictions from her physicians and her ladies began to waver and then fell silent. By July it was obvious that no normal birth was in prospect, and Mary was forced to face the awful truth – her pregnancy had been a phantom. The implications of this for her health and the impact upon her state of mind were profound. The political implications were no less severe. The whole regime had suddenly lost credibility. Instead of a safe Catholic succession, extending the Queen's proceedings into the indefinite future, the prospect was now highly uncertain. If Mary were to die, would Philip ignore the treaty and bid for the Crown himself? Elizabeth was the next heir by English law, and she was a very different kind of woman. What was Philip to do? He was now, at the age of 28, saddled with a wife who was almost certainly barren. He had, admittedly, one son, the unpromising Don Carlos, but one life was a poor protection against dynastic failure, as Edward VI had just demonstrated. As soon as he decently could, the King took his mind off these problems by returning to the continent to assume the pressing responsibilities that his father was so anxious to shed, leaving Mary exhausted and depressed.

Philip officially took over from Charles in the Low Countries in September 1555 and that gave him enough to be doing for the time being. However, he did not forget the problem of England. How could he when his distressed wife was constantly writing to him urging him to return? The country needed his strong hand (in what way is not clear); they could try again for a baby. She did not put it in so many words but that was the gist of at least one of her letters. The King had no faith at all in his wife's fertility, but there was one option that he could try – he could have an English coronation. The fact that such a ceremony had not followed his marriage is indicative of Mary's double standard towards her husband. On the one hand she was anxious to please him personally and to be a good Habsburg wife; but on the other hand she was extremely cagey about giving away any aspect of her authority. This attitude was embodied in the marriage treaty, and was undoubtedly adopted on the advice of her Council. As long as there had been the prospect of an heir, Philip had been very restrained, feeling, probably rightly, that such a birth would give him most of what he wanted without any effort on his part. Now, however, the situation was changed, and the fact that Mary wanted him back gave him a hold over her. He had originally been intending to return for the parliament, which was called for 21 October, but that, he now discovered, would be impossible. In fact he might not come back at all unless he was given a more honourable position in England, and that would involve a coronation.[31] He had been advised (wrongly, it would seem) that in England the coronation was of unusual significance and that once he was crowned he would be able to find ways to ignore, or at least to circumvent, his treaty limitations.

It was precisely this fear that raised such a storm in England. Philip as a King Consort on a limited tenure was one thing, particularly now there were such grave doubts about the Queen's health, but Philip in unlimited possession was something else entirely. A potentially serious conspiracy was raised, passing under the name of the adventurer Henry Dudley, which would have involved a small invasion by English exiles presently in France, and a major rebellion among the West Country gentry. Its declared purpose was to 'send the Queen overseas to her husband' and replace her with her sister Elizabeth. It was detected in March 1556, and came to nothing but it was a sinister indication of the way opinion was moving. At the same time the Cheshire agitator John Bradford published a scurrilous attack upon the King entitled *The copye of a letter ... sent to the erles of Arundel, Derbie, Shrewsbury and Penbroke ...* in which he accused the nobles named of seeking to obtain the King's crowning by force or fraud:

> If the crown were the Queen's, in such sort that she might do with it what she would, both now and after her death, there might appear some rightful pretence in giving it over to a stranger prince; but seeing it belongs to the heirs of England after her death, you commit deadly sin and damnation in unjustly giving and taking away the right of others ...[32]

How large a constituency Bradford spoke for is uncertain but the Queen was understandably concerned – and very annoyed. The letter not only denounced the prospect of a coronation, it accused Philip of sexual promiscuity in colourful terms, and these charges were not without foundation. Bradford would have had no means of knowing it, but the King's Spanish servants were writing cautiously to each other about the need to keep Mary in ignorance of his 'amusements', 'because she is easily upset'. In a way all this anti-Spanish agitation played into the Queen's hands because she had no desire to give Philip a coronation, and was able to use the popular protests as an excuse. She would have to refer the matter to Parliament, she claimed, and Parliament would never allow it. Nonsense, he replied, quite correctly. His coronation was none of Parliament's business – it was a prerogative matter.[33] However, on this issue the Queen would not budge and Philip became first angry and then resigned.

He may also have been considering that there were other possible ways of increasing his influence. He knew that Mary desperately wanted him back in England for personal as much as for political reasons – and that gave him leverage. He could try insisting upon his right to be consulted over major appointments. The Lord Privy Seal, the Earl of Bedford, had died in March 1555, and the Lord Chancellor, the Bishop of Winchester, in November. Neither of these offices had been filled in December 1555, and the Duke of Alba urged the King to make sure that his own men were promoted, rather than 'Queen's men'. Alba was not referring here to Spaniards, but to Englishmen 'of the King's devotion', although the idea that the English council could be so divided may not have existed outside the Duke's imagination.[34] Philip certainly was consulted and William, Lord Paget, who became Lord Privy Seal could perhaps be described as his man but Nicholas Heath, who was given the Great Seal, was at best a compromise. In neither case had Philip obviously controlled the appointment. The other way of asserting himself was to involve England in his war with France. War was, *par excellence*, the 'matter impertinent to women'. Women could not be expected to lead armies, or to understand the logistics of warfare. Moreover, as Philip was well aware there was a party among the English nobility that, although it expressed a dutiful loyalty to its sovereign lady, was actually looking for male leadership. Once England was at war, the influence of that party was bound to increase and his own role would be augmented along with it. Philip had taken over the Crowns of Spain in January 1556, and one of his first actions had been to sign the Truce of Vaucelles on 6 February. It was supposed to last for five years but in fact broke down within months thanks to the provocative actions of Pope Paul IV, who has succeeded Julius III in March 1555. Paul was a Neapolitan, violently anti-Spanish, and counting on the support of France, particularly the Duke of Guise. In September 1556 his actions in central Italy drove the profoundly Catholic Philip to order his armies into the Papal states. The Duke of Alba's soldiers are alleged to have advanced on their knees. It was not long before the Duke of Guise appeared to the rescue, and full-scale war was resumed. It was at that point that Philip's English policy turned to thoughts of involvement and the advantages of that course began to grow upon him. England was not a major power in military terms, but it had a useful navy and might even be persuaded to disgorge some money if approached in the right manner.

News of this impending approach came as a relief to Mary, who had been coping on her own with the government of England since August 1555. This was not, she felt, how it was meant to be. There were no foreign policy decisions to be made because the options had been foreclosed by her marriage. The only issue was how to counter the diplomatic hostility of France, so that in a way open war and the withdrawal of all French diplomats would be welcome. She also felt that her relationship with her husband had suffered by the long separation and by the issues that had arisen between them. Her own emotions blew hot and cold. Sometimes she was longing to have him back and writing pathetic letters to Charles asking for his intercession. Some times she was (apparently) kicking his picture around the Privy Chamber in sheer frustration at yet another round of prevarication.[35] It may also have occurred to her that when England was at war her husband would have a role as a national leader that would not encroach upon her own honour because it would be uniquely masculine. Altogether, there was a lot to be said for getting England into the war and when Philip indicated that he would be quite willing to come over and lean on the English to endorse the decision, then Mary's mind was made up. Here at last was a way in which she could be a truly supportive wife without compromising her domestic authority. Unfortunately, her council did not agree. They pointed out that the terms of the marriage treaty exempted England from any involvement in the war that had been going on in 1554, and that that war had only been suspended by a truce, not broken by a peace. So the current conflict was actually the same one that had been going on then, and not (as Philip claimed), a new one. Moreover, the country could not afford to go to war, lacking both military and financial resources. When the King arrived in March 1557, to Mary's chagrin, it presented him with a *consulta*, arguing the case against war.[36] In fact, opinion in the country was divided. The merchant community, particularly in London, was deeply hostile but elsewhere gentlemen with pretensions to being soldiers were looking forward to the prospect and the French were generally even more unpopular that the Spaniards. Despite Mary's support, Philip admitted that he found negotiations with the council unexpectedly uphill work. Two factors broke the deadlock. The first was that the Council did not make decisions on issues of war and peace and although neither Philip nor Mary wanted to act without the Council's consent, they were perfectly entitled to do so. The second was that a strange raid by a small group of English exiles on Scarborough, allegedly with French support, converted some councillors because of the provocation involved.[37] The council consequently, with reluctance and several dissenters, voted in favour of war, and it was duly declared in June 1557. When Philip returned to the continent in July he was followed by an English expeditionary force under the command of the Earl of Pembroke – the only snag was that he found himself paying the bill.

Insofar as the main purpose of Philip's visit had been the declaration of war, it was successful. However his secondary purpose had been to pressure Princess Elizabeth into marriage with his trusted henchman, Emmanuel Philibert, Duke of Savoy, and in that he failed totally. The King had by this time decided that if (or when) Mary died, it would not be worth his while to press his own claim to the succession. The mood of England was such that it would involve fighting a civil war and as long as his forces were fully committed against the French that was out of the question. The next best option would be to control the English heir through a favourable marriage, but Elizabeth could see that one coming and would have none of it. Rather curiously, Mary was also opposed to her husband on that issue and it was for that reason as much as the Princess's own obstinacy that his bid failed. It may be that she simply did not want to contemplate the succession but from casual remarks that were dropped, it seems that the real reason may have been rather subtler. Mary had said some time before – even before her own marriage – that she did not want to contemplate Elizabeth as her heir 'for certain respects in which she resembled her mother (Anne Boleyn).'[38] By 1557 it seems that she had convinced herself that Elizabeth was not really her father's daughter at all but the child of one of Anne's alleged lovers. The Duke of Savoy was far too good for such a bastard. For whatever reason, she would not consent to Philip putting the screws on Elizabeth, so he left without achieving his purpose. In spite of that, his personal relations with Mary seem to have returned to the state of the autumn of 1554, before false hopes of pregnancy disrupted their sexual activity. Five months later, the Queen announced that she was again pregnant and he allowed no flicker of incredulity to diminish his congratulations. However, no one else believed her, either within England or outside of it, and the Cardinal of Lorraine is alleged to have remarked, not quite accurately, that it was eight months since her husband had left her. No preparations were made for a royal lying in and no nursery staff were appointed. Instead, in March 1558, when the child should have been due, Mary realized that she had been deceived again. She made her will later that month, refusing to admit that there would be no heir of her body but everyone else seems to have accepted that fact and wondered just how ill the Queen was.[39]

The winter of 1557–8 was depressing for a number of reasons. Not only was Mary deluding herself again with hopes of pregnancy, but the harvest failures of 1555 and 1556 had been followed by food shortages, and then by epidemic disease. The influenza of that winter was among the most deadly outbreaks of the century, carrying off between 10 per cent and 15 per cent of the population and leaving thousands more debilitated for weeks on end.[40] Equally bad was the fact that the war, which had started so promisingly with the victory at St Quentin in August, gone from bad to worse and, in January 1558, the ancient English enclave of Calais fell to a surprise French attack. The Council, which had never ceased to have doubts about the war, had been saving money by reducing the garrison and the French knew this perfectly well. Worse still, Philip, who had done his best to save the place, then found himself being blamed for its loss, which was fair only to the extent that it had been his initiative that had taken England into the war in the first place. It is not surprising that by the spring of 1558 the King was inclined to cut his losses in England. The pensions to his English supporters had long since fallen into arrears for the good reason that they were no longer supporting him. Missing her husband again, Mary had become increasingly reliant for personal support upon Reginald Pole, now the Cardinal Archbishop of Canterbury. Her stream of affectionate letters did not cease, but his responses became increasingly perfunctory. In fact, she was an embarrassment, because he was only 31 and urgently needed more children, which it was obvious to everyone (except Mary herself) that she would never bear. The French reported that he was considering an annulment but there is no firm evidence that his thinking had gone that far. The Count of Feria, who was representing him in England by this time, reported that the factions within the Council were again inhibiting good government. One of the few informal initiatives that Philip had been able to take during his stay in England from 1554–5 had been to knock heads together and persuade the council to adopt a suitable level of consensus. When he left, he arranged for a 'Council of State' or inner ring to report to him regularly on English affairs and it did so at least until the end of 1556. His second visit seems to have put an end to that arrangement, and after he left for the second and last time, new divisions opened up. Originally it had been Paget versus Gardiner, now it was Pole versus the rest. In fact there is little evidence of these conflicts, and Feria, like Renard before him, was mostly complaining that they were not acting sufficiently in his master's interests. However, that tells its own story. By the summer of 1558, Philip's grip upon England was very slack indeed and if it had not been for the war might well have disappeared altogether.

The Queen's religious devotions had always been a bulwark of her life, and an ever-present comfort during times of affliction – which had been only too frequent. Unfortunately, the negative side of that piety had become a fierce determination to exterminate heresy. Heresy was to blame for all the ills that had afflicted England – the Church in ruins, the harvest failure, the influenza epidemic, the social disruption. In fact the positive work of Catholic restoration had gone ahead very well since 1555. Parish churches and cathedrals had been restored, clergy recruitment was booming and good works of Catholic instruction were being published and used. Even a few new monasteries and chantries had been founded. However, the aspect of this restoration that will always be remembered is the fact that nearly 300 Protestants, men and women, humble and gentle, were burned alive and dozens more died in prison. This was not necessary and in the eyes of most bishops not desirable, but Mary's sense of duty drove her on. Perhaps her biggest mistake had been to make a martyr out of Thomas Cranmer when he had been on the point of recanting, but the whole policy was extreme and quite at odds with everything else that we know about the Queen.

She was a great supporter of what she called 'good preaching', using one of the heretics' main weapons against themselves and was an enthusiastic promoter of clerical education, in which she agreed wholeheartedly with Cardinal Pole. She read her Bible, both in English and in Latin, and seems to have protected the former from the assaults of more radical sacerdotalists. She was in every other respect a gentle, merciful soul and her personal servants loved her dearly but she had this one terrible blind spot, and it earned her the name of 'Bloody Mary' by which she has been known to generations of English schoolchildren.

In August 1558, Mary was ill, perhaps with a mild version of the lethal influenza, but appeared to shake it off. Then in early October, she fell ill again, and this time anxiety swiftly mounted. Philip wrote anxiously, because her usual regular letters had ceased but he did not come. Realizing that this illness might well prove fatal, he had no desire to be caught in England at the time of her death. This was not callous indifference but a realization that if he was in the country, his honour would require him to take control of the situation, and that might inhibit the lawful succession. So he stayed away, sending the Count of Feria back to England as his special envoy. By the time that he arrived, on 9 November, the end was visibly approaching:

> I ... found the queen our lady's health to be just as Dr Nunez describes in his letter to your majesty. There is, therefore, no hope of her life, but on the contrary, each hour I think that they will come to inform me of her death, so rapidly does her condition deteriorate from one day to the next ...[41]

He then went on to describe the nervous condition of the council, who received him 'like one coming with bulls from a dead pope', and to speculate about how Elizabeth would handle the situation. When he wrote, on 14 November, Mary was still clinging to life, but she died early in the morning of 17 November, and within hours Elizabeth had been proclaimed in London. We cannot be sure what killed her. It could have been a return of the influenza but contemporaries spoke of a 'dropsy', which seems to indicate a tumour. Probably the most likely explanation is that she died of cancer of the womb, a disease of which her false pregnancies had been advance warnings. She was interred with full traditional rites at Westminster on 14 December, and Bishop John White of Winchester pronounced the encomium:

> She was a king's daughter, she was a king's sister, she was a king's wife, she was a queen and by the same title a king also. What she suffered in each of these degrees before and since she came to the Crown, I will not chronicle; only this I say, howsoever it pleased God to will her patience to be exercised in the world, she had in all estates the fear of God in her heart.[42]

The chief mourner was Margaret, Countess of Lennox. Mary had wanted Margaret to succeed her, in preference to her bastard and suspect half sister but towards the end had recognized the inevitable – her people would have no one but Elizabeth. So her life ended in bitter failure and her kinsman and great supporter Reginald Pole followed her to the grave within hours. As we shall see, Elizabeth had a remarkably clean start, because Feria had already assured her of Philip's goodwill and within months he was proposing marriage to her.

It could be argued that Mary's failure was due primarily to circumstances outside her control, particularly her early death at the age of 43 and the fact that her successor was so different. However, that would be to ignore some very important factors. She did not fail simply because she was a woman. The statute of recognition took care of that disability but her marriage was a serious mistake and from that flowed much of her misfortune. Marriage was necessary if the succession was to be secured and there was no way in which she could have known how that would work out. But why Philip? He was a Habsburg, represented the traditional Burgundian alliance and was a good Catholic. But in other respects he was a disaster waiting to happen. The Spaniards were seriously unpopular, thanks largely to the 'black legend' which was spreading from Italy and the Low Countries. Philip spoke no English, had no knowledge of the country, and was inclined to be contemptuous of its nobility, whom he regarded as venal. He was also the immediate heir to Spain and to its empire in the New World. He would soon have little enough time for England, whatever the expectations. Being married to so great a Prince also undermined Mary to some extent; she was so anxious to please him and yet so conscious of her duties to her own realm. The emotional tensions seem to have torn her apart – and that could (and should) have been foreseen. The answer is that she married Philip largely to please his father, her ancient protector, and that no man would have done. Nor would any man have suffered the role conflict that Mary had to endure. She was in many ways an intensely conventional woman, brought up to be a consort and to fulfil a supporting role, if circumstances had not thrust her in to the spotlight. Whatever she might pretend in public, she always regarded her sex as a liability and accepted that there were 'matters impertinent to women'. She complained of having to shout at her Council and suffered periods of almost hysterical emotional collapse. In fact her duty to God, her realm and her husband were in constant tension and the stress may well have shortened her life. She worked like a slave and both Philip and Pole worried about the effect that this was having upon her health. In short, she never reconciled her power with her gender, or thought of the two as being truly compatible. It would require a woman with a much more original mind to see that sex could be a weapon, and one to which the masculine world could find no ready answer.

10

The Unmarried Sovereign: Elizabeth I

The best known fact about the first Elizabeth is that she never married, but 'lived and died a virgin'. Whether she was actually a virgin is an interesting speculation but irrelevant in this context. For many years she ignored or evaded the pressing advice of her council – particularly William Cecil – and her parliament, to marry and secure the succession. She drove the political nation wild with anxiety on the latter score and her failure to act was almost universally condemned as irresponsible. With the benefit of hindsight, it looks like a successful strategy. For over 20 years she was able to use the integrity of her own body as a symbol for the integrity of her realm and, when the time came, to hand over her throne to an adult and Protestant king, who was also the hereditary heir. It is not, however, certain that it was a strategy at all. The chances are that Elizabeth never made a policy decision not to marry. It was just that she was well aware of the risks that such an undertaking would involve and every time a negotiation came to the point of decision, she found a reason to back off. The personal cost of such withdrawals may well have been high, but Elizabeth had no desire to be caught in the trap that had so afflicted her sister – whether to be a good wife or a good Queen. In order to understand Elizabeth's attitude to marriage, it is necessary to go back a step and to try to assess how she saw her overall position. Like Mary, she believed that God had called her to the throne but unlike her sister she did not feel any compulsion to right the wrongs of an afflicted generation. Instead God, in his mysterious way, had called her to the Royal Supremacy, and put into her hands the government of His Church. God had created her as a woman but, instead of regarding that as a liability, she saw it as an exciting challenge, because God had also given her wit, and a sexuality that enabled her to manipulate the rather conventional males with whom she had to deal. As far as Elizabeth was concerned, there were no matters 'impertinent to women'; it was just that a woman had to manage things rather differently.[1] She could not imitate her father's masculine and martial image and she did not try. The female equivalent was beauty and mystery – particularly mystery. So she set out to play the 'femme fatale' and to baffle and bewilder the councillors whom she could not dominate by more conventional methods. Perhaps she was often genuinely unable to make up her mind, but much of her celebrated procrastination and indecisiveness was deliberately intended to demonstrate her control. She was well aware that only the monarch could make certain important decisions and she had no intention of being taken for granted.

In order to understand Elizabeth, it is necessary to look at her mother. She was only 3 years old when Anne Boleyn was executed, so we are not looking at questions of example and upbringing, but at what was in her genes. Her sharp intelligence could have come from either parent but Henry was not noted for his cool rationality when under stress and her capacity for intellectual detachment came from her mother. She also inherited the feisty sexuality that had served Anne so well in the years of her courtship and so badly when she was Henry's queen. Elizabeth, like her mother, was an inveterate flirt, and like her mother used this quality to manipulate men. When Mary spoke of 'certain qualities in which she resembled her mother', the chances are that she had a proclivity for heresy in mind, but it was a shrewd observation, none the less. Mary had used the metaphor of marriage to her kingdom but when she took a natural husband that image lost its force.[2] Elizabeth used it from the beginning, and it became more telling as time went on. When the House of Commons petitioned her to marry in the spring of 1559, at which time she had been on the throne barely six months, she replied:

> … when the public charge of governing the kingdom came upon me, it seemed unto me an inconsiderate folly to draw upon myself the cares which might proceed of marriage. To conclude, I am already bound unto a husband, which is the kingdom of England, and that may suffice you …[3]

She then showed her coronation ring, as the pledge of that marriage, and concluded 'reproach me so no more that I have no children, for every one of you, and as many as are English, are my children and kinsfolks …'

It was magnificent rhetoric, and if it was ever uttered in that form, it was probably received simply as such. We know of it only from Camden's *Annales*, published many years later but it is true to the spirit in which she was acting in 1559, and the sentiment, if not the words, is probably authentic. At the time the speculation ran on whom, not whether, the Queen would marry and many years of fruitless political activity was to be predicated upon that notion until time finally foreclosed the option of children in about 1580.

It has been frequently noted that Elizabeth was a consummate actress, and extremely conscious of her image.[4] With Mary what you saw was what you got, and her best known portraits show her magnificently dressed but grim of face, advancing relentlessly into middle age. Elizabeth was always the Fairy

Queen, her face beautiful and mask like, unchanging for decades. How many people ever saw these portraits is not known, but they proliferate, often in poor contemporary copies, and it is likely that every gentleman's gallery and every livery hall displayed one as an expected token of allegiance. So conscious was Elizabeth of their importance that she even drafted a proclamation in 1562, when her real beauty had been marred by the smallpox, prohibiting any further portraits, and Nicholas Hilliard was later given the monopoly rights over the royal image to forestall any unflattering representations.[5] When Mary shouted at her Council, as she complained, they paid no attention, no doubt putting it down to a touch of hysterics. When Elizabeth threw a tantrum, she boxed a few ears and everyone around her quaked. When they were out of her presence, they no doubt put that down to female eccentricity also but the trouble with Elizabeth was that no one ever knew whether her royal rages were genuine or simulated and if you tested a theory it was liable to cost you dear. Apart from her youth (she was 25 at her accession) and undoubted good looks, Elizabeth had also one other advantage over Mary, which she was at pains to emphasize. She was 'mere English'. This mattered in 1558, when anti-Spanish feeling was strong, and Mary was (as was pointed out by her enemies) half Spanish by blood and more than half by sentiment.[6] The fact that she had never set foot outside England, and that her spoken Spanish was distinctly inferior to Elizabeth's did not matter at all. Despite all her struggles to avoid it, her marriage had led to her being represented as a Spanish dependent. It is not surprising that Elizabeth, as Feria put it, 'gloried' in her father; he had been a great and English king who had (it could be claimed) defeated the French in three successive wars and dismissed that interfering foreigner Pope Clement VII. But Elizabeth's mother had also been English. Although trained in France and devoted to peace with that country, she had been purely English by blood – and that was important.

Whether any reluctance to impair this image impeded her marriage negotiations with foreign princes, particularly the Archduke Charles and the two separate Dukes of Anjou, is not immediately apparent. However the last of these, with Francois d'Anjou, was clearly targeted for Francophobe reasons in John Stubbs, *The Discoverie of a Gaping Gulf* of 1579, which enraged the Queen as much for its implications of 'selling out to the foreigner' as for the suggestion that she was not in control of the situation.[7] Nevertheless the measure of her rage was the measure of its accuracy and its sentiments corresponded with much of the advice which she was receiving from her council. When it came to the point, the two factors which derailed all these negotiations were a reluctance to reintroduce any element of foreign control over England and its affairs, and an extreme sensitivity on Elizabeth's part to any loss of her own sovereignty. If, at the end of the day, it was impossible to be both a wife and a Queen – then Elizabeth would always choose to be a Queen.

There was, however, the possibility that she might marry one of her own subjects. That would eliminate one problem and ease the other. In the first weeks of her reign the Earl of Arundel was thought to fancy his chances, although Feria dismissed him as joke and he turned out to be right. Lord Robert Dudley, however, was not a joke at all. Unlike his foreign competitors he was a known quantity. He was around the Court – Elizabeth knew him well – and so did many others who were less favourably inclined. Unlike her sister, Elizabeth had not reached adulthood without any kind of sexual experience. At the age of 14 she had tangled with Lord Thomas Seymour, the brother of the then Lord Protector. Seymour was a married man at the time, and his wife was pregnant. Both were highly sexed and Seymour was a notorious womanizer, but how far their entanglement went is not known. Soon after there were rumours that 'she was with child by the Lord Admiral' but Elizabeth herself always denied intercourse. Of course she would have said that anyway, once it was clear that she was not pregnant, but the chances are that it was true.[8] Recently it has been argued that intercourse did indeed take place, and it was the fact that she did not fall pregnant that convinced Elizabeth that she was 'a barren stock'. However, that is pure speculation, based on a remark that the Queen made in 1566 on being informed of Mary Queen of Scots safe delivery. What does seem clear is that the young Elizabeth was thoroughly 'awakened' by the experience and knew thereafter that she was sexually attractive to men – a quality that Mary never possessed.

Her reaction to Lord Robert built on that experience. That she was in love with him in the conventional sense seems certain. In the summer of 1560 she showed every sign of being infatuated and William Cecil, whose great success in Scotland she had virtually ignored, talked seriously of resigning his office. There was, however, one serious snag. Robert was already married and hostile rumours were circulating that he intended to do away with his wife in order to marry the Queen. In September 1560 Amy was found at the bottom of a staircase at Cumnor Park with her neck broken and the obvious conclusion was drawn. So obvious, indeed, that we can be reasonably certain that Lord Robert had no hand in his wife's death. Elizabeth was devastated. For a few months it had looked as though the woman in her was going to overcome the Queen but this tragedy acted like a bucket of cold water. Her Council, and particularly William Cecil, had been unanimously opposed to Lord Robert's pretensions, pointing out his lack of experience in government and the fact that, although he was the son of a Duke, his father had been a parvenue who had been executed for high treason. If she had found a way to marry him, she would have been inviting kindred rivalries and feuds and an endless battle to define (or limit) the powers of the Crown Matrimonial. All this negative advice now impinged upon her. She managed to get her lover formally acquitted by an inquest but the prospect of matrimony rapidly receded, to the relief of everyone except Lord Robert, who was to maintain his suit, with diminishing prospects, for another three or four years. Elizabeth had wanted Robert, as she was never to want any other man, and the brutal way in which political sense was forced to triumph over emotion, probably scarred her forever. It was not only that he was sexually attractive – she also probably calculated that she could manage him in a way which could not be guaranteed of any of his international competitors. His inexperience in that context was an asset. Perhaps he was so in love with her that he would hardly notice if the Crown Matrimonial meant virtually nothing. Perhaps ...

That Robert wanted Elizabeth in the same way that she had wanted him is quite probable but unprovable. He also wanted the dignity and power of being the Queen's husband, and might very well have found some way to dispose of Amy that would have been short of murder. There would still have been a scandal, of course, but it might have been more manageable. As it was, he had to settle for the long running status of 'best friend'. His chemistry continued to have an unsettling effect upon her, even when she was so angry with his mismanagement of the Low Countries business in 1585, but politically he gradually became less of a loose cannon. His admission to the Privy Council and elevation to the earldom of Leicester in 1564 made him a conventional magnate and courtier, rather than the Queen's lover, whose access to the royal ear could never be predicted or controlled. Whether she ever slept with him during those infatuated months in 1560 will never be known but when Elizabeth believed herself to be at death's door in 1562, in addition to naming him 'protector' of the heirless kingdom, she denied that anything of that nature had ever occurred between them. Given the seriousness with which she took her relationship with God, her words on that occasion can probably be trusted.

Elizabeth always swore that she could never marry a man whom she did not know and that adds an air of unreality to the suits of Eric of Sweden, the Earl of Arran, the Archduke Charles and Duke Henri d'Anjou, none of whom she ever met. The only one of her later suitors with whom she had a personal encounter was Duke Francois, whom she met twice, and it was on the second of those encounters in 1581 that she gave one of her most problematic performances. She was 48 by this time and heavily dependent upon cosmetics to repel the advancing years; he was 25, erratic and ambitious. He came to England in a last-ditch attempt to save a marriage negotiation that he urgently needed to succeed for his own reasons but which was already apparently on the rocks. Without the slightest warning, Elizabeth 'entered into amorous discourse' with her guest, kissed him passionately and gave him a ring, declaring that she would marry him forthwith.[9] The Court was scandalized, especially the Queen's ladies, who were rather a staid bunch by this time, and after a sleepless night of self-examination, she changed her mind and withdrew her pledge – to his infinite chagrin. The incident is well attested, and of no ultimate significance, but it does reveal that Elizabeth was as vulnerable to 'hot flushes' as any other woman. It also gives a brief and rather sad insight into what it cost the Queen to keep her political priorities constantly in view when her emotional needs might have pointed in quite a different direction. Elizabeth reigned long and successfully but ultimately at the price of never marrying, and remaining unfulfilled in that dimension. She never (unlike Mary) considered marriage to be part of her duty to the realm. It could be that, but fundamentally it was a matter of personal inclination against political responsibility, and political responsibility always won.

As we have already seen, this was largely a question of control. Elizabeth knew perfectly well, and if she had forgotten John Knox's *First Blast* would have reminded her, that it was considered unnatural (and even unscriptural) for women to exercise control over men.[10] The Queen never accepted that, nor its accompanying notion that women were intellectually inferior. She had, and knew that she had, the intellectual edge on all the men about her, which was one reason why she felt confident about appointing the ablest servants she could find – even if she knew that she would disagree with them. At the same time, she could not overawe them as her father had done but rather had to invent her own methods for keeping them in their place. Women were supposed to be indecisive so she took advantage of that by delaying important decisions far longer than any of her advisers thought wise. Sometimes this was done in the hope that some last minute change in the circumstances would either need to be taken into account, or might make any decision unnecessary. Thus she procrastinated over intervening in Scotland in 1560, in the hope that the Scots would be able to manage without her, and even instructed the navy, which she eventually sent north to act as though independently of her instructions – a subterfuge with which the Admiral, William Winter, would have nothing to do.[11] She dithered and procrastinated about sending official assistance to the rebels in the Low Countries after William of Orange's assassination in 1584, both in the hope that it would not be necessary and because she disliked rebels, but moved eventually when the whole rebellion appeared to be on the point of collapse. Despite the reams of advice that she was given, Elizabeth always reserved the decisions in such matters to herself, and ultimately played her cards close, because it was not in her interest to reveal the workings of her mind to anyone. That was one of the main reasons for her success – no man was really able to follow her thought processes, and that gave her the degree of control that she needed. It is difficult to say how consciously this strategy was adopted and at this distance simulated indecisiveness and real uncertainty are very hard to tell apart. Her councillors had to accept what they could see. Her behaviour over the signature of the death warrant for Mary Queen of Scots sums up nearly two decades of ambiguity and hesitancy, most of which seems to have been genuine.[12]

At first, when the Scottish Queen had arrived in England in 1568, Elizabeth had wanted her restored on certain conditions. For example, she had to ratify the Treaty of Edinburgh of 1560, upon which the whole state of Anglo-Scottish relations depended. However the Earl of Moray, the Scottish Regent, had gone too far to retreat. Mary had been deposed in favour of her young son and no English interference could be allowed to overturn that situation. Without ceasing to press her case, Elizabeth accepted this situation, and took refuge in a verdict of 'non-proven' over the charges against Mary in respect of her husband's death, in order to keep her options open. The Scottish Queen's involvement in the Ridolfi plot in 1571, however, cooled Elizabeth's enthusiasm for her restoration, and in 1573 she intervened on behalf of the then Regent, the Earl of Morton against the 'Castillians' as Mary's party in Scotland were called. From then on a battle of wills developed between the Queen, who did not cease to regard her guest as the lawful Queen of Scotland, and her council led by William Cecil, and later by Francis Walsingham, who wanted her put on trial and preferably executed. She was, as Cecil repeatedly pointed out, the focus and figurehead of every Catholic plot, a danger to Elizabeth's life and to the stability of her realm. At first Mary had campaigned hard to be recognized as Elizabeth's heir and that the Queen never specifically rejected, but as the years passed, and she came to rely more on Philip of Spain and less upon her Guise kinsfolk in France, the focus of her ambitions changed. Mary never specifically claimed to be the lawful Queen of England – she was in no position to do so – but in countenancing plots such as those of Francis Throgmorton and Anthony Babington, she made the real nature of her target clear enough. At length, and following the Babington plot of 1586, Elizabeth was no longer prepared to fight against the logic of the evidence, and agreed to put her on trial.[13] She also proclaimed Mary's guilt when the verdict went against her but never ceased to regard her as a kinswoman and an anointed Queen. What then happened is reasonably clear. Elizabeth became reconciled to the fact that Mary must die but was desperately anxious not to have to answer for her death before the forum of European opinion. She tried every expedient to evade the responsibility, even (apparently) suggesting privy assassination.

When that did not work, she signed the death warrant, allowed it to be issued and then used every trick in her histrionic repertoire to pretend that she hadn't. She sulked and stormed, committing the faithful William Davidson to the Tower and rusticating her oldest and most trusted adviser, Lord Burghley, from the court and council. She may have been genuinely distressed at the course that she had been compelled to take, but it was a distress caused by a feeling that she was no longer in control of events, rather than by any particular sympathy with Mary. She also, of course, had an eye on the young King James of Scotland, who might well be distressed by his mother's fate and whom the Queen had already identified as her likely successor.

When it came to myth making, Mary won that particular contest hands down. Her exit from the world was as dignified and as emotive as her most ardent admirer could have wished and, despite her uncertain relations with the Church, she was soon enrolled as a Catholic martyr. Elizabeth was completely upstaged. However, it would be an exaggeration to say that Mary was more dangerous dead than alive. Because her son was of the reformed faith, her particular brand of Catholic legitimacy died with her and James's claim was, quite specifically, not affected by the manner of his mother's death. Although Mary may have won the romantic battle, Elizabeth won the political one because the residual Catholic claim then devolved upon the Infanta Clara Eugenia, Philip II's daughter, who had much less appeal to the recusant constituency, especially in view of the fact that England and Spain were at war.

Elizabeth hated war. Whatever she might think of her gender limitations in other contexts, war was not a woman's world. It was not that she did not understand the issues but rather that she had to concede strategic command to the men who were actually leading the fleets and armies that operated in her name, and she disliked that intensely. It made sense to do as much of the fighting as possible at sea, because Scotland was (roughly) friendly and in every other direction the sea was a moat, but there was also another reason. Men like Hawkins, Drake and Frobisher, who commanded at sea, were not magnates and they did not pretend to military resources of their own. They showed an infuriating tendency to ignore instructions but they always did so at a safe distance and they had the measure of their Spanish enemies in a way which none of her soldiers could pretend. Although it was necessary to hold musters from time to time, and to organize the counties for their own defence – field armies were best kept small, best sent overseas, and best commanded by professional soldiers of the second rank. In spite of her tendency to keep these commanders short of resources, there was sense in this strategy. Both Sir John Norris in Brittany and Lord Mountjoy in Ireland were reasonably successful, whereas when the Queen yielded to the pressure of circumstances and used noblemen abroad, they regularly failed. The Earl of Leicester made a complete mess of his tour of duty in the Low Countries in 1585–6, and so did the Earl of Essex in Normandy in 1591. Essex in Ireland in 1599 was even more of a disaster and if he had not been so comprehensively inept might have posed a threat to the Crown. Only the same Earl's role in the successful raid on Cadiz in 1596 provides a partial exception, and then the fleet was under the command of Lord Charles Howard.

Elizabeth contrived to fight a long and reasonably successful war without ever yielding entirely to military priorities. Military men like Essex and Howard became important in the council, but management remained in the hands of civilians – first Lord Burghley and then his son Sir Robert Cecil. This was a balancing act of considerable skill, considering the financial demands that the war was making and the constant need to resort to Parliament for subsidies. By 1601 Elizabeth's combination of 'Virgin mother' rhetoric and gendered posturing was wearing a little thin but it continued to serve her and she did not have to meet another parliament in the last two years of her life. The supreme test of the Queen's mettle had come in 1588, when an invasion by the Duke of Parma from the Netherlands was generally expected. The field army raised to oppose him amounted to no more than 12,000 or 14,000 men, either because the great majority of able men were held back for local defence, or because, even in an emergency, Elizabeth was reluctant to have a larger army present on home soil. Their effectiveness may well be doubted, but not their loyalty, and when she acted the part of commander in chief, they cheered her to the echo. She is alleged to have said:

> My loving people, I have been persuaded by some that are careful of my safety to take heed how I committed myself to armed multitudes for fear of treachery, but I tell you that I would not desire to live to distrust my faithful and loving people. Let tyrants fear! ... I am come among you at this time ... being resolved in the midst and heat and heat of battle to lay down for my God and for my kingdom and for my people mine honour and my blood even in the dust. I know I have the body of a weak and feeble woman, but I have the heart and stomach of a king, and of a king of England too ...[14]

It was all stirring stuff and given point by the fact that she was dressed in armour, like a latter day Joan of Arc. The words are reported and may not be strictly authentic but the sentiment is and it is consistent with her whole approach to her monarchy. By the time that she spoke at Tilbury the battle of Gravelines was over and the main danger had been averted but she may not have known that and her audience certainly did not.[15] Elizabeth's military strategy, like this speech, was broadly defensive. Tactically she might be the aggressor, as against Cadiz, but her purpose was always to protect the integrity and interests of England. The only exception to this generalization had come early in the reign, when she had allied with the Huguenots in France in an attempt to recover Calais. That uncharacteristic adventure in 1562–3, has been largely ascribed to the influence of Lord Robert Dudley, who was still much about the Queen at the time, and that may be so, because both William Cecil and the Marquis of Winchester are known to have advised against it. It ended in disaster and the lesson (if it was needed) was not lost upon Elizabeth. Thereafter she followed the double policy of allowing (and even encouraging) her seamen in their acts of piracy, while blandly denying any complicity and professing her continued desire for friendship with her 'good brother' of Spain. It is not surprising that he privately railed against such duplicity, which he attributed to her sex, ignoring the fact that his own great grandfather, Ferdinand of Aragon, had been even more adept at such tactics.

Elizabeth improvised her methodology of government because the only available model, her sister Mary, was so unsatisfactory, and central to that improvisation was her religious faith. Nothing could be further from the truth than the traditional assumption that Elizabeth was a mere opportunist when it came to her relations with God.[16] She had conformed during Mary's reign because there was no sensible alternative. Her sister had subjected her to relentless pressure, which she resented bitterly, for the same reason that Mary herself had been pressed by Edward's council. Her profile as the heir to the throne was very high, and she might well have served as a focus for overt resistance. Moreover after the summer of 1555 it appeared to be a question of when, rather than if, her time would come. Her friend and confidant William Cecil did the same, with slightly less excuse because neither of them could see the point of making martyrs of themselves when the long-term prospects looked so promising. Both were therefore what John Knox disparagingly dismissed as 'Nicodemites'. It was all very well for him; he was safely in Geneva! No one really believed in Elizabeth's conversion. Her sister certainly did not and was unremitting in her hostility. However, conformity was conformity, and that had to suffice. The Protestants, meanwhile, continued to look to her as their white hope. When a monarch was unpopular, for whatever reason, the expectations of all the disgruntled focused upon the heir and Elizabeth became the recipient of all sorts of hopes, not only of orthodox Protestants but also of radicals, of gentlemen out of service and of disaffected London merchants who felt cheated of their legitimate ambitions in Africa and the New World. She was, as one dissident observed, thought to be 'a liberal dame, and nothing so unthankful as her sister'.[17] When her time came, therefore, in November 1558, a great weight of expectation hung upon her. So great indeed that the religious persecution, which had still been blasting ahead in the summer, came to an end without a word spoken. Although she made no policy statement and insisted upon the status quo being observed, no one had any doubt that Elizabeth's settlement would be very different from her sister's. The Protestant exiles began to return, and the incumbent catholic bishops rightly expected to have a fight on their hands.

The real nature of the Queen's intentions have been extensively, and rather unnecessarily, debated. She was not committed to her father's settlement, as Mary had claimed to be. She was a Protestant, brought up in the same schoolroom as her brother Edward, and as convinced as he was of the truth of reformed doctrine. On the other hand, she was quite well aware that the majority of her subjects did not share her views and the safest thing to have done would have been to restore 'religion as king Henry left it'. This she did not do, because her sense of duty to God was stronger than her political caution. A campaign of advice was carefully orchestrated by Sir William Cecil to reinforce her resolution in this respect, because Cecil was in wholehearted agreement with his mistress on this issue. A Protestant church was a *sine qua non* at the beginning of 1559. The real questions were, exactly what kind of Protestant Church, and how was it to be achieved? In a sense the answers were clear. The church of Edward VI had operated under the Royal Supremacy and that agreed well with Elizabeth's sense of personal responsibility. Not all Protestants had been happy with that in the past and some would not be so now, but in the circumstances a bill of Supremacy was inevitable. Resort to Parliament was equally certain. Not only had both Henry and Edward carried out their reforms by statute but even Mary, who would have had every excuse for ignoring such Acts, had carefully repealed them before instituting her own settlement. Elizabeth, however, was a woman, and the Supremacy as Henry had exercised it was not only personal but quasi-episcopal. Under Edward the Council had exercised it, but both they and the king in whose name they acted, had been male. Mary had borne the title for a few months but without conviction and had got rid of it as soon as was practicable. There was simply no precedent for a woman to bear such a responsibility and much anguished debate ensued. Eventually Elizabeth decided to take the title of 'Supreme Governor', implying an administrative rather than a spiritual function. In a sense this was a distinction without meaning, because the powers of the Queen to govern the Church were unaffected but it was a conciliatory gesture to those (Protestants as well as conservatives) who did not believe that any woman could exercise any sacerdotal function, even by deputy. Elizabeth did not allow herself to be inhibited by this limitation. She governed the Church through High Commission (which was, of course, entirely made up of men) but implicitly reserved to herself the final decision on all matters, whether administrative or doctrinal. Woe betide any misguided clergyman or pamphleteer who tried to teach her her business in that respect! Elizabeth soon demonstrated that just as it had been her duty to God to make such a settlement, it was a similar duty to defend it against any attempt at 'further reformation'.

The bill of supremacy passed the House of Commons almost without argument, which is an interesting comment on the supposed strength of Catholic sentiment in the country at the time and passed the House of Lords with only a handful of lay peers supporting the bishops in their dissent. The bill of uniformity, however, was a different matter, because in truth it satisfied nobody except the Queen and a handful of her councillors. By reintroducing the 1552 Prayer Book it offended all those who looked to Henry's Church for their model, while by making some small conservative concessions and leaving the way open for the retention of minimal vestments it contrived to offend the 'hotter sort' of Protestants just as much. This time there was argument in the Lower House but not sufficient to cause the measure to be withdrawn or redrafted. In the Upper House, however, the opposition was resolute, and some 20 lay peers backed the bishops. Sir Nicholas Bacon, who presided as Lord Keeper, did not put the Bill to a vote so close was the division and the Queen took advantage of the approach of Easter to prorogue the sitting. What was she to do? Could the Supremacy be accepted without the Protestant Uniformity? It is clear that Elizabeth decided that it could not and that the issue must be tried again. During the recess a disputation was set up between the 'old sort' and the 'new' and some sharp practice was resorted to in order to remove two of the Catholic bishops for contempt. This was managed by William Cecil, and it is not certain that the Queen was privy to the device; but when the parliament reconvened, Bacon put the controversial Bill to a vote and got it through with a majority of one!

Thus were the Queen's wishes fulfilled. By the summer of 1559 she had her own Church, and a royal visitation set out on the task of implementation. One by one the conservative bishops refused to subscribe and were deprived, much, it would appear, to the Queen's disappointment, although why she should have expected anything else is not clear. Nearly a dozen sees were vacant by earlier deaths and Elizabeth therefore had a golden opportunity to shape her Church in accordance with her own wishes. She had deliberately chosen an Episcopal form of government because that corresponded to her own notions of propriety and always thereafter treated the bishops as her servants and agents. She had no concept of *iure divino* episcopacy, and made it clear – to archbishop Grindal in particular – that she expected obedience, even where the liturgy and teaching of the Church were concerned. There was nothing simulated about this sense of unique responsibility. Elizabeth knew perfectly well that you did not pose in front of God, even if you were the Queen of England. For a woman who is accused of constant dithering, her defence of her ecclesiastical settlement was determined and consistent. William Cecil, who for many years tried to nudge her in the direction of further reform, eventually came to understand this, and even to respect its wisdom. For ten years the Queen concentrated on getting as many of her conservative subjects 'on board' as possible and this worked remarkably well as the Catholic leadership debated how best to confront this remarkable woman. Then in 1570 the Pope made up their minds for them by excommunicating her and absolving her subjects of their allegiance.[18] This had the very useful effect of making allegiance and Protestantism co-terminous and thus uniting the majority of her subjects behind the Church settlement. Whatever the English may have felt about women exercising spiritual jurisdiction, it had become the national way of doing things and was doubly useful in distinguishing the English Church from that which was run from Rome. God no doubt moved in mysterious ways, but England was – after all – the New Israel.

It was precisely because the bishops were her servants that she took such pains in selecting them. It was not easy because so many of the best candidates had dubious backgrounds in terms of dissent and serious doubts about the royal supremacy. At first William Cecil drew up endless lists of likely candidates, only to find that some were unacceptable to the Queen and others declined the preferment. Both Cecil and the Queen were anxious – for different reasons – to 'unlord' the bishops. Elizabeth wanted their revenues and Cecil wanted to persuade them to concentrate on pastoral priorities but it soon transpired that the best candidates were not willing to serve on those terms and the policy was rapidly modified to include attractive financial packages for those approached. Cecil did his level best to secure the reduction or remission of first fruits and usually succeeded, a method that must at least have had Elizabeth's tacit approval. Once Mathew Parker had been selected for Canterbury – and had accepted the offer – then his opinion also had to be taken into account and the whole process became still more complicated. Cecil was also not the only patron with the Queen's ear and although his advice usually prevailed he knew better than to presume upon that influence. There were often long vacancies. Oxford was famously without an incumbent (save for one year) from 1557 to 1589. That was an extreme case, and the average vacancy was about a year but it underlines the difficulty that the Queen and Council had in finding suitable candidates. There is no evidence that Elizabeth's gender had any influence at all on this process, although it is possible that some of the early candidates may have balked at the idea of serving a female Supreme Governor. Nor is it true that the Queen was particularly averse to married bishops. She is alleged to have snubbed Mathew

Parker's wife and to have expressed a general discontent with married clergy, but it is safe to say that she never allowed any consideration of status to inhibit the promotion of a man who was suitable in other ways. It is quite probable that she preferred her clergy celibate, just as she preferred a modest level of ornamentation in churches, and liked Church music, but none of this inhibited her firm commitment to a bench of bishops who often held very different views.[19] The one thing that was not negotiable was her personal control over the Church which she had done so much to create.

There were very few biblical images of female power. The Virgin Mary was traditionally the principal female role model in the Church, but she was a symbol of submission and dependence rather than authority. Moreover she was seriously out of fashion in Protestant theology, because of a late medieval tendency to elevate her role as an intercessor – even to equate her with the Godhead. Although it is possible that the Queen's 'personality cult' may have taken over the role vacated by the Virgin in the minds of some laymen, it is safe to assume that that was never part of Elizabeth's intention. It was consequently the figure of Deborah, the Judge of Israel, who was drafted in to serve the Queen's need of a godly image. This happened very early. During her coronation entry into London in January 1559, one of the pageants portrayed 'Deborah, with her estates, consulting for the good government of Israel' and the verses that the child presenter spoke bore obvious reference to the regime change that had recently taken place:

> Jabin, of Canaan king, had long by force of arms
> Oppressed to Israelites; which for GOD'S people went:
> But GOD minding, at last, for to redress their harms,
> The worthy Deborah as Judge among them sent ...[20]

This was clearly an attempt, soon to be supported by John Aylmer's *Harborow for True and Faithful Subjects*, to fight the biblical fire of Knox's *First Blast* with an equal and opposite fire drawn from the same uniquely authoritative source. The Queen's own attitude to this imagery can only be guessed, but she never attempted to inhibit its use and it must therefore be concluded that she approved. Her own taste in symbolic figures ran in a more courtly and classical direction. She was Astrea, Belphoebe, and above all Gloriana – the Fairy Queen of Edmund Spenser's courtly imagination.

> She is the mighty Queen of Faerie,
> Whose fair retrait I on my shield do bear,
> She is the flower of grace and chastity,
> Throughout the world renowned far and near,
> My life, my liege, my Sovereign, my dear ...[21]

It was this kind of imagery that fuelled the Accession Day tilts, those secular celebrations of 17 November that were the creation of Sir Henry Lee in the 1570s. They were intended to be both fantasy and symbolic politics – designed to take the place of those religious festivals now banned by a Protestant government – the mystery plays and Corpus Christi processions. The German observer, Lupold von Wedel described one such joust in 1584:

> The combatants had their servants clad in different colours ... some of the servants were disguised like savages, or Irishmen, with the hair hanging down to the girdle like women, others had horses equipped like elephants, some carriages were drawn by men, others appeared to move by themselves ... Some gentlemen had their horses with them, and mounted in full armour directly from the carriage ...[22]

Elizabeth loved these celebrations, and the flattery that was laid on with a trowel. The Count of Feria had observed at the very outset of her reign that she was very vain, and loved the plaudits of the multitude. That did not change as she grew older; only gradually the genuine admiration for a clever and handsome young woman became a kind of sycophantic chorus – a ritual that every courtier was expected to observe. It is not clear that Elizabeth ever noticed the difference.

It was not that she was unaware of the passing of the years. No mean poet herself, she wrote with a kind of wry humour, at some time in the 1580s:

> When I was fair and young, and favour graced me,
> Of many was I sought, their mistress for to be,
> But I did scorn them all, and said to them therefore,
> 'Go, go, go, seek some otherwhere, importune me no more'
> But there fair Venus' son, that brave victorious boy,
> Said 'What, thou scornful dame, sith that thou art so coy,
> I will so wound your heart, that thou shalt learn therefore:
> Go, go, go, seek some otherwhere; importune me no more.'[23]

Elizabeth was always acutely aware of her femininity, and never more so than when she was lamenting the high personal cost of keeping her authority and dignity intact.

The saddest postscript to this world of lost opportunity is to be found in the career of the Earl of Essex. Robert Devereux, the second Earl, was the Earl of Leicester's stepson and was introduced by him to the court in 1584, when he was just short of 18. He was very handsome, had excellent manners and made an immediate impact. He went with his stepfather to the Low Countries in 1585 and it was there that he conceived an unwarranted conceit of himself as a great and dashing soldier. By the spring of 1587 he was clearly the coming favourite. 'When she [the Queen] is abroad, nobody is near her but my Lord of Essex;

and at night my Lord is at cards, or one game or another with her [so] that he cometh not to his lodgings till the birds sing in the morning.'[24] Later that same year he became Master of the Horse, a position that the Earl of Leicester had resigned for that very purpose, and when Leicester died in the following year, he stepped into his shoes in more ways than one. He was never the Queen's lover in the sense that Robert had been but he became what would now be known as her 'toy boy', fulfilling an emotional need in an ageing woman, and becoming in a sense the son that she would never have. Unfortunately Elizabeth's emotional tastes were never as discriminating as her political ones. In government she was served by William Cecil, Nicholas Bacon, Francis Walsingham, Christopher Hatton, Mathew Parker and John Whitgift. Only with Edmund Grindal did she make a mistake. However, those to whom she was personally attached were (first and foremost) Robert Dudley, a man of erratic judgement and more charm than good sense, secondly, and briefly, Francois duc d'Anjou, a disaster in every sense of the word, and finally Robert Devereux, a man of monumental conceit and no sense of reality.

Robert made the mistake of trying to turn his personal favour into political power. He believed that he was a great general and a powerful patron, neither of which was true. He had no success in the latter capacity because the Queen (quite rightly) did not trust his judgement but he chose to blame his failure on the machinations of Sir Robert Cecil, Lord Burghley's son, and set up a damaging feud on that basis. In the former mode his only real success was the taking of Cadiz, which he did his best to ruin by quarrelling with the Lord Admiral. He then painted himself into a corner over the appointment of a new Lord Deputy for Ireland, and got into the position where he could not avoid taking the responsibility himself. He went to Ireland in a foul mood, made a complete mess of his mission and returned to England without the Queen's leave, taking advantage of his privileged status to invade the Privy Chamber at an unseasonable hour. A more comprehensive programme of self-destruction could hardly be imagined yet he continued to blame his subsequent disgrace on Sir Robert Cecil. For years Elizabeth had been by turns intrigued and exasperated by his behaviour but this time exasperation had scored a definitive victory. She refused to renew his sweet wine monopoly, thus ruining his extravagant finances and convincing his unstable mind that he was the victim of a diabolical plot. The result was his abortive *coup d'état* of February 1601, a sequence of events that reveals conclusively how unreal his self-image had become. He seems to have imagined that London would rise in response to the appeal of one who (in 1596) had been its hero. When it did not stir he was left with no alternative to surrender – no doubt hoping that the embers of the Queen's affection might be rekindled to save him. However, he had gone too far. His offence was treason and he paid the price. It was only when he was dead and buried that regrets came flooding in upon Elizabeth. It is alleged that she never recovered from the need to execute her one-time favourite and she died about two years later.[25] Essex's fate is an extremely sad postscript to an emotional life that was constantly misjudged and constantly frustrated. It had only been her capacity, not always recognized either at the time or since, to keep her private and public lives separate, which turned Elizabeth's long reign from potential disaster to effective triumph.

It was Sir John Davies who observed that all affairs of state 'a stately form of dancing seem to bear'. In other words it was very hard to tell where the charades of courtly entertainment ended and the sober business of politics began. No man could have achieved that blend or overlap in the way that Elizabeth did. Her image, her histrionics and her whole style of government, were uniquely feminine. The men with whom she constantly had to deal were by turns fascinated, bewildered and infuriated by these methods and eventually she was living on borrowed time. By 1603 it had been 50 years since England had had a king and there was a great desire to return from uncertainty to a known quantity. James may have been a foreigner and was not at all warlike but Elizabeth had become a very tiresome old lady. Her paint and her wigs made a brave attempt to retain the beauty and mystery that had been her stock in trade, but those who knew her well were no longer deceived. The important thing is that she succeeded in doing, from the very beginning of her reign, what Mary had conspicuously failed to do and that was to create a distinctively female monarchy. Whether such an achievement could ever have survived marriage, we do not know but the indications are that Elizabeth thought not. At best, marriage would have muddied the waters by power sharing with her consort. At worst it would have turned her into a glorified housewife and mother. Mary had suffered the former fate and although there would have been some advantages in the latter – most conspicuously an heir of her body – it did not correspond with Elizabeth's sense of duty. At the end of the day, God had given her England to rule and that demanded a total dedication that overrode any personal considerations:

> But then I felt straightway a change within my breast;
> The day unquiet was; the night I could not rest,
> For I did sore repent that I had said before.
> 'Go, go, go, seek some otherwhere; importune me no more.'[26]

Perhaps, but the rewards had been considerable.

Epilogue: Queens Since 1603

With the death of Elizabeth 'the Great Queen', the monarchy reverted to its masculine mode and so remained until 1689. The queens of James I, Charles I, Charles II and James II were all consorts in the traditional sense. With the possible exception of Henrietta Maria, the consort of Charles I, their political role was negligible. Anne, the Queen of James I, was the daughter of Frederick II of Denmark and had married him in 1589 when he was still James VI of Scotland. The alliance between Scotland and Denmark was a traditional one. By the time that he succeeded Elizabeth in 1603 she had already borne him five children, of whom three were living, and was to bear him two more daughters who died in infancy. Apart from doing her duty as a mother, Anne's most significant act was her conversion to Catholicism, a move that triggered a modest fashion for Catholicism at court but had no noticeable impact on the King's public policy. She died in 1619, by which time only two of their children, Charles and Elizabeth, were surviving: he the heir and she married to the Elector Frederick of the Palatinate – a marriage later to be of considerable dynastic significance. James had wanted to use the marriage of his heir to heal the religious split in Europe that resulted in the Thirty Years' War and had already (in 1619) turned his son-in-law into a fugitive. The idea was to negotiate Frederick's restoration in return for a marriage between Charles and the Infanta of Spain. However, an 'incognito' visit by Charles to Spain in 1623 soon disillusioned him of that possibility. When James died in March 1625, his heir was still unmarried.

On 1 May, however, he wed Henrietta Maria, the 16-year-old sister of Louis XIII of France. Politically this was intended to keep France out of the Catholic Habsburg embrace, which appeared to the squeezing the life out of Protestant Germany. France did indeed remain hostile to the Habsburgs but not for that reason. Unlike her mother-in-law, Henrietta Maria was an enthusiastic proselytizer for the Catholic Church and that was to cause the King a great deal of difficulty and embarrassment, made worse by the fact that he loved her deeply. She bore him six children, three sons and three daughters and, when the civil war broke out in 1643, went to her home country to mobilize support for him. In that she failed, but she remained in France when Charles was defeated and received her children as fugitives from the Commonwealth regime. She did not return to England when her son regained his throne in 1660 but died in France in 1666. Her daughter, Elizabeth, and son Henry were both dead by 1660, and daughter Mary was married to William II, Prince of Orange. Charles returned as King, and his brother James as Duke of York. Her remaining daughter, who shared her name, was married to Philip, Duke of Orleans in 1661. Once he was established on his throne, Charles II followed the precedent of his father and grandfather and contracted a diplomatic marriage – to the Portuguese Princess Catherine of Braganza, the daughter of John IV. Although she was a Catholic and a member of an ancient house, her impact on England was virtually confined to the fact that she remained childless, which resulted in the Exclusion Crisis over the rights of the King's Catholic brother, James, to succeed him.

James II, who became king on 6 February 1685, married twice. As Duke of York, and still nominally at least a Protestant, he wed Anne Hyde, daughter of the Earl of Clarendon, in September 1660. That union produced eight children, but only two, Mary and Anne, survived beyond infancy. His first wife died in March 1671, and in September 1673 (by which time he had revealed himself to be a Catholic) he married for a second time, his bride on this occasion being Mary of Modena, the daughter of an Italian Duke. James's catholicizing policies made him deeply unpopular but at first he succeeded in crushing rebellions both in England and Scotland. However, the birth of the couple's first son, James, on 10 June 1688 focused minds against him. In November the husband of James's daughter by his first wife, William III of Orange, was invited to replace the Catholic monarch – who now had a Catholic heir. James fled, taking his wife and infant son with him. In 12 years of exile, before his death in 1701, Mary bore him seven more children, but only one, a daughter, survived infancy. While her husband had been king, Mary had kept the style of a queen but her only importance in the political life of the country was due to the belated arrival of her first son.

William of Orange, who was accepted as King on 13 February 1689, had a claim in his own right, derived from his mother, Mary, the sister of Charles and James, while his wife (also Mary) was, as we have seen, the daughter of James by his first, and Protestant, marriage. They had married in 1677 and because of the unique circumstances, were proclaimed jointly King and Queen. Mary II thus became England's third sovereign lady. However, the circumstances were quite different from those of 1558. Although William and Mary were granted the sovereignty for their joint and several lives, it was William who possessed the sole and full exercise of the royal power. When he was in Ireland, or the United Provinces, she acted on his behalf, but in virtue of the statute of 2 William and Mary c.6, rather than in her own right. In fact it is somewhat misleading to describe her as a ruling Queen. No doubt that would have happened if she had outlived her husband but in the event she died childless in 1694 and William ruled on his own (in theory as well as in fact) until his death in March 1702. Anne, Mary's sister, had withheld her claim on Mary's death, allowing the statutory settlement to prevail until William died when she succeeded in her own right, and thus became England's fourth sovereign lady. She had been married since 1683 to George, the son of Frederick III of Denmark but he was not accorded the Crown Matrimonial, remaining simply as consort until his death in 1708. She famously became pregnant no fewer than 18 times but bore only one son who survived beyond infancy and he had died aged 11 in 1700, two years before she became Queen. Anne exercised very considerable political influence but was not a personal ruler in the same sense that Elizabeth had been. By this time the monarchy was constitutional in the sense that executive decisions were made by her council and ministers rather than by the Queen. The 'party' system in Parliament was still undeveloped, but it was necessary that her chief ministers should be able to command a majority for all those numerous issues that required a parliamentary decision. It was a period of military success and great commercial expansion, but little of this was due to the Queen's personal initiative. With the passage of the Act of Union with Scotland in March 1707, she became the first sovereign of a united Great Britain. This was a period of constitutional development, which might have proved more difficult with a man on the throne, particularly one concerned to defend his position. Anne's passivity was gently satirised at the time by Alexander Pope who wrote:

> Here thou, great Anna, whom three realms obey,
> Doth sometimes council take – and sometimes tea.

When Anne died in 1714, her Francophile cousin James being a strong Catholic, the political arbitrators delved into the past and remembered that George, the Elector of Hanover, was the grandson of that Elizabeth who had married the Elector Palatine in 1617. Although his accession was not undisputed, he became king in succession to Anne in August 1714, and the constitutional procedure for determining the succession was vindicated. The 'Old Pretender' as James came to be known, was defeated in the following year.

George had married in November 1682, without reference to his English prospects, which did not exist at that time. His wife was Sophia Dorothea, the daughter of the Duke of Luneburg-Celle but, apart from producing a son and a daughter within the space of five years, the marriage was a failure. Both partners embarked on affairs and in 1694 Sophia's lover was murdered. George then divorced and imprisoned her in Germany, so by the time he came to Britain he was effectively unmarried (although not unaccompanied). In fact the Act of Settlement of 1701 had named his mother, the Electress Sophia as next heir after Anne, but she had died in 1713, devolving her claim upon her son. Thus England had narrowly avoided having another ruling queen but was left without a first lady until George died in 1727. He had succeeded his father as Elector of Hanover in 1698 and held both titles thereafter, paying altogether seven visits to his German lands during his time as King, on the last of which he died. The first George never learned to speak English, his son (also George) acting as his interpreter, but it did not matter greatly as executive decisions were by that time firmly in the hands of the office that would shortly be known as that of the Prime Minister. The second George had married in 1705, naturally among the German princely families, his wife being Caroline, the daughter of John Frederick, the Margrave of Brandenburg-Ansbach. By the time that he succeeded, at the age of 43, George and Caroline had had nine children, of whom seven survived infancy. He chose to be crowned jointly with his Queen and the ceremony took place at Westminster on 11 October 1727.

George II reigned until 1760, dying at the age of 77 and outliving both his wife and his eldest son, Frederick, who died in March 1751. His reign saw several wars, important colonial expansion, particularly in India, and the Jacobite rebellion of 1745. The latter, which briefly looked dangerous, was the last attempt to replace the exiled and Catholic Stuarts on the British throne. Its leader, the grandson of James II, known as 'bonny Prince Charlie', died an alcoholic wreck in Italy in 1788. For a number of years George was notoriously at odds with his eldest son, whose 'Leicester House set' contributed significantly to the development of party politics. By this time the King's political power was reduced to influence and he was no more effective as a personal ruler than Anne had been. As became the wife of a constitutional monarch, Caroline confined herself very largely to social and domestic duties. When George II died he was succeeded by his grandson, George III, who at the time of his accession was 22 and unmarried. This latter deficiency was remedied within a matter of weeks, when he took to wife yet another German princess, this time Charlotte of Mecklenburg Strelitz. At first George intervened a good deal in politics, attempting to manipulate Parliament in a way to which neither his grandfather nor his great grandfather had aspired. His immensely long reign (he lived until 1820) saw the loss of the American colonies, the consolidation of the second British Empire in India, and the wars against the French Revolution and Napoleon. Charlotte proved to be an exemplary Queen, having no political ambitions (except on her husband's behalf) and falling pregnant about every 18 months from 1760 to 1783. The couple had altogether 15 children, of whom only two died young, and this unprecedented success rate entitles Charlotte to a special place in the chronicles of the English Queens. George, unfortunately, outlived his own wits and had become incapacitated by 1811, when his eldest son became Prince Regent, until his own succession as George IV in 1820.

George III had been a model of probity, both sexual and financial, so his son, almost inevitably, was the reverse. His debts created a scandal as early as 1783 and by the time that he became Prince Regent they amounted to the staggering sum of over £500,000. In 1785 he secretly married Maria Fitzherbert, but his nuptials were not recognized, and ten years later, much against his will, he was forced into marriage with his cousin, Caroline of Brunswick. Although she bore him a daughter, they quickly separated and lived in bitter estrangement for over 20 years. When he was crowned on 19 July 1821, Caroline attempted to gatecrash the ceremony on the grounds that she was George's lawful wife – which was true. She was ejected and died about three weeks later. By then, however, she had won one important victory, because George had publicly charged her with adultery, a charge that he was forced to abandon in the House of Lords, along with the bill of Pains and Penalties, which he had aimed against her. For the ten years of his reign there was consequently no Queen, and the monarchy as an institution was in serious discredit.

From this it was to some extent rescued by the succession of his younger brother, George III's third son, who took the title of William IV. William had embarked upon a career in the navy but in 1787, when he was 24, he was created Duke of Clarence and decided to take his seat in the House of Lords. Like his brother he had a taste for unsuitable women but he was at least faithful to his mistress. For about 20 years he co-habited with an actress named Dorothy Jordan and they produced ten children. When eventually, at the age of 53, he decided that he must marry, it meant perforce choosing a woman of his own rank, and in 1818 he wedded Adelaide of Saxe-Meiningen, yet another German princess, who was 25. In spite of the difference in their ages (to say nothing of nationalities), their marriage was a happy one but all their three children died young. William had never thought of himself as a potential king but even before his marriage, the death of George's only legitimate child, Charlotte, left him second in line, behind his older brother, Frederick Duke of York, and when Frederick died in 1827, William became the heir. Succeeding on 26 June 1830, he was crowned jointly with Adelaide in September 1831. He reigned for only seven years, but they were momentous in terms of British constitutional development, witnessing the passage of the first (and most crucial) Reform Bill. Adelaide was a faithful shadow, performing her social duties gracefully and with aplomb but making no impact outside the palace circle. When William died on 20 June 1837, she was destined for a long and placid retirement. William was succeeded by his niece, the 18-year-old Victoria, the daughter of George III's fourth son, Edward Duke of Kent, who had died in 1820, just a year after her birth. Victoria was England's fifth, and Great Britain's second, ruling queen. She presided over most of the Industrial Revolution and the zenith of the British Empire and restored the tarnished prestige of the monarchy, less by what she did than by virtue of who she was. She also enjoyed the longest reign of any English or British monarch to date, dying 63 years later at the age of 81.

Victoria's political position was entirely defined by those statutes and customs that were collectively known as the British Constitution. Her power was confined to relationships with her ruling ministries, which by this time were returned to Parliament by means of general elections, and particularly with successive Prime Ministers. In theory the Privy Council was by this time purely advisory and mainly a means of keeping the monarch informed about decisions that were being made elsewhere. In practice, as time went on, the Queen had more political experience than any of her ministers and her guidance was often sought, but her main role was that of a figurehead and symbol. This was particularly demonstrated in 1876 when she assumed the title 'Empress of India' but it was also true nearer to home. In February 1840, Victoria married Prince Albert of Saxe Coburg Gotha, and it was a genuine love match. Albert quickly established himself in favour with the British people and they produced ten children over 17 years, although it was 1857 before he was accorded the title by which he is best known – that of Prince Consort. Albert did not attempt to interfere in politics but busied himself with good works and public charities, earning a deserved reputation for acumen and good sense. When he died in 1861 the Queen was devastated, and became a virtual recluse for a number of years, until her ministers eventually succeeded in recalling her to a sense of duty. All Victoria's children lived to become adults and most married, as a result of which she became known as the 'Grandmother of Europe'. Victoria was not called upon to govern in the way that the first Elizabeth had done but her gender made her an equally potent symbol – in her case of motherhood rather than virginity. In effect she reinvented the monarchy after its years of discredit under her uncle George IV, and effectively frustrated the republican movements that were strong in England at the beginning of her reign.

Her son, who took the title Edward VII (although he was usually known as 'Bertie') had waited 60 years for his chance to rule. He had married in 1863, his bride being Alexandra, the daughter of Christian IX of Denmark. It was a happy union, despite his well-publicized affairs, and she bore him six children between 1864 and 1871, but devoted herself largely to her children and to charity work, playing no part in her husband's public life. This continued after his accession, when the Queen presided over state entertainments, but otherwise kept in the background, continuing to be mainly a patron of good causes. When Edward died in May 1910, Alexandra survived him, and he was succeeded by his eldest remaining son, who took the title George V. George had married in 1893 with Princess Mary of Teck, and was 45 when he succeeded his father. During the First World War he changed his family name from Saxe Coburg Gotha to Windsor for obvious patriotic reasons and is sometimes therefore misleadingly described as being the first ruler of a new dynasty. Mary later acquired the reputation of being something of a dragon but that was purely in a domestic context. Just as her husband was a constitutional king so she was a self-effacing queen. Her only political action came after her husband's death in 1936, when she intervened decisively against her son's plans to marry the American divorcee, Wallis Simpson. Edward VIII had won golden opinions as Prince of Wales but he came to the throne unmarried at the age of 42. A constitutional crisis followed when it became clear what his matrimonial plans were. Both his government and his family were bitterly opposed to the move on the grounds that a woman with Mrs Simpson's background and antecedents could not possibly know how to behave as Queen. The democratization of the monarchy, which had been noticeable since the death of Victoria, had only gone a certain distance. Morganatic marriage was unacceptable and it was unthinkable that so uniquely placed a lady should have been through the divorce courts. After less than a year on the throne, and without having undergone a coronation, Edward abdicated in favour of his younger brother, who took the title of George VI.

George and his wife Elizabeth, of the Scottish family of Bowes Lyon helped to steer Britain through the traumas of the Second World War and again reinvented the monarchy in a domestic mode. This was largely the work of the Queen who developed a talent for high profile family life, which set an agenda for two whole generations of Britons. George died in 1952, but his widow survived him for more than 50 years, becoming eventually the best loved as well as the most durable member of the royal family. George was succeeded by his elder daughter Elizabeth II, who thus became England's sixth and Great Britain's third ruling Queen. At the time of her accession she was already married to her remote kinsman, Philip Mountbatten. Philip was never accorded the title of Prince Consort (let alone King) but was created Duke of Edinburgh, which title he retains. The couple have four children, of whom the oldest, Charles, has been Prince of Wales since 1958. Despite the 'New Elizabethan' rhetoric of the 1950s, there is no comparison between the position of the present monarch and that of her predecessor and namesake. The first Elizabeth was the head of government as well as the head of state. As such, although she was constrained by certain laws and customs, she was answerable only to God and not in any sense to her people. The present Elizabeth is not the head of any government and her political power is largely confined to an influence based on vast experience and a shrewd understanding of the world. The profile of the monarchy is high, but it is so largely for formal and ceremonial reasons. It no longer makes much difference whether the incumbent is male or female, because the symbolism is that of the office rather than the person – which was not so even as late as the reign of Victoria. The image of the Royal family as a cosy domestic unit, so assiduously cultivated by the late Queen Mother, has now largely disappeared, as first the Queen's sister Margaret, and then three of her four children, were divorced from their partners. Paradoxically, this has brought the Queen closer to her people, for whom such experiences have become routine. The monarchy no longer has a mystique but it does have a practical utility. The Queen is still the head of the Commonwealth, that international club that evolved out of the British Empire and an hereditary succession still seems the most sensible way to fill a position which is largely symbolic. By comparison, the idea of regular presidential elections and of an executive power divided between an elected President and an elected assembly has little appeal. What the first Elizabeth might have thought of her successor's reduced circumstances does not bear thinking about. The position of Queen Consort has been untested for over half a century, during which there have been dramatic social and conceptual changes. Whether the present Duchess of Cornwall will ever become Queen Consort is a matter of uncertainty and if she does what the responsibilities of that position might entail has still to be tested. The monarchy is still evolving, but it is reasonably certain that the role of the Queen as the defender of her husband's honour has been consigned to history.

Notes

Notes to Introduction

1   Bruce M. Metzger and Michael D. Coogan, *The Oxford Companion to the Bible*, (Oxford, 1993), pp. 806–18.

2   John Knox, *The First Blast of the Trumpet against the Monstrous Regiment of Women*, (1557), f.13v.

3   E.T., *The Lawes Resolution of Women's Rights, or the Lawes Provision for Woemen*, (1632).

4   Joanna L. Chamberlayne, *English Queenship, 1445–1503*, York University Ph.D. thesis, (1999), p. 2.

5   W.E.A. Axon (ed.) *The Game and Play of Chess*, (London, 1969), p. 27.

6   J.R. Lander, 'Marriage and Politics in the Fifteenth Century; the Nevilles and the Wydevilles', *Bulletin of the Institute of Historical Research*, (1963), 36, p. 133 and n.

7   K.A. Winstead, 'Capgrave's St Katherine and the Perils of Gynecocracy', (1995), *Viator*, 26, pp. 361–75.

8   Even in France, where the claim of a woman to the throne was barred by custom, Catherine de Medici could still become regent in 1559. Mary Stuart had been Queen of Scotland without challenge since 1542.

9   Henry Ellis, *Original Letters Illustrative of English History* (London, 1824), vol. I, p. 127.

10 Diarmaid MacCulloch (ed. and trans.), 'The Vita Mariae Angliae Reginae of Robert Wingfield of Brantham', *Camden Miscellany*, (1984), 28. This was written in Latin but there were similar encomiums in Italian, Spanish and German.

11 For a draft version of the treaty (very close to the final version) see C.S. Knighton, (ed), *Calendar of State Papers, Domestic Series, Mary I*, (1998), no. 24. The original manuscript is TNA SP11/1, no. 20.

12 House of Lords Record Office, Original Acts. 1 Mary. Sess. 3, cap 1.

13 For a full, and sympathetic, discussion of her relations with Robert Dudley and their consequences, see Derek Wilson, *Sweet Robin: a Biography of Robert Dudley, Earl of Leicester, 1533–1588* (London, 1981).

Notes to Chapter 1: The Queen as Trophy: Catherine de Valois

1   Agnes Strickland, *Lives of the Queens of England* (London, 1902), vol. III, p. 110. Strickland's account of Isabella's misdemeanours is highly coloured.

2   A.R. Myers, (ed.) *English, Historical Documents, 1327–1485*, (1969/96), no. 113. Taken from T. Rymer (1704–35), *Foedera, conventiones, literae et cuiuscunque generis carta publica* (London), Vol. IV, iii, p. 179.

3   *Calendar of the Close Rolls, 1419–22*, (London), pp. 118–20.

4   *Oxford Dictionary of National Biography*, (Oxford, 2004) 'Catherine de Valois' says that they did meet, but does not cite evidence.

5   For an account of the Southampton plot, see E.F. Jacob, *The Fifteenth Century* (Oxford, 1961), pp. 146–7. Henry had also had to deal with the rebellion of Sir John Oldcastle before setting out for France.

6   Fabyan describes (among many other things) 'a subtlety called a pelican sitting on his nest, with her birds, and an image of the said [St] Katherine holding a book and disputing with the doctors, holding a reason in her right hand saying "madame le royne" …' Henry Ellis, (ed.) *New Chronicles of England and France by Robert Fabyan* (London, 1811), pp. 586–7.

7   Ibid., p. 141. *Calendar of the Close Rolls* (p. 26) on the other hand, makes it appear that lands were assigned to the Queen from the Duchy and the Earldom.

8   There was a contemporary story to the effect that Henry had warned her (prophetically) not to go to Windsor for her lying in, lest their child should turn out unfortunate. She ignored the warning and is alleged to have repented bitterly at her death.

9   Rymer, *Foedera*, vol. X, p. 204.

10 J.A. Giles (ed.) *Incerti Sriptoris Chronicon Angliae de regnis trium regum Lancastrensium* (London, 1848), Vol. IV, p. 17.

11 N.H. Nicolas, (ed.) *The Proceedings and Ordinances of the Privy Council* (London, 1834–7), vol. V. p. 61.

12 BL Cotton MS Tiberius E.VIII, f.221.

13 G.E. Cokayne, *The Complete Peerage*, (1910–49), *sub* Richmond.

14 Ibid.

Notes to Chapter 2: The Queen as Dominatrix: Margaret of Anjou

1   Jaquetta, sister of the Count of St Pol, had married Sir Richard Woodville shortly after being widowed in 1435.

2   J. Stevenson, (ed.), *Narratives of the Expulsion of the English from Normandy*, (London, 1863). vol. I, pp. 448–80.

3   A.B. Hinds, *Calendar of the State Papers*, Milan (London, 1912), vol. I, pp. 18–19.

4   *Calendar of the Charter Rolls*, (London, 1927), vol. VI, p. 81

5   C. Brown, 'Lydgate's Verses on Queen Margaret's Entry into London', *Modern Language Review*, (1912), vol. VII, pp. 225–34.

6   J. Stacey, et al., *Rotuli Parliamentorum*, (London, 1767–77), Vol. V, pp. 73–4.

7   Stevenson, *Narratives*, I, pp. 164–7.

8   Thomas Gascoigne, *Loci e libro veritatem*, ed. J.E.T. Rogers (1881), pp. 204–5.

9   Agnes Strickland, *Lives of the Queens of England*, (London, 1902), Vol. III, p. 109.

10 J.S. Davies, (ed.), *An English Chronicle of the Reigns of Richard II, Henry IV, Henry V and Henry VI*, (London, 1856), pp. 116–18.

11 Stevenson, *Narratives*, I, pp. 198–201.

12 Ibid, pp. 243–64.

13 A.L. Brown, 'The King's Councillors in Fifteenth Century England', *Transactions of the Royal Historical Society*, (1969), pp. 95–118.

14 This complaint was directed at the alleged factional use of legal process as a means of pursuing personal quarrels.

15 A.R. Myers, 'The Household of Margaret of Anjou, 1452–3', *Bulletin of the John Rylands Library*, (1957–8), vol. XL, pp. 70–113, 391–431.

16 Strickland, *Queens of England*, vol. III, p. 212.

17 Davies, *An English Chronicle*, p. 78.

18 *English Historical Documents*, Vol. IV, p. 272

19 N. Davis (ed.), *Paston Letters and Papers of the Fifteenth Century*, (Oxford, 1971–6), vol. II, p. 108.

20 C.A.J. Armstrong, 'Politics and the Battle of St Albans, 1455', *Bulletin of the Institute of Historical Reasearch*, (1960), vol. XXXIII, pp. 1–72.

21 Ibid.

22 E.B. Fryde, et al., (eds), *Handbook of British Chronology*, 3rd edn, (London, 1986), pp. 87, 95, 107.

23 Strickland, *Queens of England*, vol. III, p. 225.

24 *Rotuli Parliamentorum*, vol. V, p. 375. Davies, *English Chronicle*, pp. 99–100.

25 *Rotuli Parliamentorum*, vol. V, pp. 375–83. The judges and law lords had pronounced themselves incompetent to mediate in 'so high a matter of state'.

26 R.A. Griffiths, *The Reign of KingHenry VI*, (London, 1981), pp. 870–1. While the battle of Wakefield was being fought, Margaret was at Lincluden in Scotland, seeking the help of Mary of Geldres. Helen Mauer, *Margaret of Anjou*, (London, 2005), op. cit.

27 Davies, *English Chronicle*, p. 110.

28 Rawdon Brown, et al., *Calendar of State Papers, Venetian*, (London, 1864–98), vol. I, p. 119.

29 Philippe de Commynes, *Memoires*, ed. J. Calmette and G. Durville, (1924–5), vol. I, p. 205.

30 J. Warkworth, *A Chronicle of the First Thirteen Years of the Reign of King Edward the Fourth*, ed. J. Halliwell, (London, 1839), p. 19.

Notes to Chapter 3: The Queen as Lover: Elizabeth Woodville

1   *Rotuli Parliamentorum*, (London, 1767–77), vol. IV, p. 498. *Calendar of the Patent Rolls, 1436–41*, (London, 1911), p. 53. The Duchess had recently been granted dower provided that she did not remarry without royal permission.

2   R. Fabyan, *The New Chronicles of England and of France*, ed. H. Ellis, (London, 1811), p. 654.

3   'Gregory's Chronicle', in J. Gairdner (ed.), *The Historical Collections of a Citizen of London*, (London, 1876), p. 226.

4   Jean de Waurin, *Anchiennes Cronicques d'Engleterre*, ed. E. Dupont, (1858–63), 3 vols, vol. II, pp. 327–8.

5   J.R. Lander, 'Marriage and Politics in the Fifteenth Century: The Nevills and the Wydevilles', *Bulletin of the Institute of Historical Research*, (1963), 26, pp. 135–43.

6   G. Smith, *The Coronation of Elizabeth Woodville*, (London, 1935), *Excerpta Historica*, ed. S. Bentley (London, 1831), pp. 176–212.

7   'Annales rerum anglicarum', in J. Stevenson (ed.), *Letters and Papers Illustrative of the Wars of the English in France*, (1864), vol. II, ii, p. 783.

8   Ibid., pp. 783–5.

9   Lander, 'Marriage and Politics', p. 140.

10 *Handbook of British Chronology*, p. 271.

11 A.R. Myers, 'The Household of Queen Elizabeth Woodville, 1466–7', *Bulletin of the John Rylands Library*, (1967–8), 1, pp. 207–35, 443–81.

12 A.H. Thomas and I.D. Thornley (eds), *The Great Chronicle of London*, (London, 1938), pp. 204–8.

13 Edward Hall, *Chronicle*, ed. H. Ellis, (London, 1809), pp. 273–4.

14 Polydore Vergil, *Anglica Historia*, ed. D. Hay (London, 1950), n.s. 74, p. 125.

15 J. Warkworth, *A Chronicle of the First Thirteen Years of the Reign of King Edward the Fourth*, ed. J. Halliwell (London, 1839), p. 10.

16 Bruce, J. (ed.), *Historie of the Arrivall of King Edward IV*, (London, 1838), p. 2.

17 Ibid., pp. 18–21.

18 Ibid., pp. 32–3.

19 D. Baldwin, *Elizabeth Woodville*, (Stroud, 2002), p. 77.

20 John Stacey and Thomas Burdett, 'Croyland Chronicle' in W. Fulham (ed.) *Rerum Anglicarum Scriptores Veterum*, (Oxford, 1654), p. 561.

21 *Calendar of the Patent Rolls, 1476–85*, pp. 172–3. A petition to the parliament of 1478 by Ankarette's grandson and heir, Roger Twynho.

22 Dominic Mancini, *The Usurpation of Richard III*, ed. C.A.J. Armstrong, (London, 1969), pp. 63, 111.

23 *Calendar of State Papers, Milan*, I, pp. 235–7.

24 W.H. Black, *Illustrations of Ancient State and Chivalry* (London, 1840), pp. 27–40.

25 Mancini, *Usurpation*, p. 107. Mancini believed that he had caught a cold while out fishing. The modern diagnosis is a stroke.

26 Ibid., pp. 74–5.

27 'Croyland Chronicle', p. 566. Charles Ross, *Richard III*, (London, 1981), p. 74 and n.

28 With Lady Elizabeth Butler (née Talbot). Edward's own legitimacy was also impugned, despite the fact that his mother, Cecily, was still alive.

29 *Great Chronicle*, pp. 234, 236. The fact that Elizabeth supported the proposal to marry her daughter to the Earl of Richmond is also evidence that she believed her sons to be dead by the autumn of 1483.

30 W. Campbell (ed.) *Materials for a History of the Reign of Henry VII*, (London, 1873–7), vol. II, p. 273.

31   *Calendar of the Patent Rolls*, 1485–9, p. 302.

Notes to Chapter 4: The Queen as Helpmate: Elizabeth of York

1   Henry's claim came through his mother, who was the daughter of John Beaufort, Duke of Somerset. John was the son of the Earl of Somerset of the same name, and grandson of John of Gaunt via Katherine Swynford, his third wife. Henry IV was Gaunt's son by his first marriage. The trouble with this pedigree was that Katherine's marriage had only been recognized posthumously, with a bar on claims to the throne. Of course it was possible to argue that the marriage had been valid all along and that therefore no such condition had force. This was the line that Henry's supporters took but it was not very convincing. There was, fortunately, no doubt about Henry's own legitimacy, despite the unusual nature of his parents' wedding.

2   Richard Grafton's *Chronicle* (1568) described it as 'a wrest to the harpe to set all the stringes in a monachorde and tune ... by reason of which marriage peace was thoughte to descende out of heaven into Englande ...' (London, 1809), pp. 159–60).

3   Grafton, *Chronicle*, p. 95.

4   William Fulman, (ed.), *Rerum Anglicorum Scriptores* (London, 1684), pp. 567–8.

5   Ibid., p. 572.

6   *Rotuli Parliamentorum*, VI, p. 278.

7   *Calendar of State Papers, Venetian, 1202–1509*, p. 158.

8   *Calendar of the Papal Registers*, XIV (1960), pp. 1–2, 14–28. The Ricardian statute declaring (among other things) Elizabeth's bastardy, had been quietly repealed.

9   *Rotuli Parliamentorum*, VI. *Calendar of the Patent Rolls, 1494–1509*, p. 8.

10   *Calendar of the Patent Rolls, 1485–1494*, p. 369.

11   Ibid.

12   N.H. Nicolas, (ed.), *The Privy Purse Expenses of Elizabeth of York*, (London, 1830).

13   Jasper was Chief Justice of North Wales at the time.

14   John Skelton, *Works*, ed. Alexander Dyce (1843), I, p. 129.

15   T. Rymer, *Foedera, conventions, literae et cuiuscunque generis carta publica*, (1704–35), XII, p. 303.

16   Ibid, pp. 420–8. G.A. Bergenroth, *Calendar of State Papers, Spanish*, (London, 1862) I, p. 21.

17   Ibid, pp. 714–9.

18   A.H. Thomas and I.D. Thornley, *The Great Chronicle of London*, (London, 1938), p. 306.

19   C.L. Kingsford (ed.), *Chronicle of London*, (1905), p. 255.

20   Polydore Vergil, *Anglica Historia*, ed. Hay, p. 133.

21   Ibid.

22   Rymer, *Foedera*, XII, pp. 635–6. S.B.Chrimes, *Henry VII*, (London, 1862), p. 284.

23   Ibid, p. 803.

24   Ibid, XIII, pp. 76–86.

25   In 1506 Ferdinand came to the rescue by formally accrediting her as his ambassador in England, thus giving her both status and function. It is not clear that her financial situation was much ameliorated.

26 J. Gairdner (ed.), *Memorials of King Henry VII*, (1858), pp. 223–39.

27 Rymer, *Foedera*, XIII, pp. 259–61.

28 Ibid, cited from the Venetian Ambassador.

Notes to Chapter 5: The Queen as Foreign Ally: Catherine of Aragon and Anne of Cleves

1   The ceremony itself created only a bar of what was called 'public honesty', which the dispensation did not cover. Wolsey later tried to exploit this omission.

2   *Calendar of State Papers, Spanish*, I, pp. 375–440.

3   De Puebla was intelligent and immensely experienced but he was now becoming elderly and infirm. However, his real weakness was his lack of aristocratic status. Garrett Mattingly, 'The Reputation of Dr De Puebla', *English Historical Review*, (1940), 55, pp. 27–46.

4   Fuensalida eventually fell out with Catherine, much to his disadvantage. Duke of Alba (ed.), *Correspondencia de Gutierre Gomez de Fuensalida*, (1907).

5   Henry was created Prince of Wales on 18 February 1504, but after Arthur's death the Council in the Marches became moribund.

6   Edward Hall, *Chronicle*, p. 507.

7   *Correspondencia de Gutierre Gomez de Fuensalida*, pp. 518 *et seq.*

8   Ibid.

9   Hall, *Chronicle*, p. 507.

10 Hall, *Chronicle*, p. 52

11 *Calendar of State Papers, Spanish*, II, p. 44.

12 Grafton, *Chronicle*, p. 238.

13 *Calendar of State Papers, Venetian*, ed. Rawdon Brown, et al. (London, 1864–98), II, p. 26.

14 Polydore Vergil, *Anglica Historia*, p. 163.

15 Hall, *Chronicle*, p. 532.

16 *Calendar of State Papers, Spanish, Supplement*, pp. 36–41.

17 *Letters and Papers*, I, no. 2391 (BL MS Cotton Cleopatra C.v, ff.64). J. Scarisbrick, *Henry VIII*, (London, 1968), p. 37.

18 Alfred Spont (1897), *Letters and Papers relating to the War with France, 1512–1513*, Navy Records Society, documents 53, 54, 55.

19 BL Harleian MS 3504, f.232.

20 From an eyewitness account. *Calendar of State Papers, Venetian*, II, p. 385.

21 *Letters and Papers*, III, nos 2333, 2360.

22 The banking house of Fugger was extremely important in this election because they were prepared to supply Charles with almost unlimited funds, which he used for the purpose of bribing the electors. They were repaid with the grant of silver mines in Silesia.

23 The More was one of Wolsey's residences, near Rickmansworth.

24 BL Cotton MS Vitellius C.i, f.23. D. Loades, *Mary Tudor: A Life*, (Oxford, 1989), p. 36.

25 MS Vitellius C.i, f.23. She was under the supervision of the Countess of Salisbury as Lady Governess.

26   BL Cotton MS C.x, f.185. J. Sturtz and V. Murphy (eds), *The Divorce Tracts of Henry VIII*, (Angers, 1988), p. xiii.

27   George Cavendish, *The Life and Death of Cardinal Wolsey*, ed. R.S. Sylvester, (London, 1959), p. 83, citing the King's testimony to the Legatine Court in 1529.

28   Nicholas Pocock, *Records of the Reformation, The Divorce 1527–1533*, (London, 1870), 2 vols, Vol. I, p. 11.

29   Guy Bedouelle and Patrick Le Gal, *Le 'Divorce' du Roi Henry VIII*, (Geneva, 1987), pp. 35–41.

30   Bedouelle and Le Gall, *Le 'Divorce'*, pp. 31–41.

31   Catherine directed a barrage of complaints over these delays to the Emperor, who became seriously irritated in consequence.

32   *Letters and Papers*, VI, no. 1296.

33   Ibid., VI, nos 89, 332, 311, 461, 495–6, 525, 529, 661. Cranmer's decision had been anticipated by Convocation on 5 April.

34   P.L. Hughes and J.F. Larkin, *Tudor Royal Proclamations*, (London, 1964), vol. I, no. 140.

35   *Letters and Papers*, VII, no. 1208.

36   Ibid., VI, no. 807 and Appendix 3.

37   Statute 25 Henry VIII, c.22. *Statutes of the Realm*, III, pp. 471–4.

38   *Letters and Papers*, XIV, I, no. 62.

39   Hughes and Larkin, *Tudor Royal Proclamations*, I, no.190.

40   *Letters and Papers*, XIV, ii, no. 400. Her words were reported by the informer George Constantine.

41   Ibid., no. 286.

42   J. Strype (1822), *Ecclesiatical Memorials*, (London, 1822) vol. I, p. 459.

43   Ibid, II, p. 462. D. Loades, *Henry VIII; Court. Church and Conflict*, (London, 2007) p. 96.

44   Her last appearance in a court document came when she exchanged new year's gifts with the Queen on 1 January 1557. BL MS RP 294.

Notes to Chapter 6: The Domestic Queens: Anne Boleyn, Jane Seymour and Catherine Parr

1   For the Boleyn pedigree, see J.C. Wedgewood and A. Holt *History of Parliament: Biographies*, (London, 1936), pp. 90–1. S.T. Bindoff *Hours of Commons, 1509–1558*, (London, 1982), vol. I, p. 456.

2   *Letters and Papers*, III, no. 1762.

3   Hall, *Chronicle*, p. 631. *Letters and Papers*, III, no. 1559.

4   *Calendar of State Papers, Venetian, 1527–33*, p. 824.

5   Eric Ives, *The Life and Death of Anne Boleyn*, (Oxford, 2004).

6   S.W. Singer (ed.) *The Life of Cardinal Wolsey by George Cavendish*, (London, 1827), pp. 424–5.

7   Ives, *Life and Death*, p. 85.

8   The matrimonial history of Anne of Brittany had been even more complicated. She married Charles VIII of France in 1491, despite both of them having been betrothed before

and in 1498 married his cousin and successor, Louis XII. The Pope dispensed all these impediments without difficulty.

9   When the King unburdened his conscience to the City Fathers of London in November 1528, '… some sighed and said nothing … others that favoured the Queen much sorrowed that this matter was now opened.' Hall, *Chronicle*, p. 755.

10   *Calendar of State Papers, Spanish*, IV, pp. 97, 121. Hall, *Chronicle*, p. 758.

11   *Handbook of British Chronology. Letters and Papers*, IV, no. 5996.

12   Ives, *Life and Death*, p.128.

13   R. Scheurer (ed.), *Correspondence du Cardinal Jean du Bellay*, (1969), vol. I, 44 [p. 113].

14   J.E. Cox (ed.), *Miscellaneous Writings and Letters of Thomas Cranmer* (London, 1846), p. 246.

15   *Calendar of State Papers Venetian, 1527–33*, p. 870.

16   'The Coronation of Anne Boleyn' (1533) in A.F. Pollard, *Tudor Tracts* (Westminster, 1903), p. 19.

17   Ibid.

18   *Letters and Papers*, VI, no. 568.

19   *Cal. Span.* IV, ii, p. 510.

20   Statutes, 25 Henry VIII, c.19; 20, 21; 26 Henry VIII, c.1.

21   D. Loades (ed.), *The Papers of George Wyatt*, (London, 1968), p. 185.

22   *Letters and Papers*, VIII, no.1013. Ives, *Life and Death*, p. 191.

23   Ibid., pp. 192–3.

24   Or even the autumn, depending on how premature the foetus of which she miscarried in February 1536 actually was. Rethan Warnicke (*The Rise and Fall of Anne Boleyn*, (Cambridge, 1989) described it as 'of three and a half months'.

25   Abuse in common usage. See TNA SP1/88, f. 21, cited in G.R. Elton, *Policy and Police*, (Cambridge, 1972), p. 11.

26   G. Ascoli, *La Grande Bretagne devant l'opinon Francais*, (Paris, 1927), lns 209–13.

27   Henry Clifford, *The Life of Jane Dormer*, (London, 1887), p. 79.

28   *Cal. Span.*, 1536–8, pp. 84–5.

29   George Wyatt, 'The Life of Queen Anne Boleigne' in Singer, *The Life of Cardinal Wolsey*, p. 443.

30   T. Amyot (ed.), 'A Memorial from George Constantine', in *Archaelogia*, (1831), 23, pp. 23, 64.

31   Mark Smeaton (a musician) was one of those accused of having 'had a do' with Anne Boleyn. Smeaton confessed (falsely) under torture.

32   Singer (ed.), *Wolsey*, pp. 458–9. A letter from Sir Edward Baynton to Sir William FitzWilliam; both were commissioners investigating the charges against Anne and Norris.

33   *Wolsey*, ed. Singer, pp. 451, 457.

34   Charles Wriothesley, *A Chronicle of England, 1485–1559*, ed. W.D. Hamilton (Camden Society), (London, 1875), vol. I, 189–91.

35   Strype, *Ecclesiastical Memorials*, I, ii, p. 304.

36   Mary to Cromwell, 24 August 1538, *Letters and Papers*, XIII, no.174. This is a late example, but she had made her position clear the previous autumn.

37   Historical Manuscripts Commission, *Bath Papers*, II, f.8.

38   *Letters and Papers*, XX, i. no. 266.

39   John Foxe, *Acts and Monuments*, (London, 1583), pp. 1242–4.

40   *Letters and Papers*, XIX, I, nos. 864, 1035 (78).

41   Statute 35 Henry VIII, c.1. *Statutes of the Realm*, III, pp. 955–8.

Notes to Chapter 7:   The Queen as Whore: Catherine Howard

1   Lacey Baldwin Smith, *A Tudor Tragedy*, (London, 1961), p. 9.

2   *Letters and Papers*, XVI, no. 1339. TNA, SP1/168, f.155.

3   It was the usual practice for aristocratic children of both sexes to be sent to live in friendly households, or other parts of the family, at about that age. Only later did it become normal to send sons to school.

4   Mannox swore that 'he never knew her carnally', but the truth was probably otherwise. TNA, SP1/167, f.138.

5   *Letters and Papers*, XV, no. 902. A week before they were married, there was a rumour that Catherine was pregnant.

6   J.G. Nichols (ed.), *Narratives of the Days of the Reformation* (London, (1860), p. 260.

7   G.R. Elton, 'Thomas Cromwell's Decline and Fall', in G.R. Elton, *Studies in Tudor and Stuart Government and Politics*, (Cambridge, 1974), vol. I, 189–230. Susan Brigden 'Popular Disturbance and the Fall of Thomas Cromwell', *Historical Journal*, (1981), 34, pp. 257–78.

8   *Letters and Papers*, XVI, no. 1426. H. Nicholas (ed.) *Proceedings and Ordinances of the Privy Council of England*, (London, 1837), VII, p. 355.

9   *Letters and Papers*, IX, no. 612.

10   For example, TNA, SP1/167, f.14.

11   *Letters and Papers*, XV, no. 875. TNA, SP1/161, ff. 101–2.

12   John Foxe, *Acts and Monuments*, (1583), pp. 1177–91.

13   *Letters and Papers*, XVI, no. 1320. TNA, SP1/167, f.131.

14   Nicholas, *Proceedings and Ordinances*, VII, p. 353.

15   Historical Manuscripts Commission, *Bath Papers*, II, pp. 8–9.

16   *Bath Papers*, II, pp. 8–9.

17   *Letters and Papers*, XVI, no. 1339. TNA, SP1/167, f.160. Jane Rochford's confession.

18   TNA, SP1/167, f.159. Thomas Culpepper's confession.

19   Statute 26 Henry VIII, c.13. *Statutes of the Realm*, III, p. 508.

20   Foxe, *Acts and Monuments*, pp. 1236–7.

21   *Letters and Papers*, XVI, no. 1426.

22   *State Papers of Henry VIII* (1810–28), I, ii, 167, p. 700.

23   *Journals of the House of Lords*, I, p. 171.

24   Henry Ellis, *Original Letters Illustrative of English History* (1824–46) 1st series, II, pp. 128–9.

25   *Letters and Papers*, XVII, no. 63.

Notes to Chapter 8: The Queens who Never Were: Jane Grey and Mary Stuart

1 When Henry was excommunicated, the realm was placed under an interdict, which meant that no lawful marriages could be celebrated and that included the King's marriage to Jane Seymour. In the eyes of the Catholic Church, consequently, Edward was illegitimate.

2 The only realistic candidate was Catherine Grey, Jane's younger sister. However, she married the Earl of Hertford (who had been recognized in January 1559) without royal approval and was consequently imprisoned. She died in 1568.

3 Edward's Letters Patent were drawn up in due form, but there is no evidence that they ever passed the Great Seal.

4 There is no firm evidence for this shared education, but it is plausible in view of the similarity of their accomplishments, and the proximity of their upbringing.

5 Alison Plowden in *The Oxford Dictionary of National Biography*.

6 *Journals of the House of Commons* (1803–52), I, p. 9. *Acts of the Privy Council*, II, p. 262.

7 John ab Ulmis to Henry Bullinger, 31 December 1550. Hastings Robinson (ed.) (1847), *Original Letters Relative to the English Reformation*, Parker Society, pp. 425–7.

8 S. Brigden (ed.), *The Letters of Richard Scudamore*, (London, 1990), vol. XXX, p. 96.

9 W.K. Jordan (ed.), *The Chronicle and Political Papers of King Edward VI*, (London, 1966), pp. 68–9.

10 The Duke of Northumberland was Warden General of the Marches. BL MS Royal 18C 24, ff.235–6.

11 Jehan Scheyfve to the Emperor, 11 June 1553. *Calendar of State Papers, Spanish*, XI, p. 50.

12 J.G. Nichols (ed.), *Literary Remains of King Edward VI*, (London, 1857) II, pp. 571–2.

13 *Historical Manuscripts Comission, 16th Report*, MSS of Lord Montague of Beaulieu, (1900), p. 5.

14 J.G. Nichols (ed.), *The Chronicle of Queen Jane*, (London, 1850), p. 3.

15 Ibid, Appendix III.

16 Ibid, p. 12.

17 The two who were executed with him were Sir John Gates and Sir Thomas Palmer. BL Harley MS 2194, f.23.

18 *Chronicle of Queen Jane*, pp. 24–5.

19 Ibid., p. 32.

20 Ibid, pp. 55–9.

21 This appears to have been on the initiative of the Cardinal, although Mary of Guise also visited her daughter in September 1550 to make sure that this duty was being discharged. Antonia Fraser, *Mary Queen of Scots*, (1969), p. 51.

22 Letter of Nicholas Throgmorton to Elizabeth, January 1561. Cited by Antonia Fraser, *Mary Queen of Scots*, p. 110

23 B.L. Cotton and M.S. Caligula B.IX, ff. 34, 38. *Calendar of State Papers relating to Scotland, 1559–60*, pp. 413–5.

24 Although Mary was only 19 at the time of her return, she had already been declared of age in 1553, as part of the manoeuvrings that conferred the regency on her mother.

25 T. Thompson (ed.), *Diurnal of Occurents*, (Edinburgh, 1833), p. 74. The battle was at Corrichie.

26   J.E.A. Dawson, 'William Cecil and the British Dimension of Early Elizabethan Foreign Policy', *History*, (1989), 74, pp. 196–216.

27   J.E.A. Dawson, 'Mary Queen of Scots, Lord Darnley and Anglo-Scottish Relations in 1565', *International History Review*, (1986), 8, pp. 1–24.

28   Randolf to Cecil, 19 February 1565. J Bain, (ed.),*Calendar of State Papers Relating to Scotland, 1563–69*, (Edinburgh, 1898), pp. 126–7.

29   Ibid, p. 188.

30   Ibid., p. 216.

31   Bedford to Cecil, 30 December 1566. *Cal. Scot., 1563–69*, p. 308.

32   Sir James Melville, *Memoirs of his Own Life*, ed. T. Thompson, (Edinburgh, 1827), p. 177.

33   Elizabeth's instructions to Throgmorton, 30 June 1567. *Cal. Scot., 1563–69*, pp. 339–40.

34   *Cal. Scot., 1563–69*, pp. 438–40.

35   *Calendar of State Papers, Rome, 1558–71*, pp. 338, 349. Loades D., *Elizabeth I*, (London, 2006), pp. 175–7.

36   *Calendar of State Paper, Spanish, 1558–1603*, III, pp. 33–4.

37   Raphael Holinshed (ed.) *Chronicle*, (London, 1807–8), IV, p. 536.

38   Statute 27 Elizabeth I, c.1. *Statutes of the Realm*, IV, pp. 704–5.

39   The method involved the concealment of letters within the bungs of beer barrels.

40   B.L. Cotton and M.S. Caligula C.IX, f.459.

41   P.L. Hughes and J.F. Larkin, *Tudor Royal Proclamations*, (London, 1969), vol. II, pp. 528–32.

Notes to Chapter 9:   The Married Sovereign: Queen Mary I

1   The nearest in blood was Henry, Lord Darnley, aged about 8 years at this time. Darnley was the grandson of Margeret Tudors's second marriage to Archibald Douglas, Earl of Angus. Edward Courtenay had a claim derived from his grandmother, Catherine, a daughter of Edward IV. Francis Hastings, Earl of Huntingdon, had a more remote claim still, going back to a niece of Richard, Duke of York, Edward IV's father. It is not surprising that none of these was pressed.

2   Foster Watson, *Vives and the Renascence [Education of Women*, (London, 1912).

3   B.L. Cotton and M.S. Vespasian, C XIV, f.246. Count Cifuentes to the Emperor, 8 October 1536. *Calendar of State Papers, Spanish*, V, p. 106.

4   Marillac to Francis I, 3 June 1542. *Letters and Papers*, XVII, no. 371.

5   *Calendar of the Patent Rolls*, Edward VI, II, p. 20. The actual grant is dated 17 May 1548, with issues backdated to the previous Michaelmas, but there is good evidence that the arrangements were in place by the previous July.

6   Henry Clifford, *The Life of Jane Dormer, Duchess of Feria*, ed. J. Stevenson, (London, 1887), p. 63.

7   Emperor to Van der Delft (ambassador in England), 10 May 1549. *Cal. Span.*, IX, p. 350.

8   D. MacCulloch (ed.) 'Vita Mariae Angliae Reginae of Robert Wingfield of Brantham', *Camden Miscellany*, (1984), 28, p. 255.

9   'Vita Mariae Angliae Reginae', *passim*.

10   Ibid., pp. 272–3.

11   P.L. Hughes and J.F. Larkin, *Tudor Royal Proclamations*, (London, 1969), vol. II, p. 4. 18 August 1553.

12   Statute 1 Mary, st.2, c.2. *Statutes of the Realm*, IV, p. 202. See also Henry Machyn, *The Diary of Henry Machyn*, ed. J.G. Nichols, (London, 1969), pp. 38–41.

13   Emperor to Philip, 30 July 1553. *Cal. Span.*, XI, p. 126.

14   In 1549 Charles had reorganized the 17 provinces of the Low Countries, which were all in theory part of the empire, into the Burgundian Circle, which he exempted from Imperial Law. He then arranged for the succession of each province to fall to Philip after his death or retirement, thus effectively detaching them from the empire altogether. This was much resented by his brother Ferdinand, who was due to succeed him in the Imperial title.

15   *Calendar of State Papers, Domestic, Philip and Mary*, no. 24. C.S. Knighton, *Mary*, (London, 1998) TNA SP11/1, no. 20.

16   Archivo General de Simancas, Estado Inglaterra, E807, f.36 (i). *Cal. Span.*, XII, pp. 4–6.

17   Statute 1 Mary, st.3, c.1 House of Lords Record Office, Original Acts.

18   *Cal. Span.*, XII, p. 283.

19   'The copie of a letter sent into Scotlande …' by John Elder. *The Chronicle of Queen Jane*, ed. J.G. Nichols (London, 1850), Appendix X, p. 140.

20   *Cal. Span.*, XIII, p. 11. Charles had, however, created his son king of Naples and Sicily ahead of the wedding, so that the match would be between 'equals'.

21   For example, *La solenne et felice intrata delli serenissimi Re Philippo et Regina Maria d'Inghilterra* (Rome, 1555). There were similar works in Spanish, German and Dutch.

22   *Cal. Span.*, XIII, p. 33.

23   Giovanni Michieli's 'Narration of England', 13 May 1557. *Cal. Ven.*, VI, p. 1057.

24   Cardinal Pole to Mary, 2nd October 1553, *Cal. Ven.*, V, p. 419.

25   *Cal. Span.*, XIII, 63–4.

26   *Cal. Ven.*, VI, p. 10. Memorandum concerning church property. *Lords Journals*, I, p. 480.

27   For example, *Il felicissimo ritorno del regno d'Inghilterra alla cattolica unione* (Rome, 1555).

28   He prompted his confessor, Alonso de Castro, to preach against it. As de Castro had quite a record as a persecutor himself this did not carry much conviction.

29   Pole to Philip, 5 October 1555. *Cal. Ven.*, VI, pp. 205–6. Mary gave him a generous leaving present.

30   Such rumours were circulating in London as early as March. See the pardon of Alice Perwicke of London. *Cal. Pat.*, Mary, III, p. 184.

31   Badoer to the Doge and Senate. *Cal. Ven.*, VI, p. 212.

32   *Revised Short Title Catalogue* 3480, ed. W.A. Jackson et al. (London, 1976–86). John Strype, *Ecclesiastical Memorials*, (Oxford, 1820), vol. III, pt ii, no xlv.

33   *Cal. Ven.*, VI, pp. 299–300.

34   Glyn Redworth (1997), '"Matters Impertinent to Women"; Male and Female Monarchy under Philip and Mary', *English Historical Review*, 112, pp. 597–613.

35   *Cal. Ven.*, VI, pp. 401–2. Badoer had been told that she was 'beyond measure exasperated'.

36   B.L. Sloane MS 1786, which is the Latin version prepared for Philip.

37 This was staged by an adventurer named Thomas Strafford, who pretended a remote claim to the throne. There is more than a suspicion that it was abetted by Lord Paget (who supported the war) with the aid of a French free-booter called Jean Ribaut.

38 *Cal. Span.*, XI, p. 393.

39 Surian to the Doge and Senate, 15 January 1558, *Cal. Ven.*, VI, p. 1427. Philip to Pole, 21 January 1558, *Cal. Span.*, XIII, p. 340.

40 F.J. Fisher, 'Influenza and Inflation in Tudor England', *Economic History Review*, (1965), 2nd series, 18, pp. 12–30.

41 S. Adams and M. Rodriguez Salgado (eds), 'The Count of Feria's Despatch of 14th November 1558', *Camden Miscellany*, (1984), 28 p. 328.

42 Strype, *Ecclesiastical Memorials*, III, pp. 536–50

Notes to Chapter 10: The Unmarried Sovereign: Elizabeth I

1 Judith Richards (1999), 'Love and a Female Monarch; the case of Elizabeth Tudor', *Journal of British Studies*, 28, pp. 133–60.

2 Glyn Redworth, 'Matters Impertinent to Women', in English Historical Review, (1997), 112, pp. 597–613. Judith Richards 'Mary Tudor as "Sole Queen"? Gendering Tudor Monarchy', *Historical Journal*, (1997), 40, pp. 895–924.

3 The Queen's answer to the Commons petition, 1559. L.S. Marcus, J. Mueller and M.B. Rose, *Elizabeth I, Collected Works*, (Chicago, 2000), p. 59.

4 Judith Richards (1997), '"To Promote a Woman to Bear Rule"; Talking of Queens in Mid-Tudor England', *Sixteenth Century Journal*, 28, pp. 101–22.

5 Draft proclamation of December 1563. *Tudor Royal Proclamations*, II, pp. 240–412. It is not clear whether it was ever issued.

6 Anonymous, *A Special Grace Appointed to Have been Said after a Banket in York* (1558).

7 *Revised Short Title Catalogue* 23400. Elizabeth particularly resented being described as being 'led blindfolded as a poor lamb to the slaughter'.

8 Princess Elizabeth to Edward Seymour, Lord Protector, 28 January 1549. Marcus, et al., *Collected Works*, pp. 22–4.

9 William Camden (ed. 1625), *Annales*, III, p. 12. *Calendar of State Papers, Spanish, 1580–86*, p. 227.

10 Richards, '"To Promote a Woman to Bear rule"'.

11 TNA, SP12/7, nos 169–71.

12 J. Bain et al. (eds), *Calendar of State Papers Relating to Scotland, 1547–1603*, (1898–1952), vols II and III.

13 J.H. Pollen (1922), 'Mary Queen of Scots and the Babington Plot', *Scottish Historical Society*, 3rd series, 3.

14 Marcus, et al., *Collected Works*, pp. 325–6. 'Gathered by one that heard it.'

15 Ibid., n. 1.

16 W.P. Haugaard 'Elizabeth Tudor's Book of Devotions: A Neglected Clue to the Queen's Life and Character', *Sixteenth Century Journal*, (1981), 12, pp. 79–105.

17 Indictment of Lord John Bray (1556). *Calendar of Patent Rolls*, III, p. 396.

18   Christopher Haigh, 'From Monopoly to Minority; Catholicism in Early Modern England', *Transactions of the Royal Historical Society*, (1981), 5th series, 31, pp. 129–47.

19   Elizabeth's willingness to appoint bishops with much more radical views than her own was evident in the vestiarian controversy of 1566. Ibid., pp. 102–4.

20   Richard Mulcaster, *The Passage of Most Dread Sovereign Lady Queen Elizabeth, through the City of London …* (1558), in A.F. Pollard, *Tudor Tracts*, (1903), p. 387.

21   Edmund Spenser, *The Faerie Queene*, ed. A.C. Hamilton, (London, 1984) Book 2, 2, xlii.

22   G. von Bulow, 'Journey through England and Scotland, Made by Lupold von Wedel in the Years 1584 and 1585', *Transactions of the Royal Historical Society*, n.s. 9 (1895), pp. 258–9.

23   *Elizabeth I: Collected Works*, pp. 303–4.

24   William Camden (1688), *The History of the Most Renowned Princess Elizabeth*, pp. 623–4.

25   M. James, 'At A Crossroads of Political Culture, the Essex Revolt of 1601', in *Society, Politics and Culture; Studies in Early Modern England*, (Cambridge, 1986), pp. 416–65.

26   *Elizabeth I: Collected Works*, p. 304.

Additional Reading Suggestions

(Place of publication London unless otherwise stated)

Adams, Simon, *Leicester and the Court. Essays in Elizabethan Politics*, (2002).
Allmand, Christopher, *Henry V*, (1992).
Andrews, K.R., *Drake's Voyages; A Reassessment of their Place in England's Maritime Expansion*, (1967).
Anglo, S., *Spectacle, Pageantry and Early Tudor Policy*, (Oxford, 1969).
Ascoli, G., *La Grande Bretagne devant l'Opinion Francaise*, (Paris, 1927).

Baldwin, David, *Elizabeth Woodville*, (Stroud, 2002).
Bernard, G.W., *The King's Reformation: Henry VIII and the Remaking of the English Church*, (2005).
Berry, Philippa, *Of Chastity and Power; Elizabethan Literature and the Virgin Queen*, (1989).
Bradshaw, B., and E. Duffy, *Humanism, Reform and Reformation; the career of Bishop John Fisher*, (Cambridge, 1989).
Bullough, Verna L., *The Subordinate Sex*, (1973).
Bush, M.L., *The Government Policy of Protector Somerset*, (Manchester, 1975).

Calmette, J. and G. Perinelle, *Louis XI et l'Angleterre*, (Paris, 1930).
Chrimes, S.B., *Henry VII*, (1972).
Collinson, Patrick, *Archbishop Grindal, 1519–1583: The Struggle for a Reformed Church*, (1979).
Cowan, Ian B., *The Enigma of Mary Stewart*, (1971).

Davey, Richard, *The Nine Days Queen*, (1909).
Davies, R. R., *The Revolt of Owain Glyn Dwr*, (Oxford, 1995).
Dawson, J.E.A., *The Politics of Religion in the Age of Mary, Queen of Scots*, (2002).
Doran, Susan, *Monarchy and Matrimony: the Courtships of Elizabeth I*, (1996).

Dowling, Maria, *Humanism in the Age of Henry VIII*, (1987).
Duffy, Eamon, *The Stripping of the Altars*, (1992).
Duffy, Eamon, and D. Loades, *The Church of Mary Tudor*, (Aldershot, 2006).

Elliott, J.H., *Imperial Spain*, (Oxford, 1963).
Ellis, Henry, *Original Letters Illustrative of British History*, (1824).
Elton, G.R., *Policy and Police*, (Cambridge, 1972).
Elton, G.R., *The Tudor Constitution*, (Cambridge, 1982).

Fraser, Antonia, *Mary Queen of Scots*, (1969).

Gairdner, James (ed.), *The Paston Letters*, (1904).
Griffiths, R.A., *The Reign of King Henry VI*, (1981).
Gunn, S.J., *Charles Brandon, Duke of Suffolk, 1484–1545*, (Oxford, 1989).
Gunn, S.J., *Early Tudor Government, 1485–1558*, (1995).
Gwyn, Peter, *The King's Cardinal*, (1990).

Handover, P.M., *The Second Cecil*, (1959).
Harriss, G.L., *Cardinal Beaufort: a study in Lancastrian ascendancy and decline*, (Oxford, 1988).
Holmes, P.J., *Resistance and Compromise: the Political Thought of Elizabethan Catholics*, (1982).
Houlbrooke, Ralph, *Church Courts and the People during the English Reformation, 1520–1570*, (Oxford, 1979).
Hoyle, R.W., *The Pilgrimage of Grace and the Politics of the 1530s*, (Cambridge, 2001).
Hughes, Philip, *The Reformation in England*, (1954).

Ives, E.W., *The Life and Death of Anne Boleyn*, (2004).

Jacob, E.F., *The Fifteenth Century*, (Oxford, 1961).
James, Susan, *Kateryn Parr: the Making of a Queen*, (Stroud, 1999).
Jones, M.K., and M.G. Underwood, *The King's Mother*, (1992).
Jones, N.L., *Faith by Statute*, (1982).
Jordan, W.K., *Edward VI: the Young King*, (1968).

Kelly, H.A., *The Matrimonial Trials of Henry VIII*, (Standford, CA, 1976).
Kelsey, Harry, *Sir John Hawkins*, (2002).

Loach, Jennifer, *Parliament and the Crown in the Reign of Mary Tudor*, (Oxford, 1986).

Loach, Jennifer and R. Tittler (eds), *The Mid-Tudor Polity*, (1989.)

Loades, David, *Two Tudor Conspiracies*, (Cambridge, 1965).

Loades, David, *The Tudor Court*, 1986.

Loades, David, *Mary Tudor: A Life*, (Oxford, 1989).

Loades, David, *The Reign of Mary Tudor*, (1991).

Loades, David, *Henry VIII and his Queens*, (Stroud, 1994).

Loades, David, *John Dudley, Duke of Northumberland*, (Oxford, 1996).

Loades, David, *Elizabeth I*, (2003).

Loades, David, *Henry VIII, Court, Church and Conflict*, (2007).

Loades, David, *The Cecils: Privilege and Power behind the Throne*, (2007).

Loades, David, The *Life and Career of William Paulet*, (Aldershot, 2008).

MacCulloch, Diarmaid, *Thomas Cranmer*, (1996).

Maclean, John, *The Life of Sir Thomas Seymour*, (1869).

McGrath, Patrick, *Papists and Puritans under Elizabeth I*, (1967).

Mattingly, Garrett (ed.), *Catherine of Aragon*, (1963).

Maurer, Helen E., *Margaret of Anjou*, (2005).

Metzger, B.M., and Coogan, M.D. (eds), *Oxford Companion to the Bible*, (Oxford, 1993).

Muller, James (ed.), *Stephen Gardiner and the Tudor Reaction*, (New York, 1970).

Murphy, Beverly, *Bastard Prince*, (Stroud, 2001).

Otway-Ruthven, A.J., *A History of Medieval Ireland*, (1979).

Oxford Dictionary of National Biography (Oxford, 2005).

Pierce, Hazel, *Margaret Pole, Countess of Salisbury, 1473–1541*, (Cardiff, 2003).

Pollen, J.H., *Mary Queen of Scots and the Babington Plot*, (1922).

Read, Conyers, *Mr. Secretary Walsingham and the Policy of Queen Elizabeth*, (1925).

Read, Conyers, *Mr. Secretary Cecil and Queen Elizabeth*, (1955).

Read, Conyers, *Lord Burghley and Queen Elizabeth*, (1960).

Redworth, Glyn, *In Defence of the Church Catholic: a Life of Stephen Gardiner*, (Oxford, 1990).

Rodriguez Salgado, M.J., *The Changing Face of Empire*, (Cambridge, 1988).

Ross, Charles, *Edward IV*, (1974).

Ross, Charles, *Richard III*, (1981).
Russell, J.G., *The Field of Cloth of Gold*, (1969).
Ryrie, Alec, *The Origins of the Scottish Reformation*, (Cambridge, 2006).

Scarisbrick, J.J., *Henry VIII*, (1968).
Searle, W.G., *History of Queen' College ... in the University of Cambridge*, (Cambridge, 1867).
Scofield, C.L, *The Life and Reign of King Edward IV*, (1923).
Smith, L.B., *A Tudor Tragedy*, (1961).
Strickland, Agnes, *Lives of the Queens of England*, (1902).
Strong, Roy, *The Cult of Elizabeth*, (1977).
Strong, Roy, *Gloriana: The Portraits of Elizabeth*, (1987).

Theilemans, M.R., *Bourgogne et Angleterre: relations politiques, 1435–1467*, (Paris, 1966).

Usher, Brett, *William Cecil and Episcopacy, 1559–1577*, (2003).

Vale, M.G.A., *Charles VII*, (1974).
Victoria County History of England (1959), Cambridgeshire (III, 1959).

Warnicke, Retha, *The Rise and Fall of Anne Boleyn*, (Cambridge, 1989).
Warnicke, Retha, *The Marrying of Anne of Cleves*, (Cambridge, 2000).
Watson, Foster, *Vives and the Renascence Education of Women*, (1912).
Wilson, Derek, *Sweet Robin: A Biography of Robert Dudley, Earl of Leicester*, (1981).
Wormald, J., *Mary Queen of Scots: A Study in Failure*, (1988).

Index